THE SAINTS ARE COMING

GREGORY JORDAN

A rebel priest,
a daring woman
and their years
of living
dangerously

D0067704

TWENTY
THIRD 23rd
PUBLICATIONS
www.23rdpublications.com

Author's Note

This book is based upon hundreds of
interviews, archival research, letters,
and personal journals. Conversations
are replicated as precisely as possible
according to the recollections of the
participants. The internal thoughts and
musings of Kevin and Rayna result from
hours of reconstruction with the author.

Twenty-Third Publications

1 Montauk Avenue, Suite 200, New London, CT 06320

(860) 437-3012 » (800) 321-0411 » www.23rdpublications.com

COVER PHOTO: Ramon Sanchez

ISBN: 978-1-62785-012-4

Library of Congress Catalog Card Number: 2014947509

Printed in the U.S.A.

CONTENTS

Hic locus est: "Here is the place," or simply hic, is a refrain that runs through the inscriptions on the early martyrs' shrines of North Africa. The holy was available in one place, and in each such place it was accessible to one group in a manner in which it could not be accessible to anyone situated elsewhere.

PETER BROWN, *The Cult of the Saints*

They really loved this life; yet they weighed it up. They thought of how much they should love the things eternal if they were capable of such deep love for things that pass away.

ST. AUGUSTINE

The saints are coming, the saints are coming
No matter how I try, I realise there's no reply
The saints are coming, the saints are coming

THE SKIDS, "THE SAINTS ARE COMING"

FATHER KEVIN MULLINS KNEW THEY WOULD COME FOR HIM, BUT HE HAD EXPECTED, EVEN HOPED, THAT THEY WOULD COME WITH LESS CLICHÉ. Not a big truck rumbling outside in the moonlight; not the sounds of machismo echoing off the cinder block shacks; not the knock on the door that he heard now.

Nine years prior, in 2001, when he had started to work in the Rancho Anapra colonia, the dirtiest and poorest pop-up barrio in Juarez, Mexico, he had realized that he would have to deal with some tough customers. But God is a tough customer, he always told himself, tougher than the rest. And they obviously do not realize I am an Aussie, not a Yanqui, he would sometimes mutter under his breath before quickly reminding himself of the Christian virtue of humility.

But as his years passed in Anapra—and big guns attained the stylistic equivalence of male jewelry and grotesque murder the cultural equivalence of fistfights—the tough customers seemed to multiply and expand before his eyes. Puffed-up arms, thicker necks, chunkier bodies...though they still followed the Mexican soccer clubs, the thugs started to look more like the burly lads from one of Father Kevin's native Australian rugby clubs.

Lately the calls had started to come to priests on Sunday evenings, the day of the big collection. As pastor for the past nine years of the parish of Corpus Christi, the only Catholic church in Anapra, he had given his telephone number out generously from the very beginning. He wanted to be easy to find. Marital quarrels, stillbirths, dinner invitations even to the most hungry homes, drug-addicted sons, disappearing daughters—if they called, he went.

But these days the bad guys were calling priests for money, and they had started to call him because, as any narcotraficante could surmise, the Sunday collections were growing…solely because the size of his congregation was growing…largely because Anapra was the cheapest place to live in one of global capitalism's poorest boomtowns. But the calls were still just a nuisance, an interruption in what Father Kevin thought of as his perfect poverty at night in his threadbare home alongside all the adobe shacks and concrete hovels in godforsaken Juarez. He would listen, laugh, hang up, and return to the totalitarian quiet—but for the occasional chain reaction of barking dogs—of the Mexican desert that he and his neighbors were occupying.

But tonight, as he sat there afraid—yes, he admitted, finally afraid—he imagined the playing out of the cliché: take the keys off the hook on the wall as they hold a gun to his head; stumble down the dirt road to the church with a gun to his side; unlock the church, fumble with the lock to the sacristy, fumble with the lock to the safe until they push the gun into his neck; finally get the code right, open the safe, step back to show its perfect emptiness; and then either be shot or pistol-whipped in the face or, if they have a sense of irony, beaten repeatedly with the brass chalice that they would then carry off in hope that it might just be gold.

He had taken to hiding the collections—behind pews, under his desk, behind the toilet. Anywhere but the safe.

He stood up and pondered whether he should urinate before opening the door. The increasingly complicated relationship between his prostate and his bladder, he was sure, would worsen with nerves, and better to piss now before all the commotion began. But the next knock was softer, more like the tapping of a child than the banging of a thug, and he grew curious. He could still hear the voices in the street, he could still hear the big car rumbling, but the gentleness of the knock had undermined the cliché. He stood up, put on his robe, and walked to the door. The lock was meek, so he chuckled at the formality of having to open it.

He prepared himself to see the barrel of a gun pointing at his chest, but instead he saw kindly Juan Pablo, the one man he had met in this town who would build you a building without robbing you blind. Juan Pablo had built, almost single-handedly, the extension onto Corpus Christi in 2006 after years of crooked contractors and hard-won donations. He had built it cheaply and well, and when he had completed it, he had given money back to the parish.

The crown of his head only reached to the midpoint of Kevin's barrel chest. Juan Pablo pushed at Kevin's stomach and closed the door, fumbling for the lock.

He looked up at Father Kevin.

Juan Pablo's face instantly showed that he grasped the absurdity of locks in Juarez. Nevertheless, Father Kevin felt the urge to apologize to him, as if he owed the fellow who had come scurrying down here to risk his life for him at least the courtesy of a proper dead bolt.

The voices outside grew louder, closer, but they still were calling to each other. Were they searching for the right house? Were they that stupid? Maybe they weren't drug cartel guys after all. So who, then? The many shadowy faces of evil in Juarez made the answer less clear-cut than Kevin had used to suppose.

Sure, the narcos kept calling priests for money. But who was to say petty crooks weren't following suit? Then there was Pedro Zaragoza, the oil and milk magnate with whom Kevin had had a few tiffs, and with whom Kevin's colleague, Father Billy, had virtually waged war. Zaragoza wanted to redevelop Anapra to serve his new factory city, but he was too smart, and perhaps even too Catholic, to threaten a priest directly. The junkies, well, that seemed more likely: the collection could buy them all the drugs they would need for weeks. But they would never pull up in a big monstrosity like the one rumbling below. But the old-guard narcos wouldn't either. They were quiet, stealthy. These guys, the garish types, had to be some renegade branch, some uncouth offshoot of one of the cartels.

When he had first come here, the same mission he had begun repeating to himself at age 17, when he entered the Columban order back in Sydney, had stayed intact: "My duty is to praise our Lord by serving others." So clean, so rote. The searing Juarez sun had not bothered him for long, used to it as he was from Australia; the poverty had appalled him, but it also appealed to his urge for simplicity. For the first time in his life, here in this sprawling dump in the desert, his faith and his work and his own needs had merged harmoniously.

But now, over the past year and a half, it was changing. All those devils abounding out there, slaughtering teenage boys and young women, writing messages in blood on their torsos, cutting off their heads or fingers or feet. Ministering was turning into a war against evil itself, against the various faces of Satanás, and he was turning into the brawler he used to be as a boy. Yet no one could ever pin down who the bad guys were. That was the trick, the most devilish thing about Mexico. Nothing, no one, was obvious. He surely had some in his parish, some sons of Satanás, but they would show up to Mass with clean hands and pray and sing and trick everyone into thinking they were normal blokes.

Their name for the devil here sounded even more fearsome that the simple Anglo-Saxon of Satan. Satanás—the word gave him chills, and Satan was having his heyday here. Anger at this devil, not faith, was becoming Kevin's motivator. He lamented that shift some days; other days he relished it. And how appropriate to be brawling with the devil here in devil-may-care Juarez. Some nights, after a rum too many, he half-wanted the devil to come banging through the door.

After both men sat down, Juan Pablo put his hand on Father Kevin's leg and raised his other hand to his lips. He smiled slightly, and Father Kevin smiled back. I knew you were the kind of man one would choose to get blasted to hell with, Father Kevin felt like saying. I knew you were the sort to stay and go down with the ship.

The doors of the car banged shut one by one even though the rapid exchanges in Spanish kept on. An old woman who lived across the dirt road was speaking the most now, and Juan Pablo suddenly let out a laugh that he muffled immediately with his own hand.

"Dice la mujer que eres un borracho y no vales nada," Juan Pablo translated for Father Kevin. She says you are a good-for-nothing drunk.

Father Kevin was momentarily tempted to go rushing outside to defend his reputation. A drunk, that I will accept. But good for nothing? Then he laughed, too, and didn't try to stop himself. He heard other female voices calling at the visitors. The barrio was shielding him, he knew, and he felt a warm, caressing gratitude come over him.

The car grumbled into the distance, but Juan Pablo's hand stayed on Father Kevin's knee for a good while, and suddenly the priest felt again like Juan Pablo was the protector, the minister.

"Hijos de la chingada," Juan Pablo said.

Father Kevin smiled at him. Sons of bitches. But it sounded so much better in Juan Pablo's bitter Spanish. More literally, he knew, it meant "sons of the fucked." Father Kevin wanted to say it back to Juan Pablo in agreement, say it like an old, angry Aussie with a bad prostate: hijos de la chingada. But he caught himself. He would muzzle his own devil inside. He would at least maintain the veil of holiness in front of his flock. But he said the phrase over and over to himself, and it sounded so right in his inner ears that he wanted to go out and shout it down the street through the dust at the knuckleheads as they rumbled off into the dirty Juarez night.

PART I
Baptism
2001-2004

CHAPTER ONE

◆

Kevin

ON THE THIRD MONDAY NIGHT IN SEPTEMBER 2001, FATHER KEVIN DECIDED THAT THE WHIRLING SOUND OF THE DUST STORM OUTSIDE WAS THE SOUND HE WOULD CHOOSE TO ACCOMPANY THE APOCALYPSE. He had been sleeping poorly after five weeks working in the heat and dust and noise of Rancho Anapra, and had taken to spending Sunday nights, and even the occasional Monday, across the border in El Paso just to catch up from the week's insomnia. He didn't like that he had to retreat once a week; he admitted it felt like a small concession to defeat. So he soon decided to limit himself to Sunday nights only and to try to pray himself out of his funk. Earlier in the evening, as he had stepped through the door of the house that he had learned only after renting it had recently served as Anapra's most popular brothel, he had felt the sleeplessness stirring inside. Now, he stared at the moonlit concrete walls and saw, repeatedly, just as he had seen each prior sleepless night, one of three visions.

First, the lush valleys and green, snow-topped peaks of rural Chile, where his mind would race to whenever he dipped into sleep for a few seconds. Now 47, he had spent the past twelve years of his life ministering to the peasant poor in Araucania, the volcanic region of southern Chile where the natural beauty insistently eased, ever so slightly, the pain of the widespread poverty of the indigenous people Kevin served.

Second, the ghosts of the clients and whores who, until recently, got and gave in this room and smaller bedroom adjacent. These images would attack him whenever the sound of the roaring trucks or howling dogs quickly stirred him from his momentary sleep.

Third, the cataracts of the rivers in Chile. This vision was prompted, several times each night, by the hiss and splatter of drunken passersby pissing on the wall the house shared with the main street.

His visions, he quickly realized, all had their auditory triggers within the overarching rage of the storm.

The rare moment of silence—when no truck was passing, no man was pissing, or no dog was barking—would elicit the sweet, almost aromatic, vision of the Chilean countryside. That image would last as long as it could, inevitably jarred by a drunk, a truck, or a bored dog inciting all the other dogs of Anapra.

So he had turned to the Rosary. He remembered his adoptive father's rosary, wrapped around his fingers all evening long after he came home from his work as the local magistrate in the Queensland State Justice Department in northern Australia. Kevin saw him dozing one afternoon, his Saturday Aussie siesta, his father used to call it, and not only was the rosary still in his hand, but he swore his father's fingers were still moving the beads and, what's more, his lips were still moving as he slept. This was the man who said to Kevin, when at age 17 he notified his father that he wanted to become a Columban priest, "Are you sure they'll take you? Yes? Well, we'll take you back when they confirm their mistake."

As Kevin aged, and served, and saw the range of human suffering in the places he had worked, from Australia to Bolivia to Chicago to Chile, he came to appreciate his father's habit. There was a method to the madness of that chain of beads. So Kevin had taken to getting up, cursing the rude sounds and ruder darkness, pacing the floor saying the Rosary, and then laying down with the rosary in his hands, feeling himself falling asleep after two cycles of saying it, and waking with the still lethal September sun streaming through the tiny window at the top of the concrete wall across from his bed.

This night, he got up, felt for his rosary on the nightstand, and lay back down instantly, the image of his father already pleasing him. He felt his body accepting sleep more quickly tonight as his fingers passed the beads. He felt the storm diminishing and heard the sounds fading, and finally God granted him sleep.

The next morning, he laughed as it took a few seconds to unwind the chain that by now had twisted around his fingers and hand. He got up, opened the cheap curtain onto a desert street that was incompetently doubling as a city street, and walked out into the brothel's former barroom.

The rat that greeted him was bigger than his size 14 feet, he was certain, because it darted out and immediately sat atop his left foot. He felt it try to nose up his pants leg, but the bugger was too big to squeeze in.

He kicked it, and he would swear from that day forward that the rat paused, looked at him with disdain, then pranced over to a hole in the cabinet under the sink, and disappeared.

Father John Wanaurny, his new housemate who had been put in charge of reviving a tinier chapel a few minutes up the road in Anapra from the more central and larger church that Kevin was attempting to resurrect, stood laughing at him. He had been watching the whole spectacle, Kevin realized, and looked like he had slept just as poorly as Kevin had. Their superior in the Columban order, based in Ireland, had sent them to Anapra to bolster the work of Father Billy Morton, another Columban missionary who had moved to Anapra in 1996 to build houses for the poor and assist the diocesan priest in the adjacent colonia of San Marcos. Indeed, they had come not so much to reinforce Billy's work but to formalize it. Kevin was to rebuild the parish of Corpus Christi and repopulate it with Anaprans who were being recruited heavily by all sorts of American evangelical churches setting up shop here; John was to rebuild the tiny chapel up the road as part of the comprehensive effort to geographically and spiritually reassert a church that many residents here in Rancho Anapra saw as either too corrupt or too cowardly to minister to them.

Kevin and John stood there shaking their heads at one another. John was in his late 60s, drank tall beers, ate a bowl of ice cream at lunch and at dinner, and, legend had it, still weighed the same as he did when he entered the Columban order forty years prior.

"Bloody hell," Kevin said.

"Indeed," John said, his Chicago guttural, an odd counterpoint to Kevin's Aussie brogue. "Morning has broken. They don't make nooses big enough to get around that bugger's neck."

Kevin went back into his room, nearly lunging for the rosary again to calm his nerves, but then decided, at the last second, on a cigarette instead. Cigarettes in the daytime; rosaries at night.

◈ ◈ ◈

HE HAD GROWN TO LET HIMSELF LOVE HIS ROOMS, RATHER THAN HIS HOMES. The spaces into which he retreated during his missionary's life had become, for him, a sort of captain's cabin, a retreat from the hurly-burly of life above deck. The surrounding structure's location did not matter, nor its exterior architecture, nor its kitchen, living area, or view. But the lighting, mementoes, and the one comfortable chair, that perfect reading chair, became a soothing antidote to his rootlessness.

But here, where? The one chair in his bedroom, straight-backed and made of cheap, creaky wood, prohibited comfortable reading of the *Economist* and the local rag. Pacing his concrete floor, rats and drunken ghosts rambling about, all he could think of was how to find that perfect chair and lamp.

He walked back into the kitchen for more coffee and looked out the window above the sink. There were no sidewalks here. When the trucks and cars rumbled past, he could see their exhaust shoot into the room through the window. Sometimes he felt he could reach into a passing car and pluck someone's Coca-Cola.

He lit a cigarette, having learned long ago that a smoke fostered irony, the key to a missionary's survival. The chair, the chair. He needed to find a flea market or two, sit in a few, find the one chair that would at least make this place adequate to read—maybe even the Bible a bit, too—all the while sucking on a rum. That one luxury of a comfortable chair in which to drink and read.

Then he stopped. What are you doing? You have been awake for half an hour on your whatever-it-is day in the desert, and all you have done is think of yourself, your own needs. A smoke— yes, you're entitled to think of that first thing in the morning, that and its accompanying cup of coffee. But come on, mate, the chair. Forget about the chair for a while. Get on out there and do your work; you'll find a bloody chair soon enough.

There was no one in the streets as he walked to Corpus Christi this morning, only dogs. Indeed, a stray dog had already bitten John in the fanny the day before as it chased him down the street, and he had to get antibiotics or a tetanus shot or whatever

the hell it was the local doctor at the closest clinic had insisted
he take. He felt for a moment like the town was playing a trick
on him. Then he passed a bodega and saw a group of men gathered around a television, watching the unending coverage of the
September 11th terrorist attacks in New York. Kevin paused to
watch men watch the footage of the planes again, each man sitting mesmerized in front of the small set. He had decided that
the fixation on the attacks around here was best explained by
the fact that few Anaprans could conceive of the idea of such
suffering across the border.

One of the men suddenly turned to him.

"Buenos días, Padre," he said.

Kevin never wore a collar—he joked that the last time he wore
one was at his ordination—and he liked to simply be called by his
first name. So, how this bloke knew he was a priest, and had ad-
dressed him as such, perhaps with slight flippancy, peeved him.

"Llámame Kevin, sólo Kevin," he said. Though he took to
"Father" well, at this moment he thought a bit of assumed familiarity might help him break the ice.

Call me Kevin, only Kevin. He walked off, looked back, and
realized the men had paid him no heed. He lit another cigarette.
I came here to Juarez for the first time two years ago and left running, he thought. I loathed it. And I still do. But I thought there
was need here. I came here because I thought I was needed. But
I'm not. I'm wandering around here like the village idiot of Anapra.
They are laughing about me when I turn my back, these chaps
watching the destruction of their favorite neighboring country.

He lit another cigarette and stood in front of Corpus Christi,
knowing he would be the only man to enter the church today.

◈ ◈ ◈

HE HAD SEEN THE MOVIE *CHINATOWN* WHEN IT FIRST CAME OUT BACK IN AUSTRALIA, and realized quickly that the history of water in Anapra put the evil that the liquid had once spawned in Los Angeles to shame. Here, despite Anapra being an inexorable extension of Juarez for the past decade, there was still no running water save for the main street on which he lived. And that was intentional. Back in the early '90s, there were legendary street battles between police and Anapran squatters who marched on downtown in their quest for water. Back then, the city fathers didn't want Anapra to exist. All the maquiladora factories had clustered in the east side of Juarez, and the city wanted immigrants from the interior of Mexico to cluster there, too. The infrastructure was better; transport to work was easier; police patrols were more effective and economical. But the city didn't understand that poor people clustered where it cost the least to live, and that was in Anapra, way out here on the western edge of the desert. Here land was free, and squatting in the Mexican desert legally turned into ownership of that piece of the Mexican desert with little ado.

Father Billy, when he wasn't helping Anaprans repair their self-made shacks or building new ones with the special adobe and straw mix he had perfected, had devoted himself to the challenge of bringing water to Anapra. Kevin loved that about Billy, how he so dexterously weaved his work around an issue at all its levels. He would be downtown one day petitioning the water company, filing charges in court, meeting with urban planners and plumbing experts. Then the next day he would be installing a waterless toilet in a home which, without one, would quickly and literally become a shithole, given the desert sand's inability to hold waste.

One morning in early October, as he walked up the steep hill toward Lomas de Poleo, the southernmost part of Anapra extending into the Chihuahuan desert, Father Kevin still marveled, as he did every morning he walked the streets, at the women carrying the big water jugs on their shoulders. There were only two water dispensaries in Anapra, and for people in Lomas, the walk to the closest one was still a good mile. How these women lugged the big jugs atop their shoulders and walked steady in the horrific sun baffled him. He followed one of the women up the final, steep hill that led into Lomas, and saw Billy's truck outside her home as she walked up to it.

Billy had masterminded and had almost single-handedly raised the financing for Anapra's waterless toilet project. And he was focusing it on Lomas, the fringe of Rancho Anapra, which itself was the fringe of Juarez. Billy loved the fringes, Kevin thought, and envied the man's single-mindedness. Billy had convinced Kevin to move to Anapra, even though, all during that three-day visit two years ago, all Kevin could think about was getting back to the greenness of the Chilean countryside. Yet Billy, and the people and their need, had haunted him so during those two intervening years that he finally capitulated. And each day now he was regretting it.

He came upon Billy on the side of the house, completing the installation of an overhead water tank that would give the woman's pack of children their first baths in a proper tub since they were born.

"Billy, I'm still cursing the day I met you," Kevin said, watching Billy begin to laugh even before he finished his sentence. Indeed, Kevin was increasingly appalled at his own inability to take root here and had begun to wonder if he had succumbed to a sales job. It had become apparent to him that very few people here had any interest at all in returning to the Catholic fold. They wanted help of the practical, not spiritual, sort. He was spending entire days alone at Corpus Christi, as was John at the chapel. They both felt like they had been assigned here in jest, or that Billy had overestimated their talents for anything beyond leading Masses and communion classes—activities he realized Anaprans considered, he had declared to John the night before, nonessential.

"You see, we've lost our sense of the practical," Billy said, turning on the water and smiling as the children inside the thin wall shouted in glee. "These kids will get hot showers, at least in the summer, and the house won't smell like feces now that they have a proper toilet, and soon, I promise you, they and others will be knocking down your door on Sundays."

Billy turned off the water, the kids shouting for more.

"Now help me gather up these tools, and we'll go next door and get you a few more parishioners," he said.

Kevin did as he said and, in the meantime, had already gotten what he had wandered up here for. Billy energized him. He energized everyone, the indomitable Billy Morton. And though he didn't have Billy's handiness with tools nor his patience for petitions and jurisprudence, Kevin resolved, whenever he was with him, to imitate, at least, the man's gumption. Today he resolved to stop questioning his coming here, once and for all, at least for a little while. He would give himself a year. If no one came, if the parish hadn't grown by then, well, then it was God's will. That was his mother's favorite expression. He could hear her saying it in her tiny kitchen back in Brisbane now, and he wished right now he shared her sort of fatalistic faith. But being around Billy made him think sometimes a man's will was almost as strong as God's, and to succeed in Anapra would require that sort of nearly sacrilegious will.

But neither man could realize yet that Anapra would find itself smack in the middle of a shift in city master planning. The city fathers, and a handful of plugged-in real estate speculators on both sides of the border, would soon spring a plan to build a maquila city out here, in the desert west; they would soon be making offers for this land in Lomas de Poleo that seemingly had no value whatsoever, and water would soon flow with generosity. Land, not water, would soon become the resource in dispute. And Lomas would get her water but would have the land pulled right out from under her.

◈ ◈ ◈

HE HAD BOUGHT HIMSELF A SEVERELY USED PICKUP TRUCK AT LEAST TO START LOOKING THE PART OF A PRACTICAL, SETTLED MAN but had a flat on his third day driving it and now another a few days later. This time the wheel started to rattle as he rode down the hill, and he knew the tire was so deflated that the metal disc was touching the road. There were tire repair shops all over the place, more like in Africa than Latin America, he thought. Flats in Chile had been relatively rare, even in the slums of Santiago, where he had ministered for six years prior to moving to Araucania. Despite the gnawing poverty in southern Chile, infrastructure was divine compared to the dirt roads of Anapra. In Chile, there was the regular pothole. Here there were what he could only call pits or desert sinkholes, tire traps that jarred his body whenever a wheel lunged into one and heaved its way out.

He stopped a few shops short of the closest tire shop to his house, steering so hard that he felt like he was dragging the car to the side of the road. He got out, and a boy jumped out in front of him from under a car parked on the side of the road.

The sun was so hot Kevin thought it would set gasoline on fire when he smelled the fumes from burning rubber clogging the air. He watched as the boy popped a tire as tall as he was off a big truck and rolled it with one finger over to the wall where a small barrel sat with steam coming out of it. The boy lit a torch under the barrel, and instantly the smell of burning rubber made Kevin start to cough. He took out his handkerchief to cover his mouth but noticed the boy, with smoke all around him, didn't even turn his head from the rubber he was burning a foot below his face. He placed the tire on a short pole, spun it, took what looked like the tool painters spackle with, and pasted rubber on the tire in several spots.

Suddenly he looked up at Kevin and smiled. The smiles of the children around here are the only flowers in Anapra, Kevin had thought several times already. They are the only beautiful thing, the only thing you stop to breathe in, in the landscape.

"¿Cómo te va, Padre?" the boy asked, still smiling.

Kevin had ceased to be surprised that everybody in Anapra seemed to know him, but he did not expect it from children.

"Bien," Kevin said, dropping his handkerchief out of solidarity with the boy. "¡Sufriendo del calor! ¿Cómo te llamas?"

"Me llamo Saúl," the boy said, popping the tire off the pole and spinning it back toward the truck.

"Tienes un flat malo, Padre," the boy said as he put the tire back on its mount.

"Sí," Kevin said. "I almost made it but..."

He pointed at his truck a half block up the road.

"Está bien, Padre," Saul said. "¡Un segundo!"

He tightened the bolts on the tire, gave the thumbs up to the fat truck driver, and stuck out his hand. The driver dropped a few pesos in Saul's hand, slapped him teasingly on the face, and got in his truck. As he pulled off, Saul watched the tire, even as the truck's exhaust shot up into his face. Then he nodded, turned to Kevin, and smiled.

"Let's go," Saul said, in prideful English, and laughed.

They walked up to the truck, where Saul got down on his knees and squirreled under it on his back. Kevin saw the deep, permanent scratches all over his legs and stomach, lines that ran up and down and crisscrossed his shirtless back, and looked away. This child's skin has lost all sensation, he thought. His skin isn't leathery, it's the texture of the rubber he slops around all day long.

In a few seconds, Saul had popped off the tire and spun it toward the stewing rubber. Kevin followed him but stopped a few feet away this time. He felt himself begin to marvel at this boy in front of him, wondering at what age he began to live this life of rubber. Smoke rose up around him, and Saul bent even closer to the tire as he pasted the hole. He nodded to himself, kept mumbling to himself.

"Ya está," he said, looking up at Kevin.

Kevin smiled and then started to laugh.

"How do you always find the hole in the tire? I couldn't see that hole!"

Saul laughed and pointed to his nose with his index finger, as if to say, I can smell the holes.

But that can't be, Kevin thought. He's playing games with me.

Saul rolled the tire back up the road to the truck and placed it back on the wheel mount.

Kevin reached into his pocket, taking out all the pesos he had, and handed them to Saul when he finished.

Saul looked at the pesos in his hand, then up at Kevin, and started to shake his head. Kevin instantly felt his blood rush. I've insulted the boy, but how could I know the going rate for repairing tires here in my new home?

"Lo siento, Saul, I will bring you more tomorrow."

"No, no, no, Padre, toma," Saul said.

Kevin could tell the boy struggled with mathematics, for he was counting out loud and very slowly, his brain's gears grinding. Then he handed back to Kevin half the pesos he had given him.

"Un descuento para el Padre Kevin," Saul said.

Kevin stepped closer to him.

"No, no, una propina, a tip!" Kevin insisted, handing the pesos back to him. But Saul kept his hands at his sides, shaking his head exaggeratedly and smiling.

"¡Trabajas para Dios, Padre, no te puedo cobrar tanto!" he said, laughing and walking up to another big truck that had pulled up. You work for God, Father, I can't charge you that much! Kevin repeated the line to himself, marveling even more at the boy.

He turned and watched Saul studying a tire on the truck, the driver beside him. Was this boy mocking him, repeating a line his father might have had said about Kevin as he passed by one day? Was he capable of irony at this age? He couldn't have been serious, that line about working for God! Why do I feel like everyone here, even this child, speaks to me with irony?

Next time I will call him Paul and see if he gets it, Kevin thought. Pablo. A little irony right back at you. He hopped back into his truck, sat there marveling some more, and then started the old, grumpy engine. He pulled out and drove down the road, feeling like he was riding higher, sturdier, though with one eye out for the broken bottles that lay shining in the sunlight, keeping Saul's father in business as much as the scores of potholes that rattled Kevin's innards. He didn't realize it yet, but young, smiling Saul would gradually become a constant for Kevin here, and a flat tire would become an opportunity to spend time with a Mexican boy who would fortify him much as the Rosary did, as much as Billy could.

◈ ◈ ◈

HE AND JOHN HAD SPENT SEVERAL MONTHS TIDYING THE CHAPEL up the hill toward Lomas from Corpus Christi, Kevin's church, the main church down near the main road leading downtown. The bishop of Juarez had granted the Columbans both buildings from the diocese in exchange for their setting up shop there. Corpus Christi had been merely a satellite for the church in the adjacent, more established, and politically accepted San Marcos colonia. But Anapra, really just a collection of immigrants from the Mexican interior squatting in the desert, was now growing by the day, shack by shack. Its residents didn't mind the two-hour bus ride to maquilas on the other side of Juarez; they didn't mind the lack of water and services and roads; Anapra was cheap, booming, and chaotic.

But Kevin and John's arrival here, on the heels of Father Billy's missionary work, was not solely about ministering to capitalism's poorest workers. The bishop of Juarez, and any other score-keepers following the competition for these souls among greater Christianity's varied sects, churches, affiliations, and cults, knew that Juarez was one of the global centers for competitive salvation. Big dollars from Dallas Pentecostals, the Assembly of God, the Jehovah's Witnesses, and the Mormons were being spent on Anapra's hyped-up religious marketplace. The Catholics were losing here, and losing big. Kevin was aggressively heedless to the gamesmanship but knew he had been recruited into the business of salvation, feeling just like a taco vendor or bus driver must feel about his cutthroat subsector of the global economy catering to the maquila workers moving here in droves.

Indeed, the clash of churches fit right in among the defining events and experiences of his first few months in Juarez. Be it the burning of religious relics in front of Corpus Christi by members of the aggressive evangelical group called Assembly of God or his being called Satan by several evangelicals whenever he passed them in the street, his counterparts were always eager to offer both menace and disdain.

Fall, and its loyalty to the summer heat, started to feel interminable, a cruel misnomer for the interminable desert season. Kevin nightly held debates with John about leaving the front window open to get some air into his bedroom at night, but, with no bars blocking it yet, any old brothel-goer and his brother, not knowing the former brothel was now a priests' residence, could climb in at night and confuse him for Carmelita.

And that is what happened one belatedly hot night in November. In a deep sleep, still a rare condition these days, he suddenly was awakened by the sound of a hand banging against the inside wall. He sat straight up and for a moment paused to cherish the sweet coolness of the air. But then he saw an arm sticking through the window. He quickly realized the arm was the fumbling, lolling arm of a drunken man. But then he recalled that a drunken man, be it an Aussie or a Mexican, tended to be a dangerous man at these hours and in these places. He got up and tried to remember where he had left the hammer he had been using to hang a crucifix and a couple of paintings the day before.

Suddenly he heard the intruder curse and keep cursing while another fellow, no doubt his tequila buddy, kept shouting at him.

Then Kevin found his flashlight and shined it on them. But as soon as Kevin tried to focus the flashlight, he heard them stumble off, still cursing, deep into the Juarez night.

Kevin walked over and inspected the wall. Handprints. The concrete walls had been roughly painted white and were now detailed with dusty handprints around the window.

If God could only conjure the allure of women, he thought to himself, we'd be packing every church in the world like Pentecostals.

He walked around in circles for a bit, relishing the cooler air coming in through the window. The handyman who was supposed to put bars in front of the windows had disappeared, his third handyman to do so already.

Go back to bed? He sat on the bed and looked up at the window. He pushed the alarm clock light. 4 AM. The window looked northeast, and he knew he would not be able to fall asleep again before the desert sun revealed to all the passersby Anapra's new snoring, sweaty priest sprawled atop his cot in his underwear.

A glass of rum to calm the nerves? He had to put in a long day at his forlorn parish building and considered himself to be sufficiently in control of his fondness for rum such that a 4 AM snip would do no one any good.

He got up and decided to go out back and climb the ladder to the roof. He had not been up above yet, really had not dared since the first handyman had suggested that the brothel's services had included a rooftop bar and dance floor for romance under the stars.

He changed into his slacks and a T-shirt, brushed his teeth with bottled water, and walked out back. First, a cigarette. He had considered himself a controlled smoker, too, but Juarez was undermining that sense of himself already. He inhaled deeply several times, burning through the cigarette in a couple of minutes. Onward, he said to himself.

The ladder had been built into the wall, but each step was rusting, so as he climbed up he kept telling himself the fall would not be far. As he reached the roof and peered above the precipice, he saw the moonlight bouncing off a shiny parquet floor.

Here they danced, he thought. He swung his legs over the edge and stood up. He saw their ghosts, imagined a mariachi band in the corner. He walked over to the bar. Where is a good bartender when you need one? he thought. Maybe I'll keep this place and ask the superior for an entertainment budget.

He turned and looked out over his new parish. Lima, he thought. Lima, Peru. The consensus among priests who rotated through the various poverty postings in Latin America was that God had left Lima for Satan to keep. Lima was the dirtiest, the poorest, the most soul-breaking place to try to minister. The old joke: the inscription on the gate leading into Lima read "Through me you go into the city of woe." Lima was the one place even the most ardent, devout missionaries lamented being assigned to.

While studying Spanish and working with the poor in Bolivia when he was 24 years old, Kevin had once gone to Lima to visit a Columban friend who had drawn the spiritual short straw and had been assigned there. He swore he would never go back, not even if God appeared to him and demanded it. And now here was his fate, his punishment for swearing off a whole city and its people.

Lima had found her match. Kevin kept his eyes on the black mountain peaks in the distance of the Chihuahua desert and thought of the snow-capped volcanic peaks where he had lived in the region of Araucania in southern Chile.

Why, he asked himself fundamentally for the first time since he had arrived, am I here? Why didn't I listen to the voice that told me never to come here again? Was it Billy's persistence? My admiration for the way Billy was fighting for the poorest of the poor, the most buggered of the buggered?

He had eaten something infected with God's brilliant bacteria when he had arrived in Bolivia for Spanish language immersion in 1979. He had had dysentery on and off for roughly three years thereafter in Chile, spending many a night alone sitting atop a toilet. And then, even then, he had never questioned what he was doing with his life. But here tonight, on a dance floor above a roach-infested brothel that at last had some ventilation at night now, he was longing to be somewhere else again. Nowhere in particular this time, and that made it even worse. Not Chile; not Brisbane; not Buenos Aires. Just elsewhere. He was already breaking his vow to not question his plight for a year, to emulate Billy, to fight.

He looked down toward his little parish, the words of the bishop echoing in his head.

"The Catholics have retreated from Anapra," the bishop had told his superior. "So we welcome your services there. But go in with your eyes wide open."

Billy had been the sole presence here for a reason, he thought, an unofficial one with no church to fly the flag from. That was just because Billy was steadfast enough to be the last of the true missionaries, to be willing to go where no one else would go. Maybe Billy was just tougher, in addition to being, by nature and talent, a solo operator, a lone wolf. Maybe I, Kevin thought, am not as tough as I had fancied myself. But this is the first time I have ever felt so lonesome in this work.

◈ ◈ ◈

HE HAD ENTERED THE COLUMBAN ORDER BECAUSE HE HAD BEEN, WELL, A BIT OF A HELL-RAISER. He was sixteen, a borderline juvenile delinquent grappling with the reality that he had been put up for adoption by a mother who was little more than sixteen herself. One night he was on a camping trip in the bush, as they used to say, with his friends and their fathers. One of the father's friends, a Columban priest from Brisbane, had joined the men. Kevin noticed how quickly the priest and his father hit it off, how the Columban, not wearing a collar, seemed just like a judge or a doctor or an insurance salesman. The men sat round the fire drinking, while the boys played hide-and-seek in the bush. The nerve got into them to steal a few beers, and as it was Kevin's turn to shuttle back near the fire for more, he crawled up to the supplies right under the men's noses. Just as he had grasped several beers in his hands, a man clobbered him and pinned him to the ground.

"Where you going with those, mate?" the priest said, his boot pressing into Kevin's chest.

Then the priest started to laugh, helped Kevin up, and nudged him off to his friends, beers in hand. He instantly took a liking to the rugged Columban, a man who had simultaneously instilled the fear of God in him, then showed him that such fear was mightily exaggerated, even comical.

That man's style, Kevin would realize, was the Columban style—rebellious, cranky, ironic. And, during all his years in Chile, he fancied that he had lived up to it. People were drawn to him; he had fine-tuned and harnessed his charisma, leveraging it to attract and succor his flock. He had been, he thoroughly considered, a success.

Yet, in the few Mexican Masses he had been to, downtown at the cathedral of Juarez or over the hill at the parish in the San Marcos colonia, he realized, calling himself stupid for stating the obvious to himself, that Mexico was not South America or Central America. Mexico was Mexico, its own mesmerizing fiasco. Poverty was quiet, noble in Chile; here, it was raucous, loose-hipped, musical, and quicker to laugh. There it was endured; here it was shaken off. After a few months here, he realized the key to his success as a parish priest might just be the fostering of a certain liturgical raucousness.

So as Kevin stood in front of 32 people for his first official Mass in Anapra this chilly November Sunday morning, he was most aware of his own stiffness. He knew these people wanted to sing and dance, and, while he loved the idea of a more soulful and less cerebral Mass, he doubted his ability to deliver it, to keep the customers satisfied. The sudden cold spell in Juarez, for it had gone from the 90s to the 40s seemingly overnight, and the lack of heat in his new home, had his body in no mood for dancing along to the day's hymns. But he felt stiff inside, too, comparatively stiff. He had gotten used to the Chilean version of liturgical celebration—not Anglo reticent, but not Mexican uproarious, either.

And for a heavy moment, just as the 32 people were moving their plastic chairs into place in front of the altar, he found himself doubting not just in his head but, for the first time, in his heart and in his gut, whether he could deliver what these people most deeply wanted. He trusted his skills to rally souls, to minster to the dying, to feed the hungry, to help people cobble together their lives. But he did not know if he could fuel these hungry spirits, these Mexican worshippers who wanted a Mass to be a gymnastics session. He always proudly emphasized to his flock that he was an Aussie, not an American—more vitality, more sun down under. But semantics were failing him here on stage.

The room grew quiet, and it felt to him like he could touch the cold air between him, standing behind the altar, and the people in the folding chairs below him.

On the previous Sunday at this hour, he had walked the streets of Anapra to get a feel for the residents' Sunday morning rituals. The streets were packed with men and women carrying morrales, the universal Latin American striped plastic bag with straps. As he turned the corner onto the street with one of the larger evangelical parishes, he heard the beating of bass guitar: then, as he walked closer and closer, he began to feel its pulsations. I don't give a rat's ass about music, but I bloody better well get some fast, he thought. The service, he knew, had begun at 9 o'clock, and it was now nearly eleven. At least fifty people were out front corralling their children as they ran around in the dust. He knew many of them knew who he was, so he didn't dare step inside the courtyard.

But then he did dare. He went to reach for a cigarette to get up the nerve, realized that would be disrespectful, so just pulled up his collar a tad and walked right up to the entrance.

He saw what must have been two hundred people seemingly controlled by the electric-bass player. The guy was about as tall as his instrument, yet whenever he would point it leftward to emphasize a note, the parish would all sway leftward, and as he would come around to the right, they would follow. The drummer, Kevin realized, was being so drowned out by the bass player that you had to enter the building itself to even realize there was a drummer on stage, too.

On stage. That was the difference, he said to himself. They've got a rock 'n' roll show here, a damn concert, and we're stuck singing poorly translated ditties about eagles' wings.

This morning at his own first Mass, he began with the Sign of the Cross, and as he lifted his right hand up, then down, then left, then right, he took pity on these poor souls about to spend a cold, hard hour with a stiff Aussie Anglo at their helm. He had decided at the age of 17 to become a priest, in response to George Harrison's concert for Bangladesh, the 1970's anteced-ent to 1985's Live Aid. The images of the devastating floods in Bangladesh, on top of the massive killings there, had mesmer-ized him, but so, too, had the way music mobilized to aid and console people. Missionaries and musicians alike were inter-viewed on television, people who spoke about devoting their lives to helping the poor as if the decision were as simple as going off to law school, and he was hooked. He remembered his father's Columban friend from the campfire, he inquired on how to join the Columbans, and his future life as a servant of the poor, and the objective of becoming a bit of a rock star to boot, was instantly in the works. Musically, he knew he was no George Harrison; he couldn't carry even The Beatles' simplest melody. But he had never imagined that being like Harrison here and now, with these people in front of him obviously craving a man who valued rhythm and melody, might just be the key to being a successful missionary thirty some years later in Juarez.

◈ ◈ ◈

HE HAD ALWAYS RESISTED THE URGE TO COMPARE—him-self, peoples, homiletic styles, brands of rum—seeing it as an inevitable symptom of dissatisfaction. But he did make excep-tions for sons of bitches and suffering. The worst sons of bitches had until this day been the enforcers who carried out Pinochet's reign of terror on the streets of Santiago. The worst suffering, oddly, had been a man in the emergency room in Chicago dying of malnutrition. He had been sent to Chicago for one year in 1984 by his superior to improve his pastoral skills.

His superior knew what he was doing in assigning him to an inner-city hospital in Chicago for a year. There he submitted to a forced immersion into death and suffering and acquired a priest's singular obligation to console in their midst. He had seen chests blown open by high caliber bullets, throats slit, bodies turned into their parts by car crashes, and yet the worst was this old black guy one subzero night whom an ambulance driver had spotted lying under the drifting snow on a street corner near the hospital.

The words of the Irish doctor were: "You're an Aussie, Father, but all you are Irish at the end of the day, right? Remember the hunger strikers in Northern Ireland? Bobby Sands and those boys? This is what their dying was like."

Their dying, not their deaths. He wondered, and still would wonder, at the doctor's word choice. The instantaneity of death versus its prolongation seemed at the root of his point. He almost detected an admiration for what used to be called The Passion, that long, slow climb up the hill.

He had tried for months to improve the musical component of his Masses and had formed a raggedy band to play on Sundays, but by spring the parish had only grown to fifty people or so. He was adjusting to the noise and dust but not to his sense of failure. This early spring Saturday he climbed back up on the roof to survey the lives of his absent flock. Attendance wasn't increasing; he wasn't connecting. The Rio Grande River—the absurdity of the sickly trickle of a river between Juarez and El Paso—was mocking him. The highway, not the fence and most definitely not the river, was the real demarcation between Mexico and America, but how easy it would be for all these people on this side, he thought, to rise up and en masse cross that highway and

squat down on the streets of those people on the other side—
disrupt their orderliness, their safety, occupy every table at every
Whataburger on the West Side and the East Side of El Paso.

It was not so much the fact of the distinctness of two cities
and the way they embodied two countries, but rather the universal acceptance of their physical separateness, that amazed him.

The bishop had said to him, with that dubious tone, "Go out
and set up shop in Anapra; there are no Catholics out there anymore."

He knew many people who would lament coming up with an
apt, pithy retort a day after a provocation or challenge. But Kevin
had always prized himself on his quick-wittedness. Retorts, well,
he thrived at them, often amazed himself with his own mental
nimbleness.

"We'll find some," he said back, his bravado making the bishop snap his head back and smile slightly.

But, after six months' worth of Masses with a handful of
attendees, he kept hearing the bishop's assessment of Anapra
more and more often in his head. There weren't any here simply
because they were disinterested. The evangelicals were giving
them food, building them houses, bribing them for their souls,
or at least their attendance, and that was good enough. Billy was
right, this was a *quid pro quo* world, and without food or toilets
or houses you've got no flock. No one really seemed to need a
pastor; no one seemed to really want hard-core spiritual help.
They wanted gifts, or, as Billy put it, practical assistance. The gift
of the word of God satisfied few needs.

He went back downstairs and picked up the morning paper
that John had left on the kitchen table. He was trying not to
admire the daily half-naked girl right there on Page 1 when a
woman started banging at his door.

"¡Padre!" she shrieked. "¡Padre!"

He knew that shriek, not from this particular woman but its

universal pitch and desperation. There was, in it, a culturally transcendent sound. Something had happened to a child.

He threw the paper down, rushed to the door, and opened it to see a woman he had passed on the street leading from his house to the church several times now.

"Padre, please come!" she said through her choking on tears, and grabbed his hand and pulled him so hard he could not even close the front door. He tugged back, pulled loose, and ran back inside for the vial of holy oil and what he called his little black book—the book of sacramental rituals that had instructions for how to handle just about every type and level of dying and death that humans could encounter.

She ran, and he ran behind her, in the direction of the church, and even though he knew he was going to give last rites to a very sick child, perhaps to a dying child, for a moment he felt needed, he felt the old rush of being needed and of being about to minister. He caught himself, as he did more and more often when his vanity jumped out of the bushes, and slowed for a moment. The woman pulled ahead of him, but suddenly the street and passersby came into an intensely clear focus.

She stopped ahead of him, at a house a couple of hundred feet before the parish and on the other side of the street. Then she fell on the ground. He ran faster now and saw other women flailing on the ground, and a few men shouting and weeping and twisting in circles in the street.

He came upon them and first saw the blood on the front tire of the car. Then he saw the boy's brains smeared on the road in front of the tire, his head now merely a bulb on the top of his torso.

Everyone stopped, frozen in their grief, and looked at him. He slowly swiveled his head, making eye contact with each of them. Then he momentarily closed his eyes as he bent down over the boy.

Thank God for Chicago, he thought. He had seen enough of

human insides at the hospital there to stomach it. But brains—
he had glimpsed them but always through the semblance of a
skull, through a bullet hole, never outside their container.

He touched the boy's wrist. He was still warm; his soul was
still lingering. Perhaps, he thought, that's what his family members were trying to catch, swinging their arms all around.

He reached into his pocket and took out the vial of holy oil.
One time at the hospital, as what seemed like a baker's dozen
of doctors and nurses were trying to resuscitate a patient in the
ER, he anointed the dying man's toes. Got the call that he was
Catholic, rushed into the room, saw no room for God at the mo-
ment, but then spotted the fellow's foot sticking out right at him.

"Improvisation is everything, Father," a nurse had turned and
said to him without even making eye contact.

He opened his eyes and studied the boy's head. There was a
little piece of forehead left, bloodless and brown and somehow
still boyish. He dipped the vial upside down onto his thumb,
then reached down and rubbed the oil on the spot.

He felt everyone gather in closer; a few people fell on their
knees. He put the vial back in his pocket, lifted up the book, and
his fingers knew exactly the page to go to for the blessing of the
recently deceased. But this was in English, this book. He had
been meaning to get a copy in Spanish from the archdiocese, but
the house and all its headaches had forced him to keep postpon-
ing his trip downtown. And now it was too late.

He lifted up the book and for the first time lifted up his eyes.
Everyone was locked in on him, needing him. Here are my parishioners, he found himself thinking. We just needed a bloody
catastrophe to bring them out of the woodwork.

He cleared his throat and tried to summon his Spanish brain,
sloppily translating as he read: "Blessed be the God and Father
of our Lord Jesus Christ, the Father of compassion and God of
all encouragement, who encourages us in our every affliction, so

that we may be able to encourage those who are in any affliction
with the encouragement with which we ourselves are encouraged by God. For as Christ's sufferings overflow to us, so through
Christ does our encouragement also overflow. If we are afflicted,
it is for your encouragement and salvation; if we are encouraged,
it is for your encouragement, which enables you to endure the
same sufferings that we suffer. Our hope for you is firm, for we
know that as you share in the sufferings, you also share in the
encouragement."

He made the sign of the cross and looked at the boy's family
again. They were calmer now, looking at him not as much with
that please-do-something face as with bewilderment. He wondered why. Are they wondering where his soul is, like I am? Are
they wondering how the hell I got into this line of work?

He stood. A man behind him started weeping again. Kevin
turned. The man started hitting himself on the head and fell
backward onto the street. Kevin wanted to figure out who the
boy's mother was, but the man's grief was so catastrophic that
he walked toward him first.

Suddenly a young woman crawled over to him.

"Tío, Tío, no, no, no es tu culpa," she said, tears coming down
her cheeks. This was her. Perhaps still a teenager, Kevin thought.
And she is thinking about her uncle, her tío, trying to keep him
from going over the edge.

Kevin stopped, raised his right hand, and blessed them. As
he did, the mother looked up at him, her eyes dreamy but her
arms clinging to her uncle. He froze on them for a second. The
God of all encouragement, he repeated to himself, the God of
all encouragement.

The mother suddenly focused, returned to this world, and
let go of her uncle. The man was calmer, dazed but somehow
present again, too.

The mother stood up, stepped toward him, and hugged him.

In the background, he could hear the sirens, still far but coming ever closer. He could feel her fingers in the backs of his ribs, almost trying to stick themselves into the ridges between them.

He hugged back. The closer and closer the sirens came, the tighter he hugged her. When the ambulance pulled up, he thought she was about to burst him, but he kept matching her, tighter and tighter until the silencing of the ambulance signaled for them to release. She looked up at him.

"God bless you," he said, quickly realizing he had said it first in English. "Que Dios te bendiga."

"Gracias, Padre," she said.

As the ambulance crew asked for the next of kin, she turned, stood taller, and raised her hand as if she were still the schoolgirl she not long ago still was. And all he could think was how she had made him feel, at last, needed here, and how grateful he was to her for her faith, or her need, or both if she possessed them. But probably just her need.

That night he sat with John recounting the day, a glass of rum in his hand as he watched John eat his dish of ice cream.

"And you know what, John?" he said. "In spite of it all, today was the first day I felt needed here. In Chile I felt needed ten times a day. This was the first time in all of my eight months in Anapra."

"We'll break through," John said. "People here talk. They'll know what you did today. We'll break through."

But Kevin, despite the paradoxical, almost diabolical uplift that the tragedy had given him as a minister, still doubted it. He didn't want any more tragedies like today. But like an actor, he said to himself, I needed my one big break. God bless that poor boy, he thought, and God bless his beautiful mother, but maybe they gave it to me. Maybe now word will spread and people will realize; maybe now they will open their hearts to me a little bit more.

◈ ◈ ◈

MANY DAYS, WHEN HE WAS THE ONLY ONE AT CORPUS CHRISTI, he would stand in the chapel's courtyard and marvel at the traffic coming in and out of the house about 60 meters from the chapel in a diagonal line across Remora Cangrejo Street. It was spring now, and after months of observing, it had become clear to him that his neighbor, an attractive woman in her late 40s, ran a drug den, and he marveled at the openness of it. Its openness is its perfect camouflage, he thought. In Chile, or in Chicago, buyers and dealers made an effort to be clandestine. There was a pretense of the rule of law. Here, the coppers themselves pulled up, walked in smiling, and walked out with their baggies a few minutes later.

She's doing better than the Pentecostals, he would joke to himself; then he'd wonder how he could ever compete with both the free food and free houses of the evangelical churches and then the drug entrepreneurs anesthetizing the half of Anapra that wasn't going the hard-core fundamentalist route.

At the end of each day, as the desert sun was setting on the house, the traffic inevitably would slow, and a woman with long black hair would inevitably emerge. After a few days of his standing there watching her, she finally caught him and waved. Not a cordial wave, or a reactive one, but a full-on, neighborly wave with her arm extended above her head and her hand moving back and forth.

Her assumption of familiarity unnerved him. The omnipresence of junkies here was worse than the worst crack barrios he had seen in Chicago. He had heard people in the street always calling out to one chap who was so skinny that Kevin thought he had eliminated all the muscle and fat from his body and kept just the bones.

"¡Roche! ¡Roche!" men would shout, and the fellow would

stumble to a stop, struggle to summon a toothless smile, and stagger onward.

It took Kevin a week to realize they called him Roche after the Swiss pharmaceutical company that ran a massive maquiladora on the other side of Juarez. Then, a few days after that, he realized there were various men called Roche, and someone explained to him that workers smuggled pharmaceuticals out of the plant and sold them on the black market. And this woman with the long black hair, he assumed, was somehow in the middle of the transactions.

A few more days, and a few more waves, and then one day she waved and came walking toward him.

"Hola, Padre Kevin," she said as she was halfway across the diagonal path from her house to the church.

"Hola," he said, his legs carrying him toward her in the street, he would realize later, because some silly impulse in him had directed him to keep her off the church grounds.

"Welcome to our street," she said, extending her hand. "It is great to see the chapel coming to life again. I was worried God had abandoned Anapra."

"Well, not God," Kevin said, chuckling. "Just the Catholics."

She laughed, too, throwing her head back, and a foot from her now, he realized that she was surely drug-free and entirely beautiful.

"You get a lot of visitors over there," Kevin said. "I am envious. Still struggling to reclaim a few souls, you know."

"You're in the wrong line of work, Father," she said. "Me llamo Lisha."

"Lisha!" Kevin said, repeating the name with exclamation as he almost always did when he met someone for the first time. "Me llamo Kevin."

"Sí, lo sé, lo sabemos," Lisha said. "Father Kevin."

Then she said nothing, and he stood there not knowing what in God's name to say himself.

"Why don't you join us on Sunday?" he said. He didn't know where it came from but reckoned she'd fit right in there with the tax collector and prostitute imagery of the Bible.

"Father, I wouldn't set foot in a church," Lisha said, her matter-of-factness, coupled with her beauty, now uncannily beguiling Kevin.

"But I need to ask you," Lisha said, "you see, my mother is old and sick. Not deathly sick, but bedridden and, well, you know, angry. She has diabetes. They have removed both her feet. Her lungs, she gasps for air merely shimmying herself out of bed and into her wheelchair. She watches you out her bedroom window. It's the one right there in the corner of the house. And we wonder if you would perhaps come and give her the Eucharist once a week. She is devout, Father, and takes such joy in watching you try to bring this place back to life."

He looked at her, looked over at the house, and instantly imagined the sight of himself walking up to the house with every skinny and toothless junkie in town.

"I, ah, I am not sure how that might be seen," Kevin said. "I haven't been here long, but I realized quickly that Mexicans, well, word spreads quickly."

Lisha laughed and followed his eyes to her house.

"Father, I am protected, and you will be, too," she said, this time her face assuming a commanding gesture that he assumed explained her success in her line of work. "We will see you tomorrow? At lunchtime?"

"Well, yes, but let's make a deal," Kevin said, the challenge bringing out the Aussie in him. "I come, and you come on Sundays."

Lisha stared coldly at him, unblinking, and started to walk back toward her house, just as a cop car pulled up.

She stopped a few feet away and turned like a dancer.

"I will tell my mother she will see you tomorrow at lunchtime," she said. "How happy your visit will make her."

◈ ◈ ◈

THE NEXT MORNING HE MET A BUILDER AT THE CHAPEL TO TALK ABOUT ITS EXPANSION POSSIBILITIES. He had decided to convert to the build-it-and-they-will-come school of pastoring. It felt like it had taken him and John until now simply to clean the place out, to get their spiritual bearings, and he now wanted to make some sort of declaration, however absurd, if he could find the money to do so. Surely the locals would see how Billy had legitimized the Catholic Church again; surely the weather would bring them out, warm them up to their old faith.

But the whole while the architect and builder walked him through the various possibilities for extending walls and shifting the altar area and installing permanent seating, he kept peeking across the street. If one gossipy soul saw him go in and out of there, would Anapra think its new priest had already turned to drugs? Ministering to the sinners, he thought, was all well and good, but the practical consequence of the stuff...even Jesus seemed to stumble into them on the street, not go walking into the opium dens or whatever the pharmacological equivalent was when Jesus walked the earth.

Lunchtime came and he said good-bye to the builder. He walked over to the sacristy and took out a few communion hosts in case another crackhead might stumble into the house seeking some nourishment.

It had not occurred to him that lunchtime might be the busiest time of day for his neighbor. The night-shift workers at the maquilas had woken up from their morning naps by now; construction workers were on their break; young mothers had succumbed to the itch to get out of the house. So as he walked the diagonal line, he saw a dozen cars parked on the street, a cop car included.

A few people were standing outside, taking a break from their baking and smoking inside, he realized. He walked up to the door and a man nodded and pushed it open for him—it hadn't even been completely shut.

When he walked in, Lisha was standing right in front of him waiting.

"Buenos días, Padre Kevin," she said, as if she were welcoming him to her trinket shop or luncheonette, he thought. Her lack of shame startled him again, and he knew she could tell he was unnerved.

"Welcome to *my* church." She said it. To cut the tension? To mock him? Sincerely? He wondered whether he was walking into a trap. She had bought off the cops with free drugs, now she was exploiting his sense of duty? Tricking him? Implicating him so that any neighbor who might risk their lives by insisting on the absurdity of a drug den operating so openly with children around would reconsider?

For the first time since he had arrived, he felt scared. Not at any imminent danger but at how bloody tricky life here could be for an outsider. At how, with almost any interaction, he was stepping into a web of shadowy commerce and tricky evil, smaller devils hiding behind corners of shacks.

"Where is your mother?" he asked, for the first time doubting whether the woman even existed.

Lisha motioned for him to follow, and he stepped over the legs of a few junkies sprawled on the floor and followed her down a hallway. She turned and looked at him again as she put her hand on the door knob. Her face was different now, softer, less confrontational. He walked into the bedroom behind her and smelled old age.

Dickens, he thought. My own version of *Great Expectations*. It's come to this. The woman was propped up on pillows, her bandaged feet sticking out from under a couple of rumpled sheets.

"Padre," the woman said, and as soon as Lisha knew her mother was awake, she exited.

"Padre," she repeated. "How long it has been. How long it has been. Thank you for coming. They treat me like a leper here. No one would come, no one would ever come. Thank you. Thank God."

The woman's face was round and chubby, so unlike her daughter's angular, thin cheeks and jowl.

"Your daughter must look more like your husband," Kevin said, chuckling, and the woman laughed, raised her hand, and dropped it, as if to say, that cabrón, I think of him every time I look at her.

"I am ready," she said.

For a moment he had forgotten that he had not come merely for a visit.

"Ah, sí, sí," he said. He took the host out of the little bag.

He blessed her and lifted the host toward her mouth. She stuck out her tongue, trembling and shockingly red. He grazed it with the bottom of his thumb as he placed the host on it. She slowly pulled her tongue back in and for over a minute slowly chewed on the wafer while she looked at the ceiling.

"Gracias, Padre," she turned and said. "I will see you next week at this time."

He wanted to ask her if she wanted to confess, too. But he realized now where the daughter had come from. These women had a way to command you, to direct you, with their eyes and heads. The mother—he decided not to even ask her name, to keep her a step removed—didn't look like the daughter, but now suddenly she did.

"Sí, next week," Kevin said. He packed his little bag, my little drug bag, he thought, and left the room. He walked down the hall, turned to walk out, and almost bumped into a cop holding a little baggy and talking with Lisha. He nodded but did not look Lisha in the eye.

"Hasta la semana que viene," he said, and as he walked out,

he didn't look either way but headed straight up the hill to make himself a sandwich. Despite the absurdity of it all, he had felt the same sort of spiritual charge as giving last rites to the boy whose uncle had run him over. Even though he didn't have Billy's practical skills to provide good services, perhaps the trick was to go out into their homes, to bring the good word to them instead of waiting for them to come to him. But he needed, he realized, an entrée, a legitimate entry point or person to give him the street cred he was trying to develop on his own. Though he didn't comprehend it yet, Kevin was already helping another woman, the curious and charismatic Rayna, who had sought the aid of Billy and Kevin when her daughter had been kidnapped. This Rayna—and soon a stocky, smiling chap named Leo who was about to befriend Kevin— would both suddenly legitimize him among Anaprans as much as his weekly foray into Lisha's drug den.

◈ ◈ ◈

ONE OF THE MOST STRIKING FACTS OF LIFE IN ANAPRA FOR HIM WAS THE NUMBER OF COUPLES WHO RESISTED MAR-RIAGE. *UNION LIBRE*, it was called, and unlike the term "civil union," its direct translation, "free union," embodied for him the crux of the problem. It was the men, he began to calculate, who wanted their union but also their "freedom," and he set out to address that as one of the first programs he established—marriage classes.

The first class that early summer night included Leo and Lydia, the couple who showed up one of the first Sundays that Kevin had opened for business and admitted to him soon after that they couldn't believe Kevin had remembered their names two Sundays later when they decided to give him another try. Leo and Lydia had been regulars at Mass since then but sat apart from the old guard—the couple of dozen holdovers from the old chapel whom Kevin was quickly realizing constituted a rather orthodox lot unfriendly to what he liked to call "liturgical innovation," namely, music and dance during Mass.

Whenever Mass ended, Lydia, tiny and calm, would practically drag Leo, pudgy and usually grinning, quickly out the door, and Kevin guessed she might be sitting there only out of dutiful convenience, not a lapsed Catholic but one frustrated by the history of this specific church yet attracted by, well, simply this church's proximity, its location. And he guessed that Leo, the fellow who smiled more than any other in Anapra, was only sitting there because Lydia made him.

At the marriage class, which Lydia had obviously dragged the poor man to, too, solely because Kevin had kept begging them to attend, Leo suddenly had stopped smiling and sat there looking at him with the look Kevin was accustomed to receive from hard men—the look that said, who is this priest to lecture me about marriage? Who is any priest to lecture me about marriage?

Kevin now considered it a global reaction, for he had seen it in Australia, America, Chile, and Bolivia. And he agreed with it. Who am I? I retreat each night to my room with my glass of rum and recuperate from the day in the tranquility of clinking ice cubes. These poor bastards have to go home after work and work all over again.

And that was the line he usually began with, self-effacing and endearing to the resistant men from the get-go.

He noticed Leo warm up slightly, as if to say, ah, this priest, at least he doesn't think he has any understanding of what my life is like...

Kevin talked, as he always did in these courses, more about the idea of sacrament in general than the sacrament of marriage in particular. He placed marriage alongside baptism and com-

munion as a way to honor God, to access God, and he watched
Leo gradually shift from peeved to tolerant to, at the end, quite
possibly interested. At least he was smiling again.

This smiling fellow could serve a purpose, Kevin thought.
The old guard of what remained of Catholic Anapra after the
onslaught of the evangelicals were an orthodox lot. They liked,
Kevin realized, the American way: a boring Mass, a stiff, distant
priest, quick services, and few programs during the week. He
needed new blood, right hands, and insurrectionists. When the
session ended, he decided to give Leo a shot. I'm coming up
on a year here, Kevin had decided, and if I don't get that entrée
soon, I might as well call the superior and tell him we've fought
the good fight.

"¿Cómo fue, Leo, no tan grave, no?" he asked, walking up to
Leo and using Leo's name aggressively.

"Bien, Padre, bien," Leo said, bemusedly, looking more at the
floor than in Kevin's eyes. And it was that gentleness, that, as
the Yanquis said, aw-shucks style, that signaled to Kevin that he
had his man.

Leo kept smiling, as if aware that he was being played.

"I need a local assistant here, Leo, part handyman, part driver, part, well, fixer," Kevin said. "You interested?"

Leo looked at the floor, still smiling.

"I can pay you," Kevin added.

"Sí, está bien, Padre Kevin," Leo said simply, extending his
right hand for Kevin to shake. And then he walked off.

But the next morning at 7:30 Kevin heard a car pull up in
front of the house. He heard someone get out of it, shut the
door, and then knock on his door. And, as he opened it, he realized that Leo was a man of few words, but a man who valued
words, too. Within two months after their handshake, stout,
smiling Leo would become that metaphorical right hand: the
first local on the payroll of the new parish of Corpus Christi;

the new daily walking companion for the suddenly less lonely parish priest from Brisbane; and, along with this woman named Rayna whom Kevin and Billy were already helping find her lost daughter, Kevin's cornerstone.

CHAPTER TWO

◇

Rayna

RAYNA HAD NOT BEEN TO CONFESSION SINCE SHE WAS A GIRL IN MEXICO CITY. The church there had no separate cubicle in which to sit. The priest simply pulled down an old black curtain hanging from a nail on a low beam in the back corner of the church and sat on one side of it while she sat on the other. Anyone who was waiting in line in the pews could hear what sin was being chronicled by anyone who could not maintain a low whisper.

As she waited in the tiny white chapel this day in Anapra, she tried to remember what she had told the old priest that day. She had not yet had two husbands, had not received compensation for sharing her body, and had not yet tried to murder the man who had tied her up and tortured her. So what did I tell him? she wondered. What was there to tell back then?

An old man walked out from the wood box, and Father Billy, who was subbing for Kevin at Corpus Christi that day, motioned to her, but at first she didn't register it because she was still trying to remember what she had confessed as a girl.

But she wasn't going to confess anything today. She had heard how insistently kind this Father Billy, Father Guillermo as the Mexicans called him, was, and how he would help anyone who asked him, how he was as close to Jesus, and as alone, as any man in Juarez. And she had decided, after weeks of deliberation, to come to seek his help. Her daughter Cristina had been missing for three weeks, and Rayna had finally confirmed that she was alive but being held in El Paso by men who trafficked women. She was not dead, nor, as Rayna had most feared, a desaparecida— one of the many missing women who were all but dead save confirmation. But when Rayna's mind went where she tried to not let it go, she feared Cristina was suffering a worse fate.

As she entered the compartment, she felt the impulse to recite a few sins—thieving at the grocery and wishing ill on a neighbor— but the sudden darkness instantly made her imagine her daughter locked in a dark, dark box even more stifling than this one.

She bit her lip, took a breath, and choked out the words in Spanish: "My daughter has been kidnapped."

She heard Father Billy sit forward in his creaky wood chair. She pushed open the door a bit with her foot, and the slightest sliver of light entered and immediately lifted her spirit.

"But I know she is not in the fields, in the desert," she said. "I know she is still alive, and everyone said you could help me. She is in El Paso. Somewhere in El Paso."

There was silence, and then she heard Billy lean even closer. "See me after confession," the voice said. "We will try to help."

She got up and walked out past the only person left, an old woman seated on a plastic chair. She looked around. She had not been in a church for years, save for funerals, and had taken only vague interest in the news that the Catholic Church was trying to reestablish itself in Anapra. For many years now, she had been simply trying to survive, a single mother whose last husband had died and who realized, or had decided, or both, that there would be no future husbands. And the church, she had calculated years ago, was worth little more than a worthless husband. But now, today, sitting here in the dusty old chapel of Corpus Christi that she would never even lift her head to acknowledge from the street, she realized this Father Billy—his calm, commanding voice making her feel suddenly stronger—might bring her back again if that were what it would take to bring her daughter back.

◈ ◈ ◈

THE POSTERS OF THE FACES OF ALL THE DISAPPEARING WOMEN IN JUAREZ HAD BEEN APPEARING FOR SEVERAL YEARS NOW on light posts and phone poles and on the sides of buildings. Rayna knew mothers who spent two week's wages on posters of their daughters. Printers were turning it into a cottage industry. She had gone to the print shop with a photo of Cristina and stood right at the door, but then she heard the confident voice of Father Billy.

"Tranquila," he had said. "Let us see what we can do."

So she refrained from spending what little money she had, saving it to feed her children. What's more, she feared she would end up putting a poster on the wall of the tiny shack she was renting, further haunting her and her children.

She could tell, each time she stopped by the chapel and saw Billy's partner, this handsome but vain Australian priest named Kevin, that they were doing something for her. They just would never tell her specifically what. They would say they were looking, that they had their sources, that she had to keep praying while they searched. Then the Australian would always suggest she come to Mass, making her feel like that was his compensation for their efforts.

One day on her way to see the australiano, she spotted a new poster of a missing girl on the fence around the corner from Corpus Christi. She had been going to wander in to let Kevin know she was going to keep after him and Billy. But she stopped in her tracks when she saw the new poster. The girl looked about sixteen. She was smiling, and a man's arm was wrapped around her—his hairy arm was the only part of him in the photo—but it was enough to unnerve Rayna to her core. She shuddered. She knew that arm. She had felt that arm around her own shoulders. It was half hug and half threat, always a little too tight along her collarbone. In the photo, the arm got cut off at the wrist, and she wondered if this man cupped this girl's breast like her husband used to do.

Cristina had had no boyfriend, so the usual culprit was not even available to accuse. Rayna knew the day Cristina came home from school with her eyes big and red that she had tried drugs for the first time, but as a mother she knew that, even at fifteen or younger here when girls started, or were forced to start, Cristina still had never been with a man. Until now, she lamented, until now. Her fear was that men were doing to her daughter what her husband had done to her when he had beaten her when Rayna had simply smiled at a neighborhood man who passed them in the street. But if these men were beating Cristina, it was worse, because they were strangers. Husbands and boyfriends didn't kill their wives and girlfriends; they only beat them and tortured them mentally and occasionally physically. Strangers were the killers, and Cristina was with strangers.

Rayna kept staring at that arm around the girl; then she turned around. She couldn't face the australiano today, couldn't summon the falseness it took for her to pretend she was going to church to pray. She walked home, seeing Cristina's face instead of that girl's the whole way home, seeing that arm around Cristina but then suddenly seeing it tighten around her neck, starting to strangle her.

◈ ◈ ◈

CRISTINA HAD BEEN THE WILD ONE; CLARA NEVER STRAYED, NOR DID ELLIE; Claudia, with her prosthetic left leg, couldn't stray even if she had wanted to, which she didn't. Rayna vehemently loved them all and saw bits of herself in all four of her daughters and even in her only son, but she saw most of herself in Cristina, saw the wildness.

This evening she sat at home with Claudia and young Rodolfo on a tiny torn sofa. She had barely made rent today, cobbling pesos from random cleaning jobs downtown.

She watched as Claudia limped into the shack from the outhouse. The government had given her a new prosthetic left leg, and her walking had improved significantly. And so had her smile. Rayna smiled back at Claudia and motioned for her to sit next to her. Her youngest daughter, Claudia barely survived multiple birth defects and now, at 12, was finally developing the self-confidence Rayna had wished, and occasionally prayed, for. Rayna lifted up her blanket and Claudia snuggled up to her, wrapping it around all of her body except her leg, which she stuck out and admired.

They dozed, Rayna only lightly, for she was troubled by a thought that had been coming to her more and more recently: if only Cristina had been born like Claudia, that would have protected her. They were raping and killing the pretty girls and the prostitutes, and no man would ever pay for Claudia, she was sure. God had given her this leg as a gift, as a shield.

Claudia was in a deep sleep now, and Rayna covered the new leg, too. She looked at her daughter's face. All three older girls were known as beauties in the barrio, but Rayna could tell Claudia was going to be beautiful, too. And then she realized she had been wrong. Men had been, and surely still will be, violent toward crippled Claudia, too. The thought crushed Rayna, pinning her against the old sofa.

Indeed, of all the cruel things men had done to Rayna, her obstetrician had done the most damage to her spirit, and the first violence to Claudia. Men had burned Rayna, slugged her, slapped her, kicked her, and worse, but this man, this médico, she thought, had tried to murder her soul. The physical actings out of men, she had come to realize, were of little consequence. A bruise could heal; a kick, a slap—she laughed at them now after receiving so many. But as she lay here with night falling, she remembered moment by moment the first assault on Claudia, and how it was an assault on both of them at once.

This médico at the hospital downtown, this cabrón, had walked into the room and looked at Claudia, this twisted, sleeping baby, as if she were vomit or shit.

He said, without even examining her: "¿Qué vida va a tener?" What sort of life is she going to have?

At first Rayna had misunderstood. At first she had thought he had said: What sort of life do you want to have for her? She had thought he wanted to discuss more surgical options, therapy, perhaps a move to a different climate.

But his gaze—disgust, repulsion—didn't change.

"This baby has no future," he had said. "You are doing a disservice to her by taking her out into the world."

Abortion was still illegal in all of Mexico, not just parts of the country, and the baby had already been born. So she was confused.

But she didn't speak. She couldn't. She thought she heard him say that the baby would probably never be able to walk with legs like that. She thought she heard him say that her life would be a disgrace, a desgracia. He surely used that word.

The next day, as her husband drove her up the road back to Anapra, she could only look at Claudia's face and feel like that médico had wanted to abort her life after birth, to kill her then and there as if he were some enforcer of which girls should leave the hospital and which should be thrown into a bin and taken out to the desert.

It was dark on the trip, and she remembered the lights from the cars going toward downtown would often seem as if they were coming straight at them when the road curved. She remembered putting her hand on the door handle and squeezing it. She pulled it ever so slightly and felt it give until it reached the point where she knew it would give way if she pulled the slightest bit harder.

And she remembered riding like that for five minutes, knowing she could decide at any second to jump out of the car into oncoming traffic and fulfill this doctor's wishes—put this child out of its assured misery and escape from men once and for all herself.

Her husband stopped at a light. He had said nothing to the doctor, and that had at first infuriated, and then crushed, Rayna even more. He had thought the same thing as the doctor, Rayna was sure. The traffic began to line up going the other way. But if I jump, she had thought, I want to be sure to die with her. I can't die and have her not die; that would be catastrophic for her. It will have to be at high speed, but even then, suppose I slip? Suppose I only hit the blacktop and damage her brain but only break my shoulder? Isn't it better to pour Clorox down her throat? But then it would be a murder, not a suicide.

As her husband accelerated, she suddenly saw the scene at her home as her children gathered crying, trying to understand what she had done and why she had done it. None of them knew what she had lived through for them just because she was a woman, just because she was a woman here in this place where women are valued for their services but not for their souls. How she had prayed for Claudia to be a boy so he could not be treated like this doctor had treated her.

As they came to the straightest stretch of the road where cars could go the fastest, she looked out the window. Suddenly, there were no cars coming the other way. She looked in the rearview mirror to see if cars might be coming that could crush them from behind if she jumped. Only darkness.

Then she looked out into the desert. This was one of the spots where they were finding women's bodies. She looked down at Claudia in her arms, and suddenly the good in this grew clear for her. By being born so deformed, she would certainly grow up free of men's attention, free of their desire. No one would ever want to turn her into a prostitute or rape her. She would suffer in her head but not at the hand of a Mexican man.

That consolation then, 12 years ago, was no consolation now as Claudia stirred beside her this night.

"Ven aquí, Claudia," she said, pulling the girl closer.

Claudia smiled but didn't open her eyes.

"Do you know how proud I am of you?"

Claudia smiled again, snuggling closer.

"Well, you are my gift," Rayna said once she sensed Claudia was dozing again. She had never been able to speak openly to any of them, to speak words of approval or pride. What's more, she had never been able to lie to them. Claudia was a burden, not a gift, she had thought more than once. But as she finished her declaration this time, as she longed to have Cristina back home with them, Claudia's warmth and smile and smell consoled her briefly. And Rayna wanted to drive right downtown to that doctor and tell him how terribly, terribly wrong he had been.

◈ ◈ ◈

A FEW OTHER WOMEN WERE GATHERED IN FRONT OF THE CHURCH WAITING TO APPLY FOR A JOB AS THE PARISH CLEANING LADY. Father Kevin pulled up in his pickup and waved to them all. He then hopped out, walked past them, and unlocked the church. He really thinks he is something, Rayna thought, knowing everyone is watching him.

"Qué guapo es," one woman said, and other women murmured. How handsome he is. Rayna said nothing, for she didn't like the women and didn't want to establish any sense of camaraderie with them. But she agreed in her head and heart. Kevin wore a brown scarf that he would occasionally pull up over his mouth when the dust swirled up on the site, but when it was down around his neck, Rayna thought he looked like John Wayne in a cowboy film.

"Sí, qué guapo," another woman said. I know why you want to work here, Rayna thought. You think you can seduce him.

The women all giggled as Kevin motioned them in. He clapped his hands and said something in Spanish, but all the women could do was laugh. He was as thick as two of them, his shining gray hair and wide, red face and shiny cheeks all seemingly there just to set the stage for his well-maintained, peppery mustache.

"¡Qué acento!" a third woman said, and then they all giggled again except Rayna. She knew he was from Australia, and she knew Australians spoke funny, but Australian-accented Spanish was worse than any gringo accent she had ever heard.

He smiled at them all and shook their hands, and to Rayna his hand felt the size of two. He had given her his hand a few times before—when Billy had introduced them and the time after that when, like this, she came by to politely linger and let her need be known—and each time she thought his hand felt like double the size of any Mexican man's hand she had ever shaken. He must know this, too, she thought. That is why he is always shaking everyone's hand, because it makes them feel like he is giving them both his hands at once.

Kevin motioned to each woman one by one to come speak with him. Each interview lasted a couple of minutes, and Rayna noticed Kevin bowing to each woman when they were done, each woman looking up at him and blushing, flirting, hoping that this man would bring her out of her messy life.

At last he abruptly motioned to her, and Rayna walked toward the chairs he had placed in front of the altar. He stood and extended his hand again, but this time she just nodded. Her head came up to his chest, and as she looked up at him, she looked under his sunglasses to see his eyes. They were a blue the sharpness of which she had only seen on television commercials, but, as much as she wanted to keep staring at them, the odor of cigarette smoke that he gave off kept making her nose twinge. She had to take a step back. She loathed the odor and wanted to tell him it ruined his whole Hollywood presentation.

Kevin suddenly slouched down toward her and put a hand on her shoulder.

"Please pray with me," he said.

Rayna stiffened. She hadn't prayed in years. She didn't want to pray; she didn't ever feel like praying; she didn't believe in prayer anymore. But if I say no, she thought, would he stop wanting to help me? I must say yes, he expects me to say yes, just as I expect him and Billy to deliver Cristina. I will come here every day for the rest of my life to pray if they find my daughter.

They sat in chairs in the middle of the church in silence for a couple of minutes. No sign of the cross; no holding hands and tightening of eyes; no sacred gesture; not a single word aloud. She could still smell his cigarette stench, making her feel even more claustrophobic than a church usually made her feel.

As he stood up, he rested his hand on her shoulder.

"We will find your daughter," he said. "Soon."

He looked at her, unblinking. She looked down, blushing. And she realized she had never believed a man so thoroughly, so willingly, in her life, even though she knew he had no basis for his confidence.

"Now I have to go pick up some paint."

He walked out, leaving her there feeling suddenly angry at him, her gratitude turning and rushing out of her faster than he had raced out of the church. Couldn't he be more specific about how they were searching for Cristina in El Paso? How often was he talking with Billy? How often were they crossing the border? Was this all just Catholic nonsense, just another priest talking about faith and hope as if they were merely words in a book and not practical, daughter-delivering steps to take?

She stood up and looked around at his empty, tiny church. Am I fooling myself, she thought? Am I just a schoolgirl Catholic with a schoolgirl faith in the church and in priests? I am, I am. I am only coming to them from now on because they are Yanquis, not because they are priests, not because they think they are closer to God. I am only going to persist because they know more people in El Paso than I do.

◈ ◈ ◈

IF MY HEART WERE MORE PURE, SHE KEPT REPEATING TO HERSELF AS SHE STOOD AT THE FOOT OF THE BRIDGE CONNECTING JUAREZ AND EL PASO. The hard-nosed approach didn't hold; it couldn't as she spent more and more time around him. Her transactional mind-set wilted whenever he asked her to pray with him. His easy laughter, his bad accent, his, she admitted, handsomeness—she couldn't help but succumb. He didn't insist that she make some space for God, he merely suggested. And something inside her obliged every time. Suggestion was more powerful than insistence. She still wanted something from them, but something, she realized, was chipping away at her. The act of prayer, begun in compliance, out of manipulation, was now turning sincere, useful in and of itself.

If my heart were more pure. She stood at the base of the

downtown bridge watching, just as she had done many nights
since Cristina went missing. Father Kevin had told her just a
couple of days ago that Billy had a source in El Paso who had
seen Cristina, who swore she was alive. They had confirmed she
was with a bad man, a man who employed women in strip clubs
and brothels and massage parlors in El Paso. But she was alive.
But for how long? Rayna kept asking herself. And she wanted to
ask Kevin and Billy, she wanted to press the urgency on them:
for how long will she be alive if we don't rescue her tomorrow?

Tonight she had brought, on a whim, her girlhood rosary to
say while she stood there. It was nearly ten o'clock; she always
went home at ten on the bus that left from the next street over.

A few days ago after Sunday Mass, Father Kevin had come up
to her and urged the Rosary on her, told her how much peace it
usually brought him in moments of great movement. Momentos
de mucho movimiento, he had said. It didn't sound right, but
the more she thought about the phrase, she wondered if he had
said it on purpose. She could not be still, not since Cristina had
disappeared. She felt like she was always moving, even when
she slept.

So she dug the old rosary out of the box of items she never
used but kept anyway, and assumed the whole thing would come
back to her like the Hail Mary or Our Father as soon as she
began. It was nothing more than that, she had remembered, a
bunch of Hail Marys and Our Fathers. But when she took it out
of her pocket and began, or tried to begin, she realized she had
forgotten the mechanics of the Rosary. And tonight she realized
that the whole process of remembering the Rosary was what
slowed you down, slowed down all the movement.

She had gone to a religious relics store down the street and
asked if they had an instruction book. They told her that women
primarily used rosaries these days as necklaces. So she returned
to her corner and kept on with her looking. The first few weeks

she had looked for Cristina; now she looked for men, faces of men capable of stealing her child.

But there were so many. A day after Kevin's news, one of Cristina's friends had admitted that they had been befriended by some drug dealers from El Paso. Then the Juarez police reported to her that Cristina might be the man's sex slave, or that he might have brought her across the border to work as a prostitute in Dallas. Or maybe not, maybe just to work for him. Trabajar para él mismo, they had said. Just work for him only. Their use of the word "work" had troubled Rayna for days.

On these winter nights, so chilly and dark so early, she tried to plan her own rescue mission to El Paso. She had told Father Kevin she was going to go over herself, but he kept making a funny gesture with his hands, pressing air toward the ground as if he could push her anger out of her body and into the desert.

If only my heart were more pure, she thought again. She didn't know where the words came from, some prayer or song she had learned as a child that came back to her as childhood words do on empty nights like this one.

If only my heart were more pure. But she would never finish the sentence. So now, in her final five minutes tonight, she decided to try to finish it. If only my heart were more pure, I would re- member how to say the Rosary. If only my heart were more pure, Cristina would never have fallen into a life like this. If only my heart were more pure, I would never have fallen into a life like this.

She had never believed, never had faith in anything, since she was a schoolgirl. But she felt somehow that Father Kevin puri- fied her heart a bit; she felt her heart was cleaner in his presence. Sometimes she would still upbraid herself for idealizing him, for thinking a priest was any more spiritual or worthy than anyone else. She had long ago stopped thinking this way and didn't nec- essarily like feeling it again, that schoolgirl feeling. But it kept popping up whenever she was around him.

She gazed one last time at the people standing at the foot of the bridge. An Indian woman clung to a baby as she begged for coins from other beggars and gringos stumbling home. A few pervertidos leered at any woman who passed. But they were not menacing enough to be Cristina's kidnapper. She knew this man was evil; she could feel his evil from across the river and through the buildings in downtown El Paso and through the desert. Her daughter was with an evil man just as she had been, and this was punishment for her own impure heart.

She could see the bus turn the corner, and she rushed down the side street. The driver stared at her as she boarded, and she could feel him staring at her backside as she walked toward her seat. There was no one else on the bus, just this man and her. But she was not afraid; she stared back at him every time he looked at her in his mirror. He could tell, she knew, that she wasn't worth the trouble...or was more trouble than she was worth.

◈ ◈ ◈

As Mass finished this Sunday, she felt dirtier than ever. If they only knew I am still completely unmoved by the ceremony, she thought. If they only knew I am only here for my daughter, I am only here selfishly. Praying is one thing; the Rosary, yes, it helps calm me; but these recitations, the communion, the readings—they brought her too close again to the superstitious, rigid world of her grandmother.

As people stood chatting afterwards in the back of the church, she stood alone near the doorway. Father Kevin walked over toward her and said, "Buenos días."

"I have a question," she said, blushing at her own manipulativeness.

"Sí, Rayna," Father Kevin said.

"I found a rosary, Father Kevin," she said, feeling ashamed at how she always told him what she thought he wanted to hear.

"Muy bien, Rayna," he said, chuckling. "It helps, doesn't it? It helps quiet all the movement?"

"Rayna?" she heard Father Kevin say. "What is your question?"

She kept looking down, even as she spoke.

"I forgot the pattern," she said.

He looked puzzled, she could tell without even looking up at him. But she also could tell she had pleased him. She was complying well.

"The pattern of the Rosary, I forget the steps," she said.

He smiled—even though she didn't look up, she could see it.

He motioned to her and she sat in the front pew beside him.

He stuck his hand into his pocket, took out his rosary, and placed it in her hand. Then his huge hands directed her fingers across each group of beads as he explained the orchestration of the Rosary.

His voice was starting to sound less funny, she thought. She didn't follow what he was saying as she focused on his accent. She got up the nerve to ask him to repeat the steps one more time, as if she almost had it down but just wanted to repeat for reinforcement.

She wanted to ask him for any more details about Cristina but was wary that he might catch on to her guile. She had decided to get up first this time, to leave him in the dust as he usually did to her.

She nodded, stood up, pretended to be saying the Rosary, and walked off. Near the exit, she turned and saw him walking over to a new family, startling them by calling out their names. He is so good at his trick, she thought, his game, remembering all these names. He is a politician recruiting votes. He should run for mayor of Juarez, not try to revive this church.

She watched him kiss a baby and cursed herself for not daring to walk back up to him and demand that he take her then and there to El Paso, to Cristina, and do God's work instead of acting like he was in competition with the evangelical pastors up the road.

◈ ◈ ◈

SEVERAL NIGHTS LATER SHE STOOD AT THE FOOT OF THE BRIDGE AGAIN, EATING AN *EMPANADA* **SHE HAD BOUGHT AT THE STAND ON THE CORNER.** The wind was blowing in sand from the desert tonight, whipping it around in sheets from different angles so that once you turned away from it, the sand got around you and came back from the other direction.

Father Kevin had that afternoon given her a key fact. An Anglo man, not a Mexican American, had, as the euphemism went, befriended Cristina. This made her, as far as the news went, happy. She knew this Anglo by now had abused her many times over, but she believed that an Anglo man would do it less violently. Anglo men were used to paying, they were less vicious, she told herself. They would not beat Cristina after the act.

She studied every face of every Anglo that walked past her from the bridge. She used to cross it herself to clean houses. A nod to the immigration officers who knew her was sufficient. And then September 11 happened, and she had not crossed since.

She wondered how an Anglo would get Cristina over there. She wondered how they met, what pimp had identified her and lured her into his truck or trunk and then sold her to this Anglo? And this Anglo? She imagined him a doctor or lawyer, tired of his middle-aged wife, the kind of woman whose house she used to clean up in the West Side hills. The wife would be away where those wives go—San Diego or Los Angeles or Dallas—and Cristina would be given a good breakfast every morning and sleep on soft sheets like she had never touched before.

Suddenly she saw a man with Anglo skin, an Anglo gait, and an Anglo jacket, new and clean and buttoned, coming down the end of the bridge. She took a step closer. He was waiting to cross the street now, right in front of her, and she knew now that Father Kevin wore his shades not only to shield the sun but to hide himself. There he was, even at nightfall, wearing the sunglasses like a bad cop or soldier on this side of the bridge.

She walked toward him as he crossed.

"Padre Kevin, you are coming back late," she said.

Kevin jumped backwards a bit.

"Rayna, good Lord, you shouldn't startle an old man like that," he said. "What are you doing out here on a godforsaken night like this? This wind and sand will blow you back down into Chihuahua!"

"I come here many nights," she said. "I come here to hope. And say the Rosary as you showed me."

"I told you that the point of coming to church on Sundays is to hope, not coming to the foot of a bridge."

"I know, I know," she said. "Father Kevin, why are you wearing sunglasses at nightfall?"

"To keep the sand from my eyes, Rayna, and to scare off the bad guys."

She looked him up and down and remembered what all the ladies said the first time they saw him. A priest should never be so handsome. A priest should be bald and ugly, she thought to herself. She felt even angrier but stronger in his presence, too.

"You are a vain man," she said, laughing disdainfully.

"You are going to stand here in the middle of the road criticizing my fashion sense instead of asking me about Cristina?" he said.

He sounds perturbed, Rayna thought. At last I speak my mind and I ruin it all. She stepped back and looked at the road.

"She is safe, Rayna," Kevin said. "Billy was with the police earlier today. I was going to come to your house tonight. They have her. They need to speak with her for a day, coordinate with immigration her transfer back here. She is fine. She is scared but healthy. You will have her back, hopefully tomorrow. God bless her."

Then suddenly he bent down toward her and hugged her. It lasted for a few seconds. She felt the stubble of his beard and his cold ear against hers. Then he let go and kept one hand on her shoulder.

He took his hand off her shoulder and smiled at her. Then he nodded and resumed walking toward his truck in the lot next to the bridge. He is always walking off, she said to herself, as tears started to stream down her face. He likes it this way, she said, as the tears now gushed. He likes the dramatic departure.

She watched him drive off and felt embarrassed at how much warmer she felt from his hug, not on the outside, but on the inside.

SHE WENT DOWN TO THE IMMIGRATION STATION NEAR THE BRIDGE THE NEXT MORNING AND WAITED THERE ALL DAY, BUT CRISTINA NEVER ARRIVED. As night was falling, she walked up one last time to the same man she had walked up to twenty times over the course of the afternoon.

"Ah, sí, lo siento," he said. "Le llevaron por otro centro. Le llevaron a casa, creo."

Ah, I'm sorry, he said. They processed her in a different center. They took her home, I think.

He walked off, and Rayna stood there watching a guard lock the door. The guard motioned to her to leave, but she couldn't move. She didn't know whether to feel rage or joy. She gathered herself, shook her head at him, and walked to the bus stop, suddenly more horrified by the system, by her police, than by the men who had stolen her daughter.

The bus was full and stopping at every stop from downtown westward, so that Rayna reached a point where she wanted to get out and just run to Anapra. When at last they came close to her stop, she did just that. She had not run since she was a girl, and she felt her knees start to hurt almost instantly. But she kept running and found herself wishing Claudia could run like this, just to know what it felt like.

When she came upon her shack, the light inside was off, and as she walked in she could see her children all huddled in the corner of the single room. She switched on the one light and dropped her bag.

Cristina was there, her arms around her sisters and Rudy, and they clinging to her as if she were Rayna herself.

"Hija," Rayna said, anger in her voice even though she had not intended it to be there.

"Mamá," Cristina said.

Claudia got up and limped over toward Rayna.

"Hija," Rayna said again, and kept looking at Cristina as Claudia hugged her.

"Help me prepare dinner," she said, stunned at her own inability to say anything but that. She hated that she was saying things she wasn't thinking, saying things a man would say, a father.

Tears were dropping down Cristina's face, but she got up and stepped toward the tiny stove.

Then suddenly they both fell into one another, and the other kids walked over and fell into them, so that they were all leaning into each other and starting to buckle at the weight.

Rayna looked up at Cristina, stared straight into her face, and saw, suddenly, herself at her daughter's age, her own face for the first time changed forever, not scarred but shadowed, saddened, by what men had done and would forever do to her.

"These men, these priests, saved you," she said. "We have to thank them."

Cristina felt thin, weak. She seemed to have disappeared even though she now officially was not one of the desaparecidas. But I will bring her back, Rayna said to herself. I will fatten her up, fatten her body and her soul. I had been brought to the verge of disappearance before by men, Rayna thought, and I am going to be as resolute in bringing my daughter back all the way as I was in trying to get her back in the first place.

◈ ◈ ◈

THAT SUNDAY SHE STILL DID NOT WANT TO GO TO MASS, BUT SHE KNEW SHE HAD TO GO OUT OF GRATITUDE, go with Cristina, at least for a few Sundays to make Kevin feel like it had all been worthwhile. So she pushed and cajoled herself and got the children dressed as well as they could be dressed and led them to Corpus Christi. But it seemed like they arrived late, because people were already leaving the building. She didn't know why—had he changed the time of Mass? Had she gotten mixed up with all the stress? And what kind of gratitude is this we are already failing to show?

She quickly realized that the exiting parishioners were carrying the faces of missing women, about to join a procession that was beginning on the main road just down from the church and heading downtown. Father Kevin came out at the end of the line, resting his folded hands on his paunch as he walked.

She looked more closely and saw his rosary in his hands. She could see him mouthing the words as he walked past in the sunlight. She stepped out of the shade after he had passed her by about fifty feet and started to walk behind them.

As they turned left on Avenida Rancho Anapra, she took her

eyes off him for the first time and realized she was surrounded by people who were joining the procession. One woman held up a Polaroid of a teenage girl; another woman wept and screamed toward the sky; a man held up a painting of a girl.

The line was dozens of people long now, and they were walking alongside the highway that split into downtown and the border crossing.

People were clapping in unison as a man sang a song called "Levántame, Dios." Lift me up, God.

Rayna had always had the best voice in her class in school. No one had ever taught her a thing about singing; she couldn't read a note. But she could hear a song once and match it note for note, and her father used to be so proud of her that he would compel her to sing folclóricas at the village festivals.

She noticed everyone was walking with matching steps now, like in the army. She sang even louder and started to sway, too. The women around her followed her movements, and before long the whole line of people was swaying as they walked, save for Father Kevin. She noticed he walked as rigidly as ever and laughed.

"Father Kevin does not like to dance!" she said to the woman next to her.

The woman doubled over laughing.

"Hay que enseñarle," Rayna said. "We will have to teach Father Kevin to dance!"

The procession regrouped in front of police headquarters, and everyone gathered in a circle. She knew for the first time that Father Kevin had seen her. He was on the other side of the circle, and he lifted his hands and raised his thumbs at her.

"En el nombre del Padre, del Hijo, y del Espíritu Santo," he said as he made the sign of the cross. The people repeated his words, and everyone said the Ave Maria together. Then they clapped. They clapped for twenty minutes and jumped and shouted and danced.

Rayna looked at Cristina, who looked at the whole spectacle with bewilderment, and wept. It was the first time she had
failed to control the impulse, and once it had begun, she felt no
compulsion to control it anymore. She walked to Cristina and
hugged her, and out of the corner of her eye, as her head rested
on Cristina's shoulder, she caught Father Kevin watching them
embrace. He started to move his leg at the knee and smiled. She
let go of Cristina and motioned for Kevin to dance like everyone
else. But he waved his index finger back and forth, a firm rejection, when she encouraged him to move his hips. She laughed at
him and motioned with her hand that he was a hard case.

The sun was straight up in the sky now, and police officers
were gathering around and scowling at the crowd.

Rayna looked at all the faces of the women on the posters and
then looked at Cristina again, alive and dancing and shouting
and raising her fist in the air. Then Rayna looked up at the sun,
straight into it, and closed her eyes. She could still see its shining
circle—and, amazingly, Cristina's face in the middle of it, ringed
by the light.

CHAPTER THREE

Kevin

OW MANY TIMES SINCE HE HAD MOVED TO JUAREZ HAD HE THOUGHT ABOUT JESUS AND THE DESERT, how the desert was the place, with all that sand and wind and nothingness, where the devil almost got him. This was a city, but it was still a desert, and Kevin wondered if that would have been the last straw for our man Jesus—a corrupt border city with the same sand and wind and nothingness. Would that have gotten him? He studied each concrete block this morning as he walked the perimeter of the foundation of the church extension. He was convinced that something was out of whack but couldn't pinpoint what.

He asked a worker.

"Así son aquí," he said. That's the way they are here.

Beams were sitting in the center of the square construction site, and men were rolling a waterproofing stain onto them. The chemical odor made Kevin wheeze, but the men wore no masks save for the fellow mixing the solution.

"For the love of God, cover your mouths when you do this," Kevin said to them as he held his white handkerchief over his mouth. But the men didn't even look at him.

That was the current thing, he decided as he paced back and forth, that bugged him most about Juarez—so many things blowing in the air. Trucks everywhere jettisoning exhaust into kids' faces; people burning tires and dead dogs and carpets alongside schoolyards, sending the smoke scattershot; women making a sport out of sending buckets of bathroom waste arcing into the street. He could take the poverty. In many ways he had come to see it through a brighter lens than during his years in rural Chile—here at least there were thousands of jobs, and the cold startled you but didn't kill you. But the chemical reality of everyday life, the smell and flow of fluids of all viscosities and colors and smoke of all textures and odors, bugged the hell out of him. He clenched his fists at the men's heedlessness.

"Stop," he said.

No one even paused.

"¡Paran, caballeros!" he shouted.

A few men looked up.

"We are building a church here, the house of God, and I'm not going to have you poison your lungs while doing it. So let's all do this!"

He walked even closer to the few who weren't looking and motioned to them. Then he took a roller out of one guy's hands and pushed him backwards. He took his handkerchief, wrapped it around the guy's neck like a cowboy, and motioned for him to pull it up over his mouth. The guy did, and then Kevin picked up a shirt another man had shed, ripped it into long shreds, and went around handing them to the men. The men all started smiling. Kevin motioned to them to imitate him as he wrapped his scarf around his mouth, and they all did, their smiling lips jutting through the cloth around them.

"Muy bien," Kevin said loudly. "Muy bien. Now we can work on getting this place off the ground without making our funerals the first Masses to be said here."

He clapped, hit two men on the shoulder as he passed them, and walked to the front of the building. He stood there and watched. These men work hard, he thought. This whole city works hard, hard like miners. And for the first time yet, he felt a sort of sneaky contentment in Juarez. He knew this time it wasn't passing, for he felt its roots. He was doing something, he was building it, and they were slowly, ever so slowly, starting to come. He had been right about Leo and Rayna. He was no Billy, he could not fix a toilet or mend a roof to save his life, but he could identify talent. And he had identified right. Leo and Rayna, his two right hands, were insinuating their way into every nook and corner of Juarez's shabby soul and bringing back parishioners for him.

He stood in the middle of the empty field and imagined the church walls around him, a parish of hundreds standing in front of him singing and clapping, and himself walking down the aisle as God's light filled the place through colored glass like in a cathedral in Rome itself.

And then he reached into his pocket and took out a cigarette, lit it, and inhaled straight to the bottom of his lungs. Praise be to God for this masterpiece of creation, he often thought when he smoked.

He pushed his shades higher up his nose and caught a few of the workers watching him imagine his future soccer field behind Corpus Christi. A few days after he had arrived in Juarez a year ago, he had bought three knock-off pairs of fancy fight-pilot sunglasses at the same shop just across the footbridge from El Paso. The guy who sold them to him kept repeating that they were made right here in Mexico and not in China.

The glasses were so tinted on the outside that he couldn't even see his finger when he wagged it behind the lens; from the inside, they obscured his field of vision with a fuzzy blackness. What's more, he knew they gave him a certain appeal. As he studied himself in the mirror, he knew no priest in Juarez was wearing shades like these. He knew they rocked; he had quickly decided that the way to beat the charismatics, the evangelicals, at their own game was by outdoing them with charisma.

The sunlight was what most shocked him still in Juarez, not the heat. Though shade was as scarce as clean water, he quickly learned it was more valuable. The light here was worse than the worst of the Australian sun. Killer light, he thought.

When he showed up in the shades, he noticed the construction workers at the church site stared at him. He hulked over them, but that never seemed to help him get them to listen to him. Burly since he was a boy, he had learned early that a little use of his God-given heft could come in handy.

But the glasses accomplished more than body leverage. Workers stopped and stared. The site superintendent actually looked him in the eye for once, even though there were no eyes to be seen.

Somehow he had begged and borrowed, and yes, in a couple of instances, pondered stealing, over $50,000 to finance the transformation of Corpus Christi into what one might properly call a church. Two builders had started, stolen from him and lied to him, and then disappeared once he had caught on to their games. At last he had found this fellow Juan Pablo who lived just up the road from the church. Juan Pablo was a bulldog who had built many of the new houses in Anapra single-handedly, and he was building the extension of the church cheaper and better and with absolute honesty. And who was his bridge to Juan Pablo? Who convinced Juan Pablo, yet another wayward Catholic wanting no truck with the church, to offer his services? Leo and Rayna, goddamit, he said to himself. Of course!

People were starting to come; he adhered to the cliché that even more would come if he built it. He knew he was right.

And here was the beginning of his extension: a square vacant lot looking out onto a vacant field full of plastic bags and plastic bottles. Beyond that, the brown, scraggly mountain called Cristo Rey. The big cross on the other side of the mountain that presided over the west side of El Paso was not visible, but everyone who looked out pointed upward and talked about it anyway. Anapra's just on the other side of that cross, Kevin would say when he was on an errand to El Paso and people would ask him where his parish was in Juarez. He could tell no one understood the appropriateness of the geography. The Cross, the Passion, the suffering—here across the border where life is cleaner and smoother, the idea that every day resembled Jesus' final days was preposterous. The idea that the Passion was a daily bloody event—no one could even begin to get their American heads around that. But a few steps away, back over there, in Mexico, well, the Cross was a way of life.

◈ ◈ ◈

A FEW MONTHS PRIOR HE HAD HEARD A FELLOW COLUMBAN PRIEST VISITING FROM HEADQUARTERS IN OMAHA CALL JUAREZ "GODFORSAKEN."
When he would awake every morning at daybreak to do his sit-ups and say his prayers, the word kept commandeering space in his brain, squeezing out the images that he always tried to summon as he said the Hail Mary or Our Father.

After a few days of the word's assault, *godforsaken*, he started to pray to God to banish the word from his brain. Very early on he noticed that the devil was a big part of his parishioners' cosmology. He had never believed in the anti-God himself, but with so much talk of the devil, he wondered what had gotten into his head. "This godforsaken place." Kevin heard the priest's tone precisely, its mix of disgust and disdain. He took it to mean God had lost, had given up, walked away. Someone or something else was running the show. Kevin took it personally; he took it as an affront.

He had always loved the desert back in Australia and, as a young man in seminary, would imagine Jesus spending his 40 days in the Outback instead of the barren dunes of Palestine. But it was precisely the desert, or, better said, the idea of a city built into the desert like Juarez, that was the rub here. The word fit, he knew deep down. When the sun was high and its power ungodly, *godforsaken* was the only suitable word one could use to describe the sensation of walking down a desert road seething with city heat.

This morning he laughed as he knelt at his bedside. At times, during his struggles of the previous year, the worst year of his life, he thought that perhaps "godforsaken" isn't even the right word. For a while, he felt like he was in a place in which God had never even set foot. But now the old bugger—God—was popping up in the laughs of the children running in the back of the church; in Rayna's gratitude and Rosary-saying; in Leo's eloquent silences and steadfast, punctual companionship; in little Saul's whistle-while-you-work resilience; in Juan Pablo's carpentry skills.

He made his coffee on a tiny stove one spring Sunday in their new shack up the road from the old whorehouse. John and he had wearied of the noise and the dust of the main street and had found a cheaper, homier place to rent that was more part of the fabric of Anapra. He sat at the only chair at a small, round table, and after a few sips of the coffee, his leg started to jump up and down. It was quieter here, less dusty, more amenable to a morning cigarette. He felt nervous every Sunday morning, but this morning, for no reason, he felt as uncertain as he did before his very first service here over a year ago. His first cigarette failed to calm him; his second smoothed the edge slightly but not enough to not smoke a third.

He waited for daybreak and then left the house. Many mornings now he would take a long walk through Anapra to try to recruit familiar faces and defy the enemy. As success was accruing to him, the evangelicals were growing more aggressive, more openly anti-clerical. The Assembly of God parish a few blocks away was doing all it could to spoil his efforts: burning crucifixes and rosaries in a tiny bonfire in front of his church one night; offering free food to entice away the Anaprans who had taken a liking to him; performing exorcisms in front of his home.

When he turned the corner onto the street where the Assembly of God churchgoers had built their building, dozens of them were standing in front of the building, seemingly waiting for him. He stopped; they saw him and started to murmur.

He took one step toward them and, for the first of many times, felt the stupid, self-conscious sensation of being in a Western. He hated it, how the West was inseparable in the subconscious from the Western. He only kept from laughing at himself so as not to provoke the evangelicals.

But part of him wanted to provoke, too. He pushed his shades up on his nose and started toward them, smiling. They stopped murmuring, and he realized he unwittingly had sent the message he should have been trying to send all along. Don't come by my church to protest us today. Don't mess with us. Why hadn't I made it clear sooner? Why had I been so accepting of your bullying? And tell your rich check-signers back in Houston or Dallas or whatever American monstrosity they hail from that I have every right to do what I am doing here!

He nodded, kept walking past them, and turned down the

hill toward Corpus Christi. A dozen people were waiting there, still half an hour before Mass. This is progress, however slight, he thought. Dozens more came as the clock ticked toward ten. This is what winning looks like, he said to himself; then he checked his pride. Rayna walked in with her children and the place lit up; Leo and Lydia walked in last but sat in the front row. Kevin loved that Lydia dragged Leo to the front; he loved front row people.

As he made the sign of the cross, he looked out and suddenly saw a group of the same evangelicals he had warned earlier now gathered outside in front of his church. They were standing silently with their hands lifted up toward him, their fingers forming crosses.

He wanted to stop, walk out, and stand and defy them.

But the first song began, and a woman new to the parish with whom he had yet to even have a conversation of more than a minute in length had suddenly distracted him. Her voice seemed to separate from the other voices and rise to a different height. He lowered his sunglasses on his nose—he had taken to wearing them even during Mass on days when the sun shot through the plastic roof and big windows. He stopped singing and watched her as he listened. He let his focus zoom out to take in the whole congregation. I have a parish, he thought. There are enough people here to respectably call it that. I have a parish.

He noticed that Rayna's long gray hair, always so clean, seemed to reflect the sunlight coming through the plastic skylight. This woman singing was one of Rayna's recruits, or one of Leo's; he couldn't keep it straight anymore. And that is good, he thought; it is good that so many new people are coming that I forget which of my deputies recruited them. There is finally life in here, he thought, emanating from Rayna and Leo and their recruits. How blessed I am to have found them, Rayna and her uncanny intelligence and steadfast manner and affable Leo and his handiness.

These blessed people here in this godforsaken spot singing on a Sunday morning, my people, he thought, are keeping me from breaking a bunch of evangelical jaws, by God's grace.

◈ ◈ ◈

AT RAYNA'S URGING, HIS FIRST BIG PURCHASE, APART FROM THE BUILDING MATERIALS, HAD BEEN A PIANO, A GUITAR, AND A DRUM SET. The new church band, composed of anyone who had the slightest musical inclination, was already jazzing up the services, and Kevin could tell that more and more people were coming simply because of the rejuvenation of the church's musical life.

But this Sunday he walked in to find the band standing empty-handed, staring at their even emptier stage. The previous Sunday the band had showed up and found all their instruments gone. Kevin had stood in front of the band's platform and watched as they all peered into the closet where they stored all but the drum set. The padlock on the back door of the building had been broken, and the thief had stolen only the instruments—not a chalice or painting was missing.

As they walked through the chapel taking inventory of what was not missing, Rayna had walked in and started to walk with them. They stopped at a rusted statue of the Virgin Mary, what Kevin would have considered a piece of junk were it not sacrilegious to throw it in the bin. But he had noticed Rayna walking closer to it, touching it as everyone walked on.

A few days later he walked into the church—Leo now had a key and was painting the walls with rollers—and saw Rayna set up in a corner with the statue of the Virgin lying on top of a big cloth. She was scrubbing at the metal with a wire brush, and Kevin could smell from across the chapel whatever substance she was using.

What is it with these Mexicans poisoning themselves? he wondered.

He walked up to Rayna and handed her his handkerchief.

"Rayna, my friend, you're breathing this stuff in!"

But suddenly he stopped. He had never been a fan of religious art, opining whenever the topic came up that it was largely dreadful stuff that turned the agony and ecstasy of our story into bad opera. But Rayna had spotted something—dirty, rusted, ready for the junk yard in Kevin's opinion—and had breathed life into it. The face of this statue, he realized, was exquisitely feminine and precise, alive. Rayna was painting it now, a perfect fleshy color spreading from Mary's chin to her ear along her jawbone.

"Where did you get that paint?" Kevin asked.

"Lo hice," she said. "Lo hice con Leo." I made it with Leo.

"Keep going, don't let me interrupt you," he said. He stepped back to give her space, walked up to the lectern, and pretended to organize some papers.

But he kept one eye on this birthing of the Virgin the whole time, Rayna dabbing the pinkish flesh color now on the statue's nose and cheeks. She stopped for a moment, studied her work, then switched brushes, and began with Mary's lips—a red not sultry but simple and strong: a perfect red for Mary. A red, he thought, that Rayna had put deep thought into. A red like her.

But suddenly an older woman walked through the church doors and motioned to him, nervously.

He had never seen her before, yet she did not introduce herself.

"My son sent me," she said. "He wants to know how much you will pay for your instruments."

"I'm sorry?" Kevin responded, not yet grasping the reality that the thief of his band's instruments had sent his mother to offer them back.

"La guitarra, los..."

Kevin held up his hand.

"Get the hell out of this church!" he bellowed in English.

The woman stared, and Rayna stood up and watched.

Then, in Spanish, "¡Vete! ¡Vete!"

The woman huffed, glared at him, and walked out.

Kevin turned to Rayna. They stared at one another. He felt suddenly ashamed at losing his temper in front of her, and he impulsively reached into his pocket for a cigarette and lit it.

She frowned at him. He knew he was breaking his own rule by smoking in the church. But the woman, her embodiment of all the thieving around here, had set his heart arace.

"I would rather have only our clapping hands than succumb to that!" Kevin shouted. "Only our own hands and our own voices! Just like I would rather build this extension myself than pay bribes and work with crooks!"

He was trembling now and, for a moment, felt his heart tipping over the edge. He breathed deeply on his cigarette and felt a charge of coolness inside.

But suddenly his eyes fixed on the face of the statue, freshly painted and almost as alive as Rayna's own face next to it. He looked at the statue, then at Rayna, then back at the statue.

"How beautiful," Kevin said, forgetting for a moment about the mother of the thief.

Rayna blushed and lowered her eyes. Then she lifted them and pointed at the cigarette.

"The smoke, it makes the smell of the paint worse," she said calmly, without any tone of correction.

But he felt corrected, properly and without shame. He looked at the cigarette, threw it on the concrete floor, and stomped on it. I can accept being corrected by this woman, he thought. Quite acceptable.

"Sigue," he said, not ordering her to continue but asking her to, knowing that watching her work would calm him, knowing, deep down, it would work even better than another smoke outside.

◈ ◈ ◈

RAYNA HAD ULTIMATELY BEEN THE HANDS-DOWN WINNER IN THE CLEANING LADY COMPETITION, TOO, even though she had not officially entered herself. Kevin had entered and selected her, thus rigging—all without her knowledge—the decision that was his and his alone. What got her the job was Kevin's accurate hunch that her gratitude would translate into a world-class work ethic, but Kevin had never imagined she would kneel and stab at paint splotches in the concrete floor that had been there for decades. That was what he found her doing one summer morning when he walked into Corpus Christi. The Virgin, the greatest work of ecclesiastical art in church history, he would stop and tell admirers, now sat on its own podium on the side of what he liked to jokingly call the nave, even though Corpus Christi was really a box growing boxier with the extension.

He stopped to admire it, as he had done every day since Rayna had finished restoring the statue, in part to tease her and in part to praise her at the same time. Today she looked up, and he realized it was her same way of looking up—her ears seemingly alert, her eyes twinkling slightly—that she had when she was seeking his help in finding Cristina. She wanted something. She was coming out of her shell, this woman, and she is going to be bossing me around before long, he thought.

He walked up to her to spare her the hunt.

"Rayna, you're a saint, the way you work," he said.

He knew she was used to his introductory declarations by now, but he kept up the game to humor himself, trying to get a reaction out of her like he used to.

Resting on her knees, she motioned to the stage next to the altar.

"When you get the instruments back, we need to form a dance club, too," she said, as if the decision had been made.

"You mean to dance?" Kevin asked, realizing that the stupidity of his response meant that this time it was clear she had disarmed him.

She laughed.

He collected himself.

"If you want this place to really blow up, trust me, you must add dancing," she said with a self-certainty that slightly irritated Kevin. "We love it. I will coordinate it for you."

"Ah, good, yes," he said. This meek woman, he thought, she is really starting to take hold here.

"And you let me know when you want to say your first Mass, too!" he said.

She looked at him quizzically.

"I'm teasing, Rayna!" he said. "Dancing it is, once I find that bugger who stole the instruments and break his knees! Did Leo find out for me where her son lives?"

"Sí," she said, lowering her eyes like she always did when she had bad news that he had to pull out of her. "He sold everything already."

Kevin slumped his shoulders. He had raised the money to buy the musical instruments from donors all over the world. He had felt guilty asking for more money on top of the funds to extend the church, especially since that was on top of the first funds he had raised but which the first contractors had run off with.

"Tell Leo to find them, then," he said, peevishly. "I don't park my car out of my sight anymore. I don't even let my shoes out of sight when I take them off at night. They'll steal your bloody soul here if you let them."

Here this woman, all she is thinking about is forming a dance club, and we can't even keep our possessions in place, he thought. But he caught his anger; he caught himself from telling her they would steal the Virgin next. He caught himself because he realized what she had said was right but also uncannily threatening to him. She wants to turn my Mass into a dance club, he said to himself. Well, I might as well let go. I might as well let these insurrectionists take over if that is what it takes to win down here.

◈ ◈ ◈

THE THIEVING CONTINUED. Most of the braces for the roof had been stolen the night before, and the construction foreman had spent the morning trying to locate some. The foreman was getting into his car when Kevin arrived. Kevin had been expecting to see the trusses in place already. He had wanted the roof up soon so the evangelicals could see them as they walked to church that evening. Several parishioners had told Kevin the evangelicals were telling them the devil was going to burn down the new part of the church before it was even finished. Kevin had always loved a good fight, and even more a good friendly fight, a recreational one, as he called it in seminary. This friendly battle for bodies, as he called it, was only just beginning. And the margin for the new priest on the block was thin. He knew the residents of Anapra were watching him, deciding on his every move whether he offered them a better shot at safety, food, and salvation than the next church up the street.

"Stay here, I'll go get them," he said to the foreman as he blocked him from entering his truck.

Kevin had his own truck, a 1986 Ford pickup that he was pretty sure was a 1970s Ford pickup. He bought it at a junk car lot on the eastern edge of Juarez, and, though he knew nothing about engines, he marveled at the shiny metal of the rebuilt motor inside. The dealer told him it would last a good ten years, but Kevin soon realized he wasn't including the tires in that projection.

After so many flats, Kevin could just intuit the next one coming, and today, as soon as he pulled out from in front of the church, he knew his first stop would be Saul. There were a few cars already lined up at the corner as Kevin pulled up, and he saw Saul take the money from one driver and immediately walk it over to his father.

As Saul turned back to the next car, he looked back and saw Kevin and waved. Kevin tooted his horn, and the car in front of him lurched forward. The driver threw his hand out the window and started cursing him in Spanish, and Saul started giggling.

Mullins watched Saul mix a bunch of fluids together in a paint can and then take a blow torch to the concoction. His older brother cranked the car up on a rusty jack. Saul got down on his knees and stuck his legs under the running car while he scraped the rubber with a stick and dabbed it onto the back tire. Then Saul dragged his legs out from under the car, stood up, slapped the door two times, and stuck his hand out to the owner. He wrapped his dirty hands around the pesos and walked them up to his father.

"¿Qué pasa, Padre Mulkins?" Saul shouted as he walked back. Saul always called him 'Mulkins,' and Kevin liked it.

When it came his turn, Kevin got out of the car and put his hand on Saul's head. Saul soft-punched him in the stomach. Saul's father walked up and shook Kevin's hand while the boys went to work on the tire.

"Tu hijo es un milagro," Kevin said. Your son is a miracle.

The man laughed.

Saul scrambled out from under the car, and Kevin handed him the money, twenty extra pesos this time.

Saul looked at it and handed the extra pesos back to him with one hand and the payment to his father with his other. But Kevin did not lift his hand. Saul kept holding it there, but Kevin shook his head.

Saul started laughing and soft-punched Kevin in the belly again. He turned, dropped the tip on the seat of Kevin's car, and opened the door for him, bowing as he did like a porter at a fancy hotel.

Kevin shook his head and laughed as he got in the car.

He reached down as he sat, grabbed the pesos with his right hand, and set them on a little bench where he assumed Saul sat down once in a while. As he drove off, he looked back in the rearview mirror, but he didn't see Saul anywhere near the bench.

FATHER JOHN TOLD HIM THAT TO DRIVE IN JUAREZ, HE NEEDED TO LEARN TO DANCE BECAUSE THAT IS WHAT THEY DID ON THE ROADS. You had to stay on your toes out there, for the Mexican propensity for swerving is unrivalled in the Third World, he would say.

All of the Western factories were still on the east side of Juarez, and so was most of the housing construction. But one plant, a massive Foxconn factory, had begun construction after years of rumors out near the new border crossing near Anapra, and Kevin wanted to track its progress. So his quest for cheap building materials took him back to El Paso by way of the western route—the always empty Santa Teresa crossing. Though the checkpoint and accompanying building gleamed, the several-mile-long road leading to it from Anapra was still predominantly unpaved. Several rich men from El Paso and oligarchs from Mexico had bought up all of the desert on either side of this road and even to the south of Anapra in anticipation of the boom that would come from the master-planned maquila city out here. But for now, still nothing but desert.

He loved this route not only because of its ease and relative safety from maniacal drivers but because it positioned his soul back into the desert. Anapra's expansion sputtered and then stopped abruptly heading west, and the transition from shacks to pure sand and scrub always gave Kevin a quick rejuvenation, the way crossing a bridge from a mainland to an island might do for the sea-loving kind.

He flipped up the rearview mirror once he got onto the dirt road they already were calling a highway. Another piece of advice from his friend: don't look around out there, just go. Wrecked cars had been abandoned all over the highway, and Kevin had come to use them as mile markers after so many trips across.

Suddenly, as if out of the ground, a white van nearly scraped him as it pulled up alongside from behind him. He gripped the wheel with both hands as the van kept nudging him. He slowed and then slammed on the brakes to try to shake it. The van backed up in front of him and stopped. He debated throwing his truck into reverse, but before he could assess his courage, seven men wearing ski masks jumped out and circled his pickup. One pointed his submachine gun at Kevin's head through the window, grazing his temple, and motioned to him to get out.

He began to pray to himself, a Hail Mary, all while slowly opening the door and holding his hands up in the air. No one had motioned for him to do so, but cinema-nourished instinct had taken over. Then, at once, they all pointed their guns at him.

Kevin stopped praying. He realized it as he did it. I want to keep praying, he thought. I should keep praying. But his brain froze along with his body. And all he could think about was lighting a cigarette.

He opened his jacket to take out a pack, but a man grabbed him by the neck and forced him to the ground, pushing his face into the dirt and dust, cursing him as all the others drew even closer.

For the first time in my life, I wish I had worn a collar, Kevin thought. I wish I had dressed like a bloody priest.

"Sólo quiero un cigarillo," Kevin said out of the side of his mouth that wasn't filled up with dust. "Aquí, in my pocket. I am a priest."

His oppressor did not lessen the force of his grip on him. Kevin reached out his arm slowly and reached into his jacket, but his fumbling fingers failed to locate the pack of cigarettes.

No one has shot me, he thought. With seven men pointing guns at me, I just reached into my jacket so I could have a smoke. And no one has shot me for my stupidity alone.

"Sí, es, es un cura," one man suddenly said.

The guy holding him down loosened his grip and lifted his gun off Kevin's head.

Kevin looked up out of the corner of his eye. His urge for a cigarette was startling even him. He slowly propped himself up on his elbows, looked up at all the masked men, and smiled slightly.

"Soy el cura en Rancho Anapra, parroquia Corpus Christi," he said. I am the priest in Anapra, the Corpus Christi Parish. He loathed using the priesthood as a shield. He never imagined saying it as if he should be included with the women and children when the life rafts were being unhooked and the bow was sinking below water level. But he could register that this event, even in the middle of it, was more terrifying than he had ever imagined it to be.

He got up on his knees, reached slowly into his jacket again, and at last felt the consoling plastic wrapper of the cigarette pack. He slowly took it out and held it up to the gunman in front of him.

"You take communion?" Kevin asked, proud that his irony was returning as his heart rate slowed.

The man chuckled and took a cigarette. Kevin took one, stuck it into his mouth with a trembling hand, and then threw the pack up to another man who passed it around. Kevin took out his lighter, lit his cigarette first, and then passed the lighter to the next man.

The man who had originally identified him as a priest took off his ski mask first; then the others followed. Kevin recognized none of them.

"So how we doing, mates?" Kevin said, but obviously no one understood Aussie English. They all stood there smoking, enjoying their individual cigarettes together as if they were old friends meeting at the bar for a drink here in the middle of the desert.

"OK, gracias," the boss said. "Lo siento."

The man turned, looked all around, and then nodded.

"Vamos," he said, and all the men followed him back into the van. It pulled off in the direction of Anapra, and Kevin kept trying to place the face of the man who had identified him and likely saved him. Have I seen him at Mass? In the street? At the bodega?

The evening desert wind coming from all of Mexico northward now pushed at his back. And then his heart rate picked up again, steadily rising to the point where it was beating so fast that he thought his chest would explode. He slowed, lit a cigarette, and then stopped on the side of the road. He started to say Hail Marys again, just sitting there smoking and mouthing the words.

The sun was setting, and he suddenly had the uncanny sense that the shoe was about to drop. If they had been brutally killing all these women for so many years, the violence had to spread. He had come to learn that about violence, whether during his time in Chile or Chicago. It spread. It infected. It caught fire. There was lots of thieving in Juarez, but little of it led to physical harm. There were more and more the junkies, but they were all drugging themselves into oblivion. But these men I have just met, Kevin thought, these men were of a different sort. The cartels run huge chunks of the interior of Mexico, he knew, and he had always been told the Juarez cartel was firmly in control, so there was little drug violence here. The cartels kept things stable, Leo told him; they run the police and army, and Juarez will always be safe, except for the women, so long as the Juarez cartel is strong.

But these men, he had never seen anything like it. He started up the car again, lit another cigarette, and resumed driving but noticed his arm shaking as it held the wheel. He didn't feel scared for himself—he had dodged bullets and come close to having his head cracked by Pinochet's bullies in Santiago many a time. But the encounter with these men scared him for this place. Why was this road so important to those men? Why was I such a threat? They were the first of their kind he had encountered, and the whole way home he could only remember their masked faces, not the faces unmasked.

He walked into their home, spotted John eating his ice cream, and poured himself a rum.

"I think things are changing here, John," he said. "I think things are going to change for the worse."

John looked up at him and smirked.

"How much worse can they get?" he said, pausing in mid-spoonful.

Kevin swallowed his rum hard, pushing it down his throat. He told John about what had happened. He told him the whole incident didn't seem to fit. He told him he sensed from these men that they wanted to control the whole highway, not that he had stumbled into a drug deal gone bad.

"Well, it wouldn't surprise me in the least," John said, and Kevin realized he should have been thinking exactly the same thing.

❖ ❖ ❖

THE CREWS OF MEN WHO ARRIVED EACH MORNING TO PUT UP THE NEW BORDER FENCE JUST DOWN THE ROAD FROM CORPUS CHRISTI LOOKED JUST LIKE ALL THE MEN ON THE

STREET and the men on the work buses that shuttled people to work at the maquiladora plants on the other side of Juarez. That is, they looked outrageously like Mexican men to Kevin. But, in this case, they were Mexican American men, no doubt, fully and rightfully citizens of a country a foot away; half a foot; whatever the width of the fence was.

As he stood watching them work, Kevin wondered if there were a Mexican fact-checker making sure the Mexican American workers didn't capture an inch here and an inch there as the fencing progressed.

He walked closer, but still no one looked up from their work. The sun was so fearsome today that to look up from the ground was a heroic act, so Kevin couldn't blame their avoidance of eye contact on fear or lack of curiosity. But part of him felt crestfallen at their refusal, or was it utter failure, to recognize him.

Then the question that would trouble him so that he would seek out a cartographer came to him: if you divided that line between Mexico and America, and kept subdividing it, wouldn't you reach a point, however microscopic, that no one could own, that would be indivisible? Would that be all that was left unowned, all that was left, say, for God?

They turned on the big rig that beat the posts into the ground. Its piston hummed, and then the arm rose, slowly at first but then shooting up; finally, the hammerhead at the bottom came crashing down, shooting a spout of dust up into the air.

He felt the urge, the deep, genetic, Australian need, to be a smart-ass. He walked closer. He wanted to tell them there was no oil here, not even water in the first 200 feet or so. He wanted to say what he had heard the night before at the marriage class at the parish. The fence bin Laden built—that is, the fence the 9/11 attacks had caused to be financed and built. But how to phrase it? You guys working for bin Laden? You guys missed a terrorist, saw him running across this morning about 5:30, started months

ago in the Sahara? When you finish driving in one of those pil-
ings, do you turn to each other and say, Mission accomplished?

You have got to stop being such a smart-ass, he said to himself. Let the drug dealers kill you, not the border patrol, for
Christ's sake. He walked closer still. At last a border patrol truck
drove up, its light-green line on the side reflecting the sun such
that even through his aviator shades it hurt his eyes. On a roll
now: who designed your logo? Last I checked, not a green thing
in sight, but you look like the forestry service down under.

The border guard pulled up right in front of him, if not in-
fringing on God's little line at that indivisible point of the border,
then certainly daring to skirt it, just to show he could.

Kevin waved and walked right up to him.

"Hiya, mate," he said.

He knew from his days in Chicago that the fond Aussie tag
of "mate" aroused suspicions of homosexuality among securi-
ty-oriented Americans, so he tried to say it in his best American
accent in case the guard would immediately write him off as an
Australian.

"Good morning, Father," the agent said, deflating his bravado
instantly.

"Buenos días," he said, his last stab at provocation.

The guard got out of the truck and stood in front of the fence
that had not yet arrived.

"You think anyone would catch me if I stopped by for Mass
one day before this thing goes up?"

He asked the question so tonelessly that Kevin was certain
the poor flunkey was sincere.

In the blinding light he thought he looked like Enrique, the
guy who showed up at the first marriage class with his wife and
then sent her alone to the next three with a scribbled note saying
he would be there the next time, then the time after that.

"You raise a good question," Kevin said. "I have been here for a year and a half, and have yet to see a Mexican customs agent enforcing the border. So, yes, you would be welcome."

The guard looked at the workers and then back at Kevin.

"How do you know who I am?" Kevin asked.

"Father, I sit up on that hill forty hours a week looking at Anapra with binoculars. I'm not the smartest guy, but things start to fit together."

"Yes, well, yes they do," Kevin said.

"Father, I wonder if you might bless me."

"What's your name, mate?"

The guy looked nervously at the workers.

"I can't tell you that, Father. I just wonder if you could bless me. I am having some troubles right now, troubles in my family. Could you bless me without making the sign of the cross? I don't want anyone to see it."

"Well, um, yes, yes."

Kevin lowered his head, and out of the top of his eyes he could see the guard do the same. He blessed him, in silence, stood there for a few seconds more to hopefully console the chap, then raised his head, and clapped his hands.

"There you go, you're all blessed," Kevin said.

"Thank you, Father," the guard said as he turned. He looked at the workers, none of whom even glanced his way, then nodded at Kevin, and hopped back in his truck. He started it, turned it roughly, with the same sort of anger that all these guys seemed to drive with, and kicked dust up into the air all around Kevin.

Kevin closed his eyes as he heard the truck drive up the hill. He peeked but still found himself in the thick of a dust storm. He felt the dust shoot into his nostrils, causing him to sneeze over and over and to cough.

As the dust settled, he looked at the workers, none of whom were even looking at him. The words of the song came to him, and it wasn't a good song to hear. "There's somethin' happenin' here, what it is ain't exactly clear..."

Corpus Christi had over two hundred parishioners; her band had new musical instruments again thanks to an anonymous donation from someone in El Paso; Rayna was forming her dancing troupe. Yet all around him Juarez felt more hostile, more dangerous. The danger before was petty, blubbering. Now things felt more evil—the finality of the new border fence, the foreboding he felt from his hijackers, rumors of murders downtown.

He ran his hand along the fence, and the clanking sound echoed slightly in the emptiness of the desert on the other side of it. What would a good Mexican say right now, right here? "Me cago en la nueva malla de bin Laden." I shit on bin Laden's new fence. But he didn't say it, even though the blossoming Mexican in him wanted to.

CHAPTER FOUR

Rayna

"WE WOULD LIKE YOU AND YOUR FAMILY TO LIVE AT THE CHURCH IN ADDITION TO YOUR WORKING HERE, RAYNA,"** Kevin said to her, matter-of-factly, one day after Mass on Sunday. She didn't react with glee solely because Leo had whispered to her months ago that she formed part of Kevin's master plan for revitalizing the parish, and she knew he was worried about the ongoing thefts lately, too.

"OK," she said, knowing already from Leo that Kevin was going to suggest she move her family into the restored room in the tiny building attached to the church, clean the place daily, and serve as a guardian of the musical instruments at night.

Indeed, this arrangement, not precisely this but certainly this sort of stability and companionship, was exactly what she had wanted. She admitted to herself that all those Masses, even the resurrection of the statue of the Virgin, were intended to impress

Kevin as much as to pay him back. Un poco de los dos, she acknowledged to her conscience. A little of each.

But his proposal to live there was more than she had hoped for. God had felt very far away for so long, but now she could not help but think he was gracing her life for the first time.

"Move in when you are ready, no hurry," Kevin said. His back was toward the sun, and as he spoke, so much taller than her, she noticed that he blocked out the sun entirely. He smiled, walked off, and left her staring momentarily into the sun, forgetting to close her eyes she was so stunned at her continued good fortune and his continued generosity.

She stood there, blinking wonder. How does he seem to sense how I have lived? The cold nights on floors of family and friends? The jobs I have lost? That I have been tempted to steal for my children? He knows nothing about me and yet he seems to know everything.

She walked into the room that would be her future home and stood there. We will be safe here, she thought, safe from what is starting to happen. A church will be the safest place to be. She knew, though she knew that he didn't know, that the Sinaloa cartel was moving into Juarez. She knew that very soon there would be war here, just as there had been in other regions that the Sinaloa cartel coveted, and that the Juarez cartel would fight them—and lose—just like the other cartels whose turf the Sinaloa cartel had co-opted.

She had always resisted but now gave in to his will for her to thank, not him, but her faith. I'll finally thank God, she thought to herself. I'll say it openly now. God gave me Cristina back. God has given us this home. God brought this crazy Australian man into my life. God will protect us now from the storm coming down upon us soon.

◈ ◈ ◈

BUT IT FRUSTRATED HER THAT, DESPITE ALL KEVIN AND BILLY HAD DONE FOR HER FAMILY, she still felt bored sitting here listening to all this talk about the Sacramento de la Comunión. She remembered her own First Communion clearly, the dress she wore in Mexico City, how all the girls compared their dresses, how that was the very first time she had a sense not of being a Catholic, but of being a girl. During the ceremony, which lasted two hours, it felt like every kid in the communion class was fidgeting, nudging someone, or staring off into the heavens behind the altar.

Never again did she feel at peace in a church, and even here today, in a class, not a Mass, she felt the same gnawing unease. They don't put clocks in churches for a reason, she thought. And the cross, well, the torture of sitting here...

But Rodolfo, who sat beside her, was her sacrificial offering. Billy and Kevin had delivered Cristina back to her, and Rodolfo would now be prepared for the sacrament. That was the quid pro quo. Kevin had never stated it explicitly, had only asked, but his way of asking for things was often more a demand than a question, she had come to realize. He added the question mark to the last word, not to the whole of his words. He always seemed to tack it on at the end, as if realizing it would be more courteous to do so.

Kevin walked into the chapel wearing something around his neck that made him look like an Englishman in the black-and-white films she occasionally saw late at night, usually involving an air raid shelter. It wasn't a scarf, for it was too thin and wavy. It was impractical; it surely was not Mexican; God knows what it was. This is theater, she thought.

She felt angry at him. This had become a pattern, she realized. He would transform her life but then act like a boob. If you are a priest, why don't you dress like one? Tu vanidad, that's why. You are one of the most vain men I have ever encountered, she wanted to say to him sometimes. I don't even know you; you helped save my daughter's life, and yet I have such distaste for your vanity.

Kevin began the communion class by calling the boys and girls up to the front rows away from their parents. Rodolfo, she could tell, didn't want to go. He knew only a couple of these fifteen or so children and was aware, as were all her children, that people were talking about them, talking about her, staring at her with the sort of open disgust at her relationship with Kevin that even a child could detect.

Rodolfo walked up slowly, and she saw Kevin spot the boy's reluctance. Kevin walked over to him, tousled his hair, and pointed to a seat. Then he sat down next to him. Now watch, she thought, he is going to try to charm him, too.

But he just sat there. The kids started to fidget; then slowly, one after another, they began to look at Kevin. He smiled and began to swing his legs like they were swinging theirs, becoming, before her eyes, one of them. He became a gray-haired, mustachioed child. Soon many of the kids were smiling, speaking to him in Spanish, making fun of his accent and his mustache. She saw Kevin suddenly lean down toward Rodolfo and whisper to him. Rodolfo leaned back, belly-laughing as Kevin patted him on the knee.

Kevin finally stood up and began to speak about the sacrament and God, and one holy word drifted into another, for Rayna was just watching him, not listening to him, the words merely background sounds to his pacing and facial gestures. The kids were transfixed, each and every one of them, not in a sacred, churchy way but as if they were watching a clown at the circus. He had won their imaginations. She had seen him do it on Sundays, but it was easier with adults. Charisma can seduce us, she thought. He startled us by remembering our names, that was his trick, and each new person who came one Sunday and then came back the next and was called by his or her first name the moment Kevin saw them suddenly felt like they had not felt, recognized, since childhood. But this poor, charismatic man who can enchant even our hard-hearted children has no idea what awaits him if the violence starts, she thought. He cannot imagine the things he will see.

Looking at Rodolfo, she closed her eyes and tried to pray for him. She had long lamented having girls in Mexico, but that was because, she knew, she didn't live in Culiacan or Mazatlan. There the boys slaughtered one another. And Rodolfo will soon be of age, she realized, just as Juarez is about to turn into a slaughter house for our young men. I have at last gotten all my daughters straight, and now Mexico comes for my son, she thought. She realized she had started to speak about her country like the priests did. Mexico, this vague, vast, incomprehensible, all-encompassing term for the bad things that were about to happen here in Juarez.

◈ ◈ ◈

THEY POSITIONED THE MATTRESSES IN SEPARATE COR-NERS OF THE ROOM, UNPACKED THEIR BELONGINGS, AND THEN STOOD THERE LOOKING AT ONE ANOTHER. Night was sneaking over the desert, but the one dangling light bulb served no purpose yet, so she turned it off to save the parish money.

"Bien, está bien," Rayna said, and she knew by the way her children looked at her and did not affirm her that it was not. But it was at least mejor, at least better, at least a roof and safety.

"Oye, you should all be grateful, this is better than most people in Anapra live," she scolded them. "When you see Father Kevin, you thank him and smile, smile wide."

The children nodded and Rayna clapped her hands.

"OK, let's fry some eggs," she said, walking over to the little stove and putting on her kitchen smock.

The children sat on the edge of the mattresses and watched her. As she beat the eggs, she could only wonder what she had done to deserve this. Billy helping her in the first place; Kevin taking a liking to her; now this, well, this home inside his church.

What did Kevin want from her? What did he see in her that made this worthwhile for him? She knew there were a few good men in Mexico, no, many, but they were fading, fewer, hiding or retreating from the bad ones dominating daily life. And most men today wanted something if they gave something. No one could want her physically now, she thought, not five children into her fifties. And Kevin had never showed that motivation, not in the least. But there had to be something, there had to be.

She flipped the eggs and lifted each one with a spatula onto little plates. She put some cold refried beans on each plate, too, and handed their suppers one by one to her children.

Our first night, she thought, but of what? Our first night of a new life? An easier life? Or another trap, traps within traps within the biggest trap of all—coming to Juarez to seek, simply, work? Maybe I should just take them all back to Mexico City now that it is safer there? I could clean houses there, become a maid if I'm lucky. I've been lucky of late, so maybe my luck has turned? But now that I've got this, now that we've finally got a proper roof and kitchen and toilet? Wait, Rayna, she said to herself. Be patient. This man and this place are in your life for a reason.

◈ ◈ ◈

SHE COULD COUNT THEIR BREATHINGS, KNEW THEM BY HEART NOW AFTER SO MANY YEARS OF SLEEPING IN ONE ROOM. She leaned up from her cot on the floor and looked across the room at her children, each curled up like they were inside her.

She could not sleep tonight. She had slept well all the nights of the first month here, but now the women of the church had found out, the women were catting her, the women had begun to do what she knew they would do. She had accosted one of her underminers, a woman from the church's old guard, today. She knew the woman had shared more than a few beds in her day, and she reminded her of that to her face. She had seen her walking up the street from church after a choir rehearsal and had crossed the street to meet her.

"Why are you speaking this way about me?" she said coolly. She knew that Father Kevin had met with the three women himself, and he had warned her not to get involved.

But she had to draw the line now that she knew they were whispering that she had her eyes on Father Kevin.

"No hay mayor desprecio que no hacer aprecio," she had told him, repeating the old refrán that she had heard her aunt assuredly state so many times back in Mexico City when she was a child. There is no better disdain than not paying someone the slightest bit of attention. She knew it didn't translate well as she watched him process the refrán, but she wished he could grasp its sweetness. Here in Mexico the refrán was like armor to a woman.

In her old, wild days Rayna would have slapped her. That was how she rationalized merely warning her with a question and a stare. The woman did not respond, and Rayna decided she would tell Kevin just that, that there was no altercation, just a simple setting straight of the record.

She got up and stepped lightly toward the window. The floor, in spots her feet gauged well now after just a week here, squeaked loudly, so she almost slid as she moved.

The church glowed. I am living in a church, she said to herself with disbelief. And yet she realized she was scared, more scared than she ever was in a home. She felt oddly more vulnerable, more visible, more known.

She heard a noise below in the courtyard, and, even though she knew it was a cat the moment she heard it, she still jumped.

One of her children stirred behind her. She looked back, heard a sigh, then silence, and then snoring.

She turned back to the church and wanted to go down inside. She had never felt such a feeling, a calling to go to a place, a pulling at her insides from cords in the center of the place.

She put on her robe and walked down the stairwell. Stepping inside the church proper, she realized she had never been alone inside a church in her life. She half-stopped, looked all around, and jumped again as a bird in the rafters swooped down and across the room.

The white walls made the space glow, and she walked toward the altar. She wondered for a moment if Father Kevin would be angry at her, if this was some sort of sin, being inside a church without a priest.

But she had come to pray. That should be okay, a good excuse, she told herself. She knelt on the hard floor in front of the altar. The concrete was cold on her knees, and protruding bits of it dug into the skin on her kneecaps. The pain, she thought, was good.

"Está bien," she whispered.

She looked up at the cross on the wall behind the altar. She blessed herself.

Thank you for letting your house be my house, she said. Thank you for giving my children a warm room to sleep in. Thank you for bringing this man, this first good man, whoever he is and whatever he wants from me, into our lives.

ANOTHER NIGHT SHE HEARD SCRATCHING IN HER HALF-SLEEP AND THOUGHT IT WAS A DOG. But then the moaning, the pleading moaning, woke her fully. She got up and opened the window. It was nearly a full moon, so she could see well, but, even though the moaning grew clearer, she still couldn't see anyone in front of the gate.

She turned and looked at her children; they were stirring, too.

"¿Qué es, Mamá?" Claudia whispered.

"No sé, no sé," she said. "There is someone in the street, but I can't see him."

Rodolfo got up and stood beside her.

"¡Dios!" the man cried.

"He is lying below the gate," Rayna said. "He is hurt. He is dying."

She turned and took her jacket off the wall.

"No te vayas, Mamá," Claudia said. "Don't go. It is a trick. Una trampa."

"He is calling for God's help," Rayna said. "Father Kevin, he would want me to go."

"Father Kevin is a man," Rodolfo said.

"Stand here and watch," Rayna said. "Take my phone and call Father Kevin if something happens. But I know that voice is sincere."

She turned and half-ran downstairs. She wanted to prove to Father Kevin that she could fulfill his expectations. She knew he knew this, but usually he would see her doing things. This time he wouldn't see it, and that was better. This, she realized, was her debut.

She felt the cold air on her bare ankles as she rushed through the door into the courtyard.

"¡Dios!" the man cried.

She peered through the gate and saw him on his back below it. His hand reached under the gate, grabbed her ankle, and startled her. She jumped back, pulling his arm into the courtyard and scraping it against the bottom of the gate.

"¡Dios, ayúdame!" he shouted.

"¿Roche?" she said. She knew it was him, one of the many Roches in particular, from the scabs on his arm.

"Roche, soy Rayna, let go, let go, I will bring you in," she said, and started gently kicking her leg backwards to try to break loose of his grip. But he kept clinging, his fingers squeezing her ankle so hard now that it hurt.

"Roche, let go, let go!"

She swung her leg forward to get more momentum and then swung it backwards as hard as she could. She broke free but ended up pulling his shoulder into the gate. He cried out.

"¡Mamá!" Rodolfo shouted.

"¡Shhh!" Rayna hissed. "Está bien. ¡Es Roche!"

She took the keys out of her pocket, unlocked the gate, and pulled it into the courtyard.

She leaned over him, studying his bloody and torn shirt. Blood was drying on his face, too, and his eyes rolled up into his head, then back down.

"Estoy muriendo, Rayna," he said.

"No, no, Roche, no estás muriendo, no te dejo," she said, dragging him into the courtyard. Claudia appeared alongside her.

"Help me drag him into the church," she said. "Pull. Pull hard."

Roche cried out as they pulled him arms first.

Rayna pulled harder and faster; she kept holding his hand when they got to the church door and she unlocked it.

They pulled him over the threshold and she flipped on the lights with her shoulder.

She bent over him. He had cuts all over his body, not deep but crisscrossing his torso and neck and cheeks.

"¿Qué te pasó, Roche?" Rayna asked, but he could not talk.

"Go fill a jug with soapy water," she said to Rodolfo. He nodded and ran toward the bathroom.

She looked at his body, cut by cut, and saw only one deep enough that it would need to be stitched.

"Hospital, no," Roche muttered. She knew he feared going to the hospital because the police might visit him there and put him out of his pain forever.

"OK, te arreglo yo," Rayna said. I will fix you.

She helped him up and took him inside, her children cowering at the sight of the wounded man. She helped him lie down on the floor. He began to whimper; her kids huddled together.

"He is harmless," she said. "Sleep."

Rayna heated water in a teapot, poured it on top of some soap she had drizzled into a pan, walked back over to Roche, and began to unbutton his clothes. She dabbed at gash after gash but soon noticed Roche had fallen sound asleep. She finished cleaning him, got another wool blanket from a box, and put it on top of him.

She wondered if she should call Kevin but decided that he did not bring her here to be calling him in the middle of the night. He wanted her to give, too, not just take. This was why he wanted her here. But this was another sign, she knew. No one would ever have slashed this poor man in Anapra a year ago. The nights are different now, the nights are darker, she thought. The nights are changing, and thank God we are in here.

◈ ◈ ◈

BUT THEY FOUND THEIR RHYTHM, LEO AND RAYNA AND KEVIN, and she knew she had established a rapport with Leo such that they could together convince Kevin what he needed to do to keep the parish growing. On Easter 2003 there were nearly 100 people at Mass; on Christmas even more; and by the following spring he told himself to stop counting heads, knowing full well he never would until there were so many to be uncountable.

One day the mother of the man who stole the musical instruments came running into the church, shouting for Kevin to come to the hospital downtown to give the last rites to her dying son. He had been shot through the eye and the neck, and when Kevin got back and told her the man had survived, Rayna asked him if he had mentioned the theft after the anointing.

"No, that hole where his eye used to be seemed to be sufficient divine justice," Kevin said, and they both looked at one another, each shocked at his own callousness.

She rarely saw Billy, whom she realized early on was not the parish priest type, needing to go to hospitals and soup kitchens; Billy preferred to work with his hands building houses and digging wells. But she realized that their different styles, Billy and Kevin, were a blessing for Anapra—Billy out in the fields and streets and Kevin here building our refuge.

But one day she heard Billy and Kevin talking heatedly outside her window in the church's courtyard. All the utilities running to Lomas de Poleo had been cut off. Some 250 or so homes on the southern bluff overlooking Anapra, now a dense bowl of shacks below Lomas, were without electricity. For the past couple of years, Billy had been ministering to residents up there, and, though Rayna had only been up on the mesa once, she knew that the land was as barren as a piece of earth could be and that the squatters there were among the poorest of Anapra's poor.

She heard each man saying the name Zaragoza repeatedly and knew they were talking about one of Juarez's richest men who came from the family that controlled much of Mexico's milk supply and now owned gas stations all over Juarez.

Billy was raging, she could tell. She stayed still, trying to understand what they were saying. Zaragoza was trying to evict the residents of Lomas; the land, and all the land from Anapra west toward the San Jeronimo, the name for the area on the Mexican side of the Santa Teresa crossing, had been purchased by wealthy Mexicans and Americans alike over the past few years; now, suddenly, Zaragoza was trying to evict the hundreds of people who had been squatting there for decades. She heard Billy keep insisting that Mexican law meant these people owned the land after so many years of living on it. That was when her happiness ended. These men have done so much, she thought, but they are not from here. They are not us. They do not understand. They have just spent five minutes talking about Mexican law. They will never be able to understand that men are the law here, either men with guns or men with money or men with both.

Several months later, Rayna rode up with Leo to watch the completion of what had begun the night before: men were literally fencing in Lomas de Poleo, white concrete fence posts now sticking out of the ground all around the area and barbed wire being rolled out and attached to the posts. Billy mobilized a protest, recruiting other Anaprans and people from El Paso to join the residents of Lomas. That afternoon, Rayna walked from the church to Kevin's home and found him pacing in the courtyard, his rosary tight in his fingers.

"They are going to force them out, aren't they?" she asked.

He looked at her and smiled gently.

"Billy wants to help them fight it out, Rayna," he said. "But it's a fight we won't win."

"No one can win against Zaragoza, not the whole of Anapra," she said.

She knew she was telling Kevin what he already knew, but she felt she had to say it anyway because these priests, she thought, as good-hearted as they are, they aren't us, they aren't from here, and there are things they will never understand even if they think they do.

But Billy would lead the fight nevertheless, she knew, and Kevin would do his best to walk the line between parish priest and peacemaker, and Lomas and Sinaloa would become words, she realized right there standing in his courtyard, that Padre Kevin wished he had never heard at all, never in his life.

PART II

Communion

2005-2011

CHAPTER FIVE

---◇---

Kevin

ROM THE FIRST TOUR HE GAVE KEVIN OF JUAREZ
BACK IN 1999, FATHER BILLY EMBODIED KEVIN'S
ORIGINAL VISION OF A MISSIONARY PRIEST—precisely the one inspired in Kevin by George Harrison's
concert for Bangladesh and by the rough and tumble Columban
priests Kevin had met when he was seventeen back in Brisbane.
Like the swashbuckling Columbans Kevin had met since then—
the clerical globe-trotters who had returned from the poorest
corners of China, India, and Peru—Billy lived entirely, authen-
tically, and zealously to serve. A dangerous, adventurous setting
only reinforced the persona. They were the guys who came back
and didn't talk about saving souls but serving the poor, improving their health, building their homes and schools, defying their
tyrants, even if it meant death. They were part John Wayne and
part Mad Max. There was a purity, an uncompromising devotion, to Billy's service that made him as authentic a radical as

Kevin had ever met. People of the Protestant persuasion, as Kevin saw daily around Anapra, conflated missionaries with proselytizing. Billy, and the Columbans, went into hellholes like doctors or nurses would—the mission was to heal. If Billy saved a soul or two along the way during his seven years living in a shack among the poorest people of Juarez, well, "bonzer, mate!" as Kevin would say whenever his Australian slang would kick in. But Billy was here more so to save lives, physical lives, by feeding and sheltering and detoxing and, well, insisting on living.

And he raged at injustice. Billy had a laser eye and a terrible stomach for it, that's why he picked Anapra over any other barrio in Juarez. The most suffering of the long-suffering lived here, a group of impoverished people attracting similar people like an urban magnet. Billy's talent for asceticism—Kevin envied that, too. Kevin relished a fine meal from time to time, a splurge. During his first two years here, Kevin felt ashamed that he had to go to El Paso to spend every Sunday night in a parish house because it was the only way he could survive the dust, noise, and deprivation of Anapra. That stuff, however, the toxic stuff, was Billy's fuel, his nourishment. His soul metabolized human and environmental toxicity. No need for Sunday night respites; no need for an occasional filet mignon. Wake up every day and go to war for life.

Kevin had heard whispers about Lomas de Poleo, that sliver of Anapra on the edge of the desert up the hill from Corpus Christi, ever since the notorious purchase of thousands of acres of adjacent land bordering Anapra by an El Paso real estate magnate, William Sanders. Sanders had founded the LaSalle part of what would become the massive Jones Lang LaSalle international commercial real estate company. What's more, the rumors about the Mexican businessman Pedro Zaragoza's offers to purchase the properties of the residents of Lomas had been spreading for over a year—and now the buyouts were actually occurring. Zaragoza, a key donor to the archdiocese of Juarez, a keeper of the bishop's company, a respectable Mexican oligarch who made his fortune in milk and now had turned to petrol stations, usually got what he wanted in this town. Indeed, he and his family usually got what they wanted in this country. He said the land on which the Lomas residents were living had belonged to his family generations ago. He would nevertheless pay relatively handsome sums of money to the current residents, Anapra's squatters, and help them relocate. Rejection of the offer would not be a conceivable response.

But Billy, Kevin saw clearly, didn't see it that way. Billy, in fact, was raging at Zaragoza's land grab. Indeed, in a legal vacuum, in a Mexican fantasyland untainted by oligarchs and corruption, Billy believed he was technically and empirically correct. Under the squatter's rights law of the Mexican desert, if a family lived on a plot of sand for many years, by law that land was theirs. Zaragoza, in Billy's eyes, was coming too late to the game. His family may have owned the sand once upon a time, but even if they had, after so many years of squatters, Zaragoza's forebears had foregone that right of ownership, and so, too, had Pedro.

One day Billy stopped by Corpus Christi, a few days after the men everyone was sure were Zaragoza's thugs took station at a makeshift gate that suddenly appeared at the newly official entrance to Lomas. The word "entrance" still sounded funny to Kevin, for until recently the shacks up on the bluff only looked worthy to be homes to rabbits or coyotes approaching from any angle in the open desert. Now, all the fencing had been put up by Lomas' new, old owner, and seemingly overnight Lomas had become, as Kevin joked, the poorest gated community in North America.

Billy, Kevin had come to realize, didn't seethe like he did. Rather, he somehow controlled his anger, focused it, harnessed it, made it his personal power plant to drive him relentlessly in his battle with the machine.

"I knew this was coming, things were getting too easy around here," Kevin said to try to lighten the situation. But Billy didn't laugh; Billy rarely laughed, especially at moments like this. And Kevin had the feeling he wasn't going to see him laugh for a long time.

◈ ◈ ◈

BUT AT LEAST NOW, IN HIS FOURTH YEAR, KEVIN HAD FIRM-LY GOTTEN OVER HIS LONGING FOR THE STUNNING VISTAS OF RURAL CHILE, his eyes and spirit having slowly adjusted to the dust and brownness of the Mexican desert. The aridness of the place had shaken him; he never knew how much he had valued the color green. But the Mexican people had helped him come to see their own beauty as more than an adequate replacement. He adored their collective upbeat mood, their outward natures, and their singing and dancing. Indeed, Leo and Rayna, his de facto team, had become his inseparable companions, too. There was no word for it in English, and for that he loved the word simpático all the more, for it described what he felt with them in a way that only their language could describe. He had come to appreciate the nuance of the word, how it captured the feelings of ease, trust, compatibility, goodwill, and good humor all in four vowel-rich syllables. They were becoming, slowly and unashamedly, family.

But their companionship could not console him when it came to the one thing here that he could not align with all the Mexican generosity, quickness to laugh, and pervasive simpático—how in this culture they regularly abused and now, seemingly, regularly slaughtered women. He heard the whispers that Rayna was a victim of some gradation of abuse, and the thought of it made him feel violent himself. Indeed, all the outrageous violence toward women kept Kevin from completely settling in here like he did with the Chileans in Araucania. He loathed that he ascribed the qualities to Mexicans in general. He loathed what he felt was becoming his prejudice. Perhaps it was the Mexican press that was culpable as much as any flaw in the cultural character. The movie stars from Hollywood had led marches in support of the disappearing women; the UN was investigating; lawyers and advocates from the United States and Mexico City were crusading for it to end. But it went on, the desert somehow complicit, offering itself up as the dump for the bodies and bones of anonymous women, of women dead only for having been alive and coming to this city from whatever village in the interior where they had been born destined to seek a better life in Juarez.

However, this woman he had known, the woman whose funeral he was about to preside at. That was a first, even though his encounters with her had been brief. Nevertheless, they had been sufficient to transform her death, and this funeral, into events that put flesh on the statistics from the morning rag. He had seen her, as a girl, come to Corpus Christi on occasion with her mother back in the early days of few churchgoers. She was now a dead nineteen-year-old mother of two whose photo in the paper reminded Kevin of a browner version of Sissy Spacek—frail, sickly, but uncannily beguiling. A string bean but a string bean with something irresistible in her glance.

But what preoccupied him most was that she didn't constitute, strictly speaking, one of the desaparecidas. She wasn't an anonymous girl dragged from a bus, or dragged from a brothel, or dragged from the side of the road, never to be seen again. She had been killed for an explicit reason, not out of meaninglessness. She had been the girlfriend of a local chap who had gotten into a drug deal gone bad, had disappeared, and had left her, in the eyes of his counterparts, as the next logical recipient of vengeance.

She had been found in a field on the edge of Lomas de Poleo, just off the new road they were perpetually building to connect the Santa Teresa border crossing with Juarez proper. Kevin knew the land would someday be a maquila or housing. It was probably another of Zaragoza's or Sanders' fields, for all Kevin knew, but, in the eyes of the barbarians, it was still just the beginning of the Chihuahuan desert of northern Mexico, a convenient dumping ground for dead women. Most of greater Juarez, he realized, before the factories and migrant workers had started arriving by the day, looked just like that field not too long ago. But this field, whatever or whoever would someday occupy it, would always be bloodier than the rest.

He castigated himself for not having done more to know this Sissy Spacek of his parish back in those early days. He had promised himself he would get to know deeply and truly the lives of each of his parishioners but had experienced such an overwhelming sense of disorientation back then that he had failed himself in a way he had not done since his first days at the hospital in Chicago. Corpus Christi had nearly 200 members now; his growing parish was the envy of all the flabbergasted evangelicals in Anapra; the church's extension had begun, construction for real this time after three years of false starts, sabotage, and corrupt contractors. He felt in tune with his flock—their tastes in music, homilies, and even post-Mass buffets.

Yet Sissy Spacek gnawed at his gut. He suddenly remembered she had arrived at Mass alone once a little over a year ago. Why that day? Had her boyfriend raised his hand at her the night before? Had she discovered his occupation? Was she moved to attend, moved to pray for help, because of some menacing secret she had discovered about him?

He tried, but failed, to remember giving her communion that day. And he beat himself up even more. You should have spotted her, he said to himself. You should have known this was going to happen.

And now, as her family and friends started filling the pews

and Kevin donned his vestments in the rear of the church, he felt suddenly alien again, the same feeling of not belonging that had cost him so much sleep during his first years here. It made him dizzy, murderous himself, having to do these Masses. He wanted to sit the perpetrators right down in the front pew and beat them after the final blessing.

As he dressed in the tiny room at the back of the church, he could only think of the man who killed this girl. What was he thinking as he pulled Sissy Spacek out of his car that night in the desert and dumped her onto the sand with not even a thud, she weighed so little. Was he drug-crazed himself, or a clean, cold-eyed dealer? Kevin felt like he wanted to slug the wall.

He turned and stepped up to the concrete altar and nodded to the guitarist and pall bearers. As if he had nodded to them, too, dozens of people in the pews immediately started weeping and moaning on cue. Some started slapping their own heads.

As he made the sign of the cross, he again caught himself not serving them in the moment but nourishing his anger at the girl's killer. Her children sat beside their grandmother in the front pew, and he looked at them once—disheveled, dirty-faced, and a haze in their gaze that told him of the troubled lives they would surely live from this day forward.

He decided not to look at the children again but the next instant chastised himself for his cowardice.

And as the mourners rose and began to sing, he felt the grief suddenly grip his chest. He was fifty-one years old, as stout and hearty as Australia herself, and a walker to boot. But his chest tightened to the point that he wanted to loosen his collar.

He struggled to the chair beside the altar and leaned into it, pretending to sit like a man in contemplation rather than cardiac arrest. He breathed deeply, unbuttoned his shirt beneath his vestments, and closed his eyes.

Then he heard Leo and Rayna singing in the pew to his left.

They came to almost every Mass now; indeed, the three of them usually came together to set up ahead of time. Their voices seemed to call to him. He looked at them, their eyes shut tightly. No one was sitting near them. He could tell they were singing louder than normal, and he could tell they were doing it for him, raising their voices to help hold him up. These fine companions, he said to himself.

He felt better. He stood straighter. He wobbled for an instant, but as the next verse of the song began, he started to sing along, too, sing for Sissy Spacek and for all the moments she would never share with her young children. But in the back of his mind, he kept grappling with her death in the context of the recent spike in murders in Anapra and across Juarez. No one was talking about it, no one seemed to see them all as part of an overall story. But he sensed, suddenly and fearfully, that poverty alone was no longer the sole enemy here. There was something afoot, something more wicked than the desperation of survival on dollars a day.

◈ ◈ ◈

THAT NIGHT LEO CAME OVER TO SIT WITH HIM AND JOHN WHILE KEVIN HAD HIS GLASS OF RUM AND JOHN ATE HIS ICE CREAM AND DRANK HIS TALL BEER. He knew Leo felt his silence. That was the only time dear Leo spoke, really, when he sensed agitation or minor despair in Kevin. He was masterful in his intuition of Kevin's needs, be it a splash of rum, an electric drill for a repair at Corpus Christi, or a few words on a night like this.

"There were a lot of surveyors out near the Santa Teresa crossing," Leo said. "I drove out there yesterday. You wouldn't believe how many trucks there were. Maybe something is finally about to happen. Maybe they are finally going to build a factory?"

He's picked one of my favorite topics, this wise friend, Kevin thought. He has heard me debate the maquilas with Billy, and he knows I come down on the side of jobs, not necessarily hearty wages and working conditions, at least not for now. We need to get jobs for these people and then fight for the better stuff later. Indeed, Billy the purist raged against the paltry wages and gulag-like working conditions of the maquilas. Kevin would sit quietly, hear Billy out, and then ask a more or less rhetorical question comparing life without the maquiladoras to life with them. But even Leo's selection of Kevin's favorite debate topic couldn't pull his brain from its recent fixation.

"Leo, have you noticed a spike in funerals, funerals for murdered people, in the past few months?"

Leo looked at him quizzically.

"No," he said, shaking his head.

"Well, maybe it's just me then," Kevin said. And at that point he said what he usually said at this juncture of the evening in this company.

"I think I'll have another, just a splash," Kevin said, and Leo nodded, smiled, and poured a wee bit more than a splash of rum for him.

"And Lomas, Leo, we are losing there; there is no way to win even if our people are right," Kevin said.

"No hay manera," Leo said. There is no way. And yet Billy fights on, Kevin thought, fighting perhaps like I should be fighting even in the face of certain defeat. He is retaining civil rights lawyers from Mexico City for the Lomas residents; he is walking through the entrance and staring Zaragoza's thugs in the eye; he is smuggling in food and water even as the thugs try to starve them and thirst them to death. And I'm here, trying to build a world made of prayers and sacraments.

"What do you think Jesus would make of all this, Leo?" Kevin said.

Leo smiled, innocently, Kevin realized.

"Paz, he would have wanted peace," Leo said.

Kevin smiled at him and didn't want to tell him he was wrong. Jesus would have been raising hell right about now, not trying to build up the church chorus and develop confirmation classes at Corpus Christi. Jesus would have been raging like Billy. Kevin had made his decision on Lomas early and clearly—that is not a fight worth fighting. The practical, necessary way to serve here is to provide these people with an opportunity for a spiritual life and with a few practical benefits—meals, camaraderie, a place to sing and dance and feel safe—whenever I can, he thought. But after a few sips of rum each night, a troubling question would always start to nag at him. He didn't want to involve happy-go-lucky Leo in it, so he grew silent and they sat there in the semi-darkness together.

But the question kept on in his head. Is the practical way also the cowardly way? And, then its corollary: At the end of the day, even when he loses, was Billy right all along?

◈ ◈ ◈

THE ARCHDIOCESES OF EL PASO, JUAREZ, AND LAS CRUCES, NEW MEXICO, HAD COME UP WITH THE IDEA TO CELEBRATE AN ANNUAL *MISA DE LA MALLA*, or Mass of the Wall, along the new and rapidly unfolding border fence that was somehow supposed to keep Islamic terrorists from crossing the desert to America. At the Mass they would pray for the souls of those who had died trying to cross, and for unity, for borderlessness, for the oneness of the human race. Kevin liked the idea in principle, but in practice, now three years running, it was flopping. The new fence, the post-9/11 fence, had gone up with an efficiency the likes of which Kevin had never imagined the border patrol capable of. The Mass, the bright idea to celebrate union and not separation, had been regularly overwhelmed by the triteness of the notion in the face of the simple, stunning physicality of the fence. Metal had demarcated a "here" and a "there," and the rest was naïve fantasy, Kevin thought. "But we'll pretend again this year," he had told Leo the night before, "just to not ruffle any feathers."

There was no one in sight on the other side of the fence when Kevin pulled up in his truck, but about ten men and women from the parish were already here on the Mexican side of the fence. Leo and his boys, struggling with the gusty wind, were setting up two tents, after gauging where the sun would be by the time Mass started.

He marveled at Leo at these moments, the way he seemed to intuit the mechanics of the cosmos. He watched him extend his arm and raise his thumb toward the sun, then walk to a new spot, then gauge the sun again, and then motion to the men where to drive the stakes. He could fix anything—that Kevin adored and needed. But it was Leo's other life—the outdoor life he lived prior to coming to the city—that intrigued Kevin. Skinning animals, bracing a dog's broken leg, sucking the puss out of a cut—that was the stuff that reminded Kevin of the uncanny talents he had seen in the aborigines back home in the Australian outback. He often realized part of his fondness for Leo was based on how much he reminded him of the aborigines that fascinated him as a boy. That code, those talents—perhaps the desert forged them, the desert everywhere.

He walked up to Leo and looked up at the sun with him.

"Feroz hoy, Kevin," Leo said.

"Ferocious every day, Leo, burning itself up like hell up there!"

They spotted the cars coming from the western road in New Mexico, a border patrol car leading them. At almost the same instant, the convoy from El Paso appeared, kicking up dust as it bumped down the mountain from the northeast.

"Who said Mexicanos are always late, Leo?"

"Real Mexicans are never late," Leo said. "It's the Mexican Americans."

Kevin laughed, but the arriving cars kicked up so much dust that he stopped and had to spit.

The functionary for the bishop of El Paso got out and stood about fifty feet from where the tents were. He looked at the tents and started shaking his head. He walked toward Kevin, and the way he walked, Kevin thought, so perfectly fit his title. The functionary's functional gait—he didn't move his arms, just legs taking tiny steps as they carried a torso in the straightest of lines to its destination.

"Here we go," Kevin said to Leo. "Time for us to be functional."

Leo laughed and then spit. Kevin walked up to the fence and smiled at the functionary, whose blank face he had expected in response.

"We have to move these tents," the man said. "They are in the wrong place."

Kevin decided to let himself lose it. This man each year for the past three years symbolized all that he loathed in the Yanquis: their prepotencia, presumptuousness, their self-certainty. He once loathed it as an Australian loathed it, but now, even more deeply—now he had begun to loathe it as a Mexican.

"The hell they are!" Kevin said.

The functionary's jaw dropped.

"I beg your pardon?"

Kevin knew he was going to say that, too.

"My guys know what they are doing, sir, and I'll bet you the collar on your neck that when the Mass begins, the shade will be binational."

"I am sorry," the functionary said. "They are in the wrong place."

"Father," Kevin said. "We are on earth. We orbit around the sun. The sun's angle shifts by minute, you'll notice if you look up."

As they stood there, more cars began to converge from both El Paso and New Mexico. These were the bishops, and Kevin turned and saw the bishop of Juarez coming up the hill. Anaprans were walking up, too, scores of them, far more than were coming from the Yanqui side, just like every other year.

"We have three bishops converging on us within five minutes, sir, and about fifty priests. You haven't even set up your own tents yet. You've got to get your act together, you Yanquis, or you're going to look awfully bad to your boss."

"We are going to set up our tents there," the functionary said, pointing.

Kevin felt the urge to slug a hole in the fence and continue straight with his fist into the functionary's jaw. That was what frustrated him most about this bloody fence right now, its prohibition of a legitimate punch.

"Let me give you some Australian clarity, Father," Kevin said. "Bugger off!"

Nothing riled him more than an officious Yanqui. In Mexico, you rarely encountered someone of this sort—a bureaucrat who exerted power not so much to justify his job, as was the case in Mexico, but to justify his very being, his unjustifiably enormous ego. He had received the same attitude from an agent at the bridge when he had crossed over to El Paso the morning prior.

He had gone to his barbershop in downtown El Paso—that was the one concession he still made to Western luxury, for every Mexican barber he ever tried had butchered his hair. The girls in the shop asked him where he lived, and he replied that he came to see them all the way from Anapra.

The three of them had stood aghast and then laughed with disbelief.

"Anapra!"

One would say the word out loud and and then laugh with

the others. Then another would utter it, and they all would laugh again.

When the girl had finished his hair, Kevin looked in the mirror, nodded, and winked at her.

"The three of you are welcome to visit us anytime in Anapra!"

They roared again as they shook their fingers at him, and he tipped each of them as much for their good humor as their expertise.

But it was what had happened prior to his barbershop visit that reminded him of this functionary. At the border crossing, an agent asked him where he had been and why he was crossing.

"To go to my barbershop," Kevin replied. "I'm attending a Mass with the bishops of El Paso and Juarez and Las Cruces tomorrow, and I want to look sharp."

"With the bishop?" the agent asked. "Why the bishop?"

Kevin dug in but knew this was the best place in the world to bite one's tongue.

"To say a Mass along the fence," Kevin replied calmly.

"Along the fence? For what?"

"To pray together, bring people together from both sides of the border, to pray that the borders between us someday go away and we all may live as God's children."

The agent paused. Kevin could see him trying to get his head around the statement, then trying to determine if Kevin was, as the Yanquis say, fucking with him.

"Are you being smart with me, Father?"

"No, I am being truthful and sincere."

"How much time you spend over there?"

"I live there. You must be new, for I cross here at least once a week. That guy knows me. And that guy."

"Don't point, please," the guard said. "Why do you live there?"

"Sir, I am a missionary priest, a Columban," Kevin said, sarcasm now ceding to anger. "I work with the poor people of

Anapra, try to help them. Now may I be on my way to my barbershop?"

"So you are an Australian with an American passport working with the poor in Juarez?"

"Yes."

"Thank you," the agent said, handing Kevin his passport.
"That was all I was asking."

"What?"

"That was all I wanted to know."

Kevin felt himself tightening his fists. The things he wanted
to say. His adoption had prevented his knowing his true parent-
age, but he assumed it was Irish at moments like this, for he was
both proud and wary of his Irish temper.

"Good day, mate," Kevin said.

The agent didn't look up.

So as the church functionary and the border agent seemed
to merge into the same frustrating person, he walked over to
Leo and watched as more cars and buses began appearing in the
distance across the border.

"Cabrón," Kevin said. That bugger.

Leo laughed and shook his head.

"You wouldn't survive over there, Leo," Kevin said.

Leo laughed even harder.

"Tú tampoco," Leo said laughing. You wouldn't either.

"Seriously, look at this priest setting things up. He's a numb-
skull. You ever see a guy like that in Mexico? Not even working
for the state, do you? Answer me, Leo, you know I'm right!"

But Leo kept laughing, seemingly knowing that the best way
to help Kevin settle his anger was precisely what he was doing.

Kevin's anger had subsided in Chile, so much so that he
thought he had conquered it. But that was merely an effect
of his surroundings, of the placid and hassle-hating Chileans
themselves. Here it came racing back like blood to his pounding

heart. At first he blamed it on the sun. Then he blamed it on the dust, for a few days. When he finally blamed it on himself, he knew he was right.

On the other side of the fence, he saw a priest from New Mexico, an American with whom he had drunk rum once after a retreat in Santa Fe.

"Hola, Father Kevin," the priest yelled. Kevin looked at him and thought for a moment that he had been sent from God, this relaxed American priest, to calm Kevin's blood pressure.

"Now there's a fine one, Leo, that fellow," Kevin said as he started to walk toward the fence. "Restores my faith in our neighbors just to see the fellow."

He stuck his fingers through the fence to shake hands, or more precisely, fingers, and the good priest scratched his hand on the wire as they struggled to find the right positioning with their fingers.

"You OK, Father?" Kevin asked. "Not worth getting tetanus just to shake the hand of a Mexican!"

"An Australian Mexican, at that!" the priest said, and they both laughed.

Another priest from New Mexico walked up and more deftly stuck two fingers through the fence.

"You just crossed illegally, Father," Kevin said, nodding up the steep New Mexican hill to a border patrol truck.

Slowly but steadily, Kevin's parishioners started walking toward the fence. He could spot three or four people on every dirt road down the valley and up the hill that was Anapra. Only a few square miles in all, and something like a bowl with Lomas at the top of the hill, Anapra looked like an ant colony at times like this.

As the buses and cars came driving along the dusty border roads on the other side of the fence, and as his parishioners came walking down the bowl and up the hill to the fence, he couldn't help but think how all these people looked alike, how this fence served as the perfect metaphor for the separation of man from himself in the Garden, and how, if he were bishop, he would make that the basis of his homily. This fence is our fence as much as the functionary's fence or the border agent's fence. It is here because of *how* we are, not *who* we are.

"Someday we'll stop meeting this way," Kevin simply said to them.

The other two priests chuckled.

"And someday you'll be the first Australian pope," his old drinking buddy cracked.

"Ah, yes, yes, my destiny," Kevin said. "My ambition."

As he took his seat, facing south, he realized he had been given the perfect view of Lomas de Poleo up there atop the bowl. Billy was now furiously leading the final battle in his heroic defense of the neighborhood, working with lawyers to try to stop the last evictions, leading protests, trying to summon celebrities to the cause just as had been done when Jane Fonda and other movie stars rallied for the desaparecidas before pop culture lost interest in the issue. But nothing was working; little by little, Lomas was becoming a ghost village. The rich men's bullies had been burning houses, beating residents, blocking entrances, and cutting off the electricity at random and terribly inconvenient times.

From here the white fence around Lomas gleamed in the sun, much more out of place than the rust-brown color of the border fence beside Kevin. Surely the American fence planners had not searched for indigenous fence architecture to respect the local architectural idiom, he thought to himself, now losing track of the Mass for the Malla altogether. But isn't it ironic, he thought, staring up at Lomas, that the American fence at least looks more fitting here than the one the rich Mexicans have built? That border looks worse than this one, he thought. And maybe it is worse, too.

CHAPTER SIX

---◇---

Rayna

DESPITE HER OBVIOUS UTILITY TO KEVIN (THE CHURCH HAD NOT BEEN ROBBED ONCE SINCE SHE HAD MOVED HER FAMILY IN)...despite her infectious joyousness as the new dance troupe director (there were now twelve women in the group and on Sundays they would stand in front of the altar and sing and dance and turn the place into bedlam)...despite the spotlessness of the church she cleaned (she had taken to using bleaches and dyes that Kevin had immediately prohibited when he heard her cough as she knelt scrubbing the altar)...despite her very apparent tall task of caring for five children and now four grandchildren (all of whom were now studying hard and staying out of trouble)—despite all these factors, the snipers within the parish continued their attacks on Rayna. Chisme, they called it, a combination of gossip and *ad hominem*, or as Father Kevin joked in his schoolboy Latin, *ad mulierem*. She knew some of them were calling her a manipulator, a kiss-up. She knew one of the women was calling her a whore. She had been called worse but never so repeatedly, so aggressively, so cohesively. What did these nagging women want? she asked herself night after night as she lay awake listening to her children sleep. My eviction from the church? The end of my friendship with Father Kevin?

But what struck her most was how a woman here could never change her past, never reinvent her fifty-year-old self from her twenty-year-old self. She wondered if women suffered this in America.

And what woman here, really, could say she was clean? The woman calling her a whore—Rayna knew she had slept with more men than any woman in the parish. She had children by at least three different men in Anapra alone, and the Virgin Mary knows how many she had left behind in Zacatecas.

She knew that at 3 o'clock the woman would be here, possibly alone at first, to set up the food tables outside the church. Rayna stood watching from her window above the courtyard, and she heard her antagonist before she saw her. She had the key to the storage area, and Rayna heard her jostling with the lock.

Rayna looked in the mirror, tidied her hair, lifted her chin, and walked downstairs. It was unseasonably warm for February, about 80 degrees, and she was happy for the families of the children who would be confirmed tonight that they would be able to celebrate in the courtyard afterwards.

That is, provided that there was no blood on the concrete slab below their feet. She was ready to be male about this, to be macho, to accost her accuser and slap her cheeks if she did not apologize. She was jeopardizing what Rayna had worked for here—a safe, relatively warm place for her family to sleep; Kevin's trust; the first job she had held in years. But in Mexico, a man had to do what a man had to do.

She stood and watched the woman coming toward her, backwards, dragging a table. Rayna walked up to her, touched her on the shoulder, and the woman jumped slightly.

"¿Cómo estás?" Rayna asked, extending the syllables to be sure the woman knew she was being as false as the day is hard.

"Bien," the woman said, looking down.

"Let me help you," Rayna said.

"No, no, estoy bien," she replied.

But Rayna, with one hand, pulled the table away from her and dragged it to its spot along the back wall of the church. She set it up, stood in front of it, and watched, aggressively, as the woman followed and set up a second table next to the first.

"Now," Rayna said, "why are you telling Father Kevin that I was a prostitute? That's what you said, not a whore, but a prostitute. As if it were my profession."

"I never said any such thing!" the woman said. "You have a persecution complex! Now let me do my work and go back into your church!"

The woman walked off, and for a moment Rayna turned to follow her but stopped after a few steps. She felt like something physically stopped her, froze her legs and brought a calm over her that she had never felt before in a moment like this. She felt suddenly sad, not angry, and didn't know whether that was good or bad, growth or weakness.

A few hours later, Father Kevin showed up and asked her in his ever-jolly tone how her day had been. She could tell that one look at her now was all it would take him to know the answer to his own question.

"God, I think, kept me from killing her today, Father Kevin," she said. "He froze me. But I don't know if he will be here next time."

"I spoke with them, Rayna. I wasn't going to tell you, but I met with the three worst offenders," he said. "I began by asking them if they'd ever heard of Jesus blessing prostitutes, for Christ's sake.

I am not going to change. But I think the best solution is to employ you as a cook up at the house and get you out of here. You have been living at the church for two years now. We now have a budget, and we can pay you to cook for us and work here, too. Pay you enough to live in your own home and not have to put up with this bullshit."

He always surprised her, she realized. Always offering, always giving. And what have I done to deserve this? Why are these men, these priests, saving us? And, catching herself, who will care for the church at night?

Of all her successes, that was the one she valued the most. No one was breaking in, despite the church being guarded by a woman and children.

She agreed to the move, reluctantly, but on the condition that she move back if or when the first nocturnal robbery occurred.

A few nights later, as she helped the children pack their things into boxes, she remembered how Kevin had looked at her when she set the condition for moving. The one thing such a vain man can never hide is his pride in a success, she thought. He sees me as his success. He sees my wanting to defend the church physically as a reflection of how I have grown into it spiritually. It would break his heart if I told him it was more because of the music and the flowers than the prayers and the Masses. But maybe it wouldn't. Maybe he knows. Maybe he knows I'm the reason, not just him, that so many more people are coming these days.

And in the morning, after they packed the boxes into Leo's car, she took one last walk around the church before leaving. She wasn't really leaving, she knew, but she was leaving today a different person than when she had moved in, and that had never happened to her during one of her dozens of moves during her adult life. She usually left a place in a worse state, both the place and her condition in the world. But this morning, she felt like she was moving up by moving out, and, for a few seconds, she stood in front of the altar and prayed. And during her prayer she called the church "my church" and realized she was calling it her own when she said it. She also promised it she would continue to care for it, to bring it life and love and cleanliness in return for the new life it had given her.

❖ ❖ ❖

HE STARTED TO EXPLAIN THE GAME TO HER AS HE SAT ON THE SOFA WATCHING SATELLITE TELEVISION AND SHE STUFFED A BIG TURKEY ON THE COUNTER IN FRONT OF HIM, but it struck her as little more than wide, white men running into each other. She could hardly say the word, rugby, could hardly get it out of her mouth without giggling. She saw one man get up, wipe blood from a cut in his face, and go diving into another fellow wearing a different colored jersey.

"Why would you play this game? Fútbol is so much more elegante, Father."

"No one has ever accused me of being elegant, Rayna," he said.

And yet, as he took Claudia's son, Ali Martin, in his arms, shook the bottle of formula, and held it to the baby's mouth, she knew she had never seen a man handle a baby with such joy. Rayna's only consolation in two of her daughters getting pregnant so young was Kevin's joy at it. He didn't judge them for their age; he didn't scold them for not being married; he embraced these babies, and when he met their fathers, he acted as if there were no doubt that they would be honorable, loyal fathers. And she saw the boys feeling the need to act up to the level of his expectation.

"Do you regret not having children?" she asked him abruptly as he sat on the brown sofa in the living room across the counter from her. She had never asked him a personal question, she was sure, but as she watched his obvious pleasure at feeding the baby, she simply could not refrain from asking this one.

Then he blinked.

She thought he was going to say something sarcastic, but he simply looked at her and then back at the baby.

Then, without looking at her, he opened his mouth, kept it open momentarily.

"This is my family, Rayna," he said with no emotion. "These little buggers. You. Your children. What else does a rapidly aging priest sworn to celibacy have?"

She stuck the turkey in the oven and left him to his game. She went into his room and started cleaning the floor but realized how clean it already was. Of course, she said, without children running around dirtying things up, with only two men living in this big house, there was surely going to be less dirt. She knew he had been adopted, but she did not know the details. A few photographs were sitting on his desk, one of an older couple who she surmised must have been his adoptive parents. She heard him shout at the game back in front of the television, and she laughed. If I have found God, she thought, or if he has finally found me, I think it was to be able to help this crazy man.

"So then Juarez has grown on you?" she asked, pridefully teasing him as she walked back out to the kitchen. "¿México te va bien?"

He smiled.

"Bien," she said. "So now the only thing left for you is for my daughter Ellie to give you dance lessons because you still look terribly out of place up there on the altar whenever we dance!"

He huffed and shook his head and returned to the rugby. She liked to keep him in his place and had learned from him to undermine any moment of sentiment with humor.

As she started to prepare the salad, Clara walked in from school and threw her book bag on a chair and sat down next to him as if she had always lived here in this home and as if he were, if not her father, her grandfather who was seated in this spot watching this channel at this hour of every day. They lived in a shack with no heat or plumbing a few blocks up the road now, but Rayna's becoming cook here naturally transitioned into her children and their children showing up when she cooked. And they naturally and rapidly became one big Mexican family, and she could tell Kevin loved it. Maybe he had his ulterior motives, too, just like I did when I kept showing up at church in the beginning. Maybe he made me cook not just to help me but to help himself, she thought. And that is good, she thought, that is what he means when he says God is good. I always thought it was the silliest thing to say, God is good, whenever something goes right. But it is going so right for all of us, we are so right for him, that I feel for the first time in my life like I wouldn't change a thing, and I think that is what he means when he says those words, God is good, all the time now.

◈ ◈ ◈

WHENEVER SHE WALKED INTO THE CHURCH AND SAW THE CHOIR REHEARSING, SHE IMAGINED THE DANCING THAT WOULD ACCOMPANY THE SONG. She had always loved music, but Kevin's growing practical devotion to it—his recognition of its necessity here—made her appreciate its power even more. But the day a few weeks prior when she saw Gabino, a local mentor to young troublemakers, standing among the choir with a guitar over his shoulder, she couldn't hear a word they were singing.

This was Kevin's fault, she thought. He insisted on his open-door policy. He loved to pronounce, "Who am I to turn a worshiper away?" It was the only time he sounded sanctimonious to her, and naïve, too. There were sons of the devil in Mexico, she wanted to tell him. Maybe not in Chile or Chicago or Brisbane. But here we don't live in la-la land. Even Jesus would have had a hard time welcoming some of the bad guys in Juarez with open arms.

And so this is what we get, she thought, guys like this Gabino. She understood ministering to drug addicts, to prostitutes, even to thieves. But Gabino was a preyer, worse than a murderer or dealer. He recruited kids to enter the dirty world, to deal or smuggle drugs or people across the border, and that was even worse. And she didn't want him here.

She called Leo, dialing him on his new parish cell phone from her new parish cell phone as she went upstairs.

"Leo, did you know Gabino is playing in the choir?"

She already knew Leo knew. She loved him as much as Kevin loved him, but she was ever outraged by his nonchalance. Leo lived and let live, but his inability to feel outrage, just like Kevin, made her want to choke him sometimes. And now, that nonplussed tone of voice, that chuckle…

"Leo!"

"Be calm, Rayna," he said. "Tranquila. You know Kevin's policy. Maybe it will change Gabino."

"He works for Alarcan," she said, knowing that mere mention of one of Anapra's baddest of bad guys, a murderer and drug dealer who lived up the hill from the parish toward the border fence, would show Leo she wasn't hopeful about Gabino's prospects for redemption.

Then she hung up. The next time she saw Leo, at Kevin's home, she didn't speak or look at him. A few days later, in the same kitchen, he walked in and sat at the table.

"Gabino is running illegals from here to Dallas. He offered me a job," Leo said.

She put down the big knife she was cutting a recently cleaned chicken with and looked up at him.

"The sinners, we've got to welcome all the sinners," she said. "But not when they are invading us, trying to eat us from inside. Not this kind of sinner."

Leo shook his head and looked at the table.

"Say something, Leo!"

He looked up at her timidly.

"I will talk with Father Kevin."

Rayna shook her head, picked up the big knife, and pointed it at him for a second.

"If I see him ever talking to one of the young people, I will throw him out of the church myself, Leo," she said, and slashed into the chicken carcass. "And if you don't speak with Kevin by tomorrow, I will stick my head into this man's business. Trust me, if I am bugging you now, I will bug the two of you to no end until he is out of here."

❖ ❖ ❖

A FEW WEEKS LATER SHE OPENED THE CHURCH EARLY ONE SATURDAY FOR A CONFIRMATION CLASS KEVIN WAS HOLDING THAT MORNING. The choir was coming to rehearse, too, so after she switched on the lights, she walked to the choir section beside the altar and began to tidy it.

When she looked up, Gabino was standing right in front of her. She jumped.

"Gabino," she said. She stepped down from the podium and walked right up to him.

"Gabino, if you ever speak with Jorge and Will, those boys in the band, again, I will kill you, do you understand?"

Gabino scrunched his face and turned red.

"I know what you are doing," she said. "If you come here, come to church. Not to recruit these boys. Father Kevin will accept you, you know that, and you know I won't. But you are not to abuse the privilege he grants you. If he lets you play music, that is his foolish mistake. But if you abuse that right…"

She seethed, as much at Kevin's innocence as at Gabino's presence. What good things these men, Billy and John and Kevin, are doing here, she thought. But how naïve they are, thinking they can summon the evil out of some of these hard hearts. How naïve they are to the sheer force of evil, its resistance to change, the regular impossibility of changing it once it has taken hold of someone like Gabino.

She noticed Gabino turn away, though, and was surprised he was not more defiant towards her. She wondered, for a second, if Kevin didn't have a deal with him that she wasn't aware of. That wouldn't surprise me, she thought. That would be just like him, reassuring Gabino that he was welcome and even telling him what a great guitar player he was. She could hear Kevin saying kind things to him in her head, his voice full of optimism and hope in humanity, his voice, here, sounding so foolhardy.

❖ ❖ ❖

GABINO DIDN'T SHOW UP THAT SUNDAY, AND WITH NO GUITAR PLAYER THE CHOIR SOUNDED OUT OF SORTS THE WHOLE MASS. Perhaps he is gone, she thought. Perhaps he realized I would never quit, that I would have my way no matter who is running this place. She refrained from saying anything to Kevin. Let it be, she thought. I've won this and I'll save my comment for the next time he brings in a devil's son to our church.

A few days later, Leo walked into the kitchen. Kevin was watching the BBC news while Rayna was preparing lunch.

"Gabino nearly died," Leo said abruptly. "Alarcan wanted to rob you, Kevin, steal your truck. They put Gabino up to it, and he refused. He said it is sacred, the truck, sacred. And they beat him up so badly that he nearly died."

Rayna looked at Kevin. He looked back at her, not with a face that said, look, I was right, but with knowing sadness.

"I would have given them my truck, the bastards," Kevin said. "Where is he?"

"I don't know. I just saw his brother. I think he is hiding."

"Jesus, what have we become?" Kevin said.

Then she didn't see Gabino for another month and found herself worrying about him whenever the choir began playing.

But one day he walked back in carrying his guitar fifteen minutes before choir practice was scheduled to begin. He limped, looked thinner. He was trying, and failing, to act as if nothing had happened. The bruises from the beating Alarcan's heavies had given him were fading but still visible. She felt ashamed. If Kevin only knew, she thought, if Kevin only could have read my cold, hard heart when I wanted to throw this man out.

Gabino carried on that way for months—silent, sheepish, moving only his wrist and lower arm now when he played and not his whole body, packing up his guitar and leaving as soon as the Mass was over. He struck her as a man who wasn't scared but sick, as if what he had suffered had altered not just his brain and heart but some other organs that he needed to function properly.

❖ ❖ ❖

ONE DAY SHE WALKED UP TO HIM, AND THIS TIME HE JUMPED WHEN SHE SPOKE HIS NAME.

"¿Estás bien, Gabino?" she asked.

He blushed and lowered his head. He started to shake.

"¿Qué? ¿Qué? Tell me!" she asked, putting her hand on his shoulder.

"Tengo cáncer," he said.

She shook him gently, trying to get him to look at her.

"¿De qué tipo?"

"Pancreático," he said, his chest almost collapsing in on itself as he exhaled.

Dios, she said to herself. This place has transformed him, God has struck him at last, and now he has struck him down.

"Gabino, cuánto lo siento," she said. "Have you told Padre Kevin?"

He shook his head, still not looking up.

"Gabino, look at me," she said. "Look up at me."

He slowly raised his head.

"Come to vespers tonight," she said. "I won't say anything to Kevin. But I am starting to see it, some people who pray here, who pray and believe hard, get better from things. A woman who had a limp, she walks better now. A boy who was very sick, his parents came and suddenly the boy recovered. Please come. We will pray together."

Gabino nodded.

An hour later, as people started to trickle into the church at sunset, she saw him sit in an end seat a few rows behind the cluster of twenty or so people.

He recited along with them, most intensely during the Magnificat. He came back for weeks, always to vespers, never to Mass, the choir managing with a new guitar player. Every time she saw Gabino he looked thinner, as if in direct correlation with the shortening days of December.

Then Gabino stopped showing up again. One night after vespers, while she was cleaning up, she caught Kevin's eye. He was talking with an old woman who always came to vespers first and inevitably left last. When vespers would end, she could barely walk out of the church. Kevin was helping her walk down the aisle. They stopped.

"You know Gabino was missing again today," Rayna said. "I think something happened to him."

He smiled at the old woman, slowly helped her to the street, and patted her shoulder as if he were winding her up for her brief trek to her home up the hill. Then he turned to Rayna matter-of-factly.

"He went back to Zacatecas," Kevin said. "Leo said he went back to die."

She thought he looked at her with slight anger, as if he did, in the end, know she had conspired to get rid of Gabino.

"I will always wonder if he knew he had cancer before sacrificing himself for the truck," Kevin said to her.

"Does it matter?" she said.

She looked closely at him and saw Kevin's eyes were moist.

"If he knew, he was heroic," Kevin said. "If he didn't know, then the kicks those bastards gave him in the gut, I think, triggered his cancer. And I might then just send his name in to Rome for canonization. The man died a minor saint in my book."

She walked him to his used truck, the one he had purchased to replace the used one that had been stolen, and waved as he drove off. He looks like a ghost, she thought. He looks weary. It is like he is seeing something here, in Gabino's beating, in the chaos up in Lomas and the construction of the border fence and the rise in violence, and what he sees is changing him, changing how he sees this place, changing how he sees us. How brief was his time of contentment, she thought. He has gone back to being the gruff Anglo man who arrived here.

The rain was coming down so hard that it felt like the roof of the Church was thundering as the double baptism of two boys—one of them the first in Anapra named Kevin—was about to begin. People had to shout to be heard, and the musty smell of everyone's wet suits and dresses filled the air so that the whole place, albeit with only thirty or so people attending the baptism, made her imagine a packed train station at rush hour on a rainy day that Kevin had described when he talked about all the people in Chicago.

She was watching him pour the water over a baby's head at the precise moment when the first car went floating down the road in front of the church. She knew she had been the first to see the car—the family members were all so focused on the baby, and Kevin, having earlier made his regular joke that he had not drowned a baby yet and wasn't about to do so, looked almost nervous as he dipped the baby's head in the water.

She motioned to him, and he did look up, and the disbelief on his face made Rayna think, "This must be the face Kevin would make were he to see a true miracle." Here, in Juarez, after a drought of God knows how many days, there were cars floating down the street.

He blessed the baby and then paused and looked at the proud parents.

"I'm sorry to have to tell you that your car is floating down the street in front of the church right now," Kevin said, his voice calm but his tense body betraying alarm. "I think the Good Lord would be fine if we pause for a bit and investigate the situation."

Kevin nodded to them, and suddenly the father turned and darted toward the door with the whole family, except the mother and baby, running after him.

Everyone froze in the doorway. Rayna stood next to Kevin and felt her jaw drop just like all the others. The rain was so thick that it was like looking through mottled glass, but even so she could see the car slowly sliding down the hill. Others were behind it, moving slowly, equidistant and orderly, in the same direction.

The father ran outside and other men followed.

"Bloody hell," Kevin said under his breath. She had heard the expression so many times that she now could distinguish it every time he said it, even in the middle of a fast-paced telephone call in English.

Then he ran out, too, and she watched as the men became mere blurs through the lens of the thick rain.

The women and children watched as the men ran down the hill to the first car, caught hold of it, and steered it atop the rushing water to the side of the road. Then they waited for the next one to arrive, grabbed it, and directed it to a spot in front of the first one. Then another, and another.

The rain slowed, and there were no more cars coming down the hill, but Rayna could see the water running down the hill like the wild rivers she had seen on the nature channels on television.

Then the men started shouting and running down the hill. Their voices weren't exasperated, like they had been when car after car was floating toward them. These voices had to do with people in trouble, not things in trouble. And she instantly registered what the men had likely seen below. The street led to one of the more recent expansions of shacks down in a tiny valley on the northern tip of Anapra, close to the border. Everything ran downhill to there, and Rayna remembered hearing the men say that only a fool would settle there, for if the one-in-a-hundred-years type of rain ever came, the whole place would become a lake.

The men disappeared, and the women all looked at one another.

"Stay here," Rayna said. "Stay here with the children. I will go out and come back to tell you if everything is okay."

She had grown to cherish her role as Kevin's proxy, particularly in moments of crisis. She found herself acting like him, as if she had watched Gregory Peck, one of Kevin's favorite actors, and tried to imitate his cool reaction when the gun was pointed at his head or the train was flying off the tracks.

The rain picked up again and looked like it was coming through chutes now, a rush of it and then a lull and then another rush. She was drenched by the time she was halfway down the hill, and she felt the water on her skin under her clothes. She tiptoed on the soggy land beside the new, rushing river that once was the dirt road in front of the church. The water was rushing so fast it made her afraid, and as she came to the midpoint of the hill, she could see cats and dogs struggling to escape the water's grips.

Then she turned the corner and saw all the houses, or, rather, saw that they were all gone. The men were helping residents up the hill, some clinging to their dogs, others to a suitcase, some to a few pieces of clothing in a bundle.

But there was nothing left. Metal roofs, plywood, beams, and cars were floating in a soup of junk and clothing. She could see the water rising inch by inch over the whole area, no bigger than a few blocks.

She spotted Kevin, half-carrying a woman and her daughter in either arm up the hill. His vestments were sticking to him, his hair was flat, pasted to his head, and on his face he wore a grimace the likes of which she hadn't seen even when he was blessing someone's brains.

She found herself thinking the worst thing, a thought so absurd and offensive she knew she would have to go to confession to purge it.

This is why they named the streets for fish, she thought to herself. It was a cruel joke after all but not because this is the desert. Because they knew this would come, the cruel men who sat downtown picking names for our little godforsaken village. They were mocking us, the city planners downtown. Streets in the poorest barrio in Juarez named after fish! ¡Cangrejo, Trucha, hasta Pulpo, se dice! Crab, Trout, Octopus even, they said!

Kevin was now twenty feet from her, staggering. Other men

were carrying people on their shoulders behind him. The rain stopped instantly, and, for a moment, everyone stopped along with it, looking up at the gray vastness, the low, gray evil thing above them moving ever so slowly now, slower than the water rushing down the street still beside her.

The men carried the victims toward the church, and the women and children waiting there instantly began to disassemble the chairs in front of the altar.

As Kevin walked in with the two victims leaning on either side of him, he called to Rayna.

"Get the mattresses from your old room, Rayna! And heat some water and run up and grab all the tea and hot chocolate and coffee you can from the house! And the bottles of rum!"

But before she could turn, a man carried in a woman who was bleeding from a gash in her arm. Rayna ran into the bathroom and grabbed the first aid box and towels. She ran back out and started cleaning the woman's wound as more and more people kept coming in, some now falling on the floor and weeping, some sitting against the wall, stunned and mute.

She saw Kevin going from person to person, blessing some, welcoming others who were not Catholic, holding a woman's hand and praying with her. When he came close to her, he looked at her and grimaced.

"The devil is raging today, Rayna," he said.

She threw the bloody towels into a trash bag and stood.

"I will start making soup," she said.

"Lots of it," he said. "Mucho."

◈ ◈ ◈

THE NEXT DAY THE RED CROSS TRUCK ARRIVED, AND THEN A COUPLE OF SMALLER TRUCKS WITH A DOCTOR AND SOME NURSES SHOWED UP. They set up their equipment in a corner of the church, and when Rayna walked in, she realized with one glance at Kevin that he had spent the night here. His clothes still looked damp, and he was coughing something worse than his usual smoker's cough. She went back out and ran up to the house to get him a change of clothes.

On her way back down the hill, she could see the remnants of lower Anapra. The water level had dropped, but there was still a pond down there full of junk and clothes. Television trucks surrounded the area, some with American lettering.

Is this what he was fearing? she wondered. Did he know this was coming? Is this what we deserved? Something biblical to get people in line, to put a halt to the violence?

She walked into the church's courtyard and heard Kevin and a woman talking with raised voices.

"I do not care if they are not Catholic!" he said, trying to stay calm. "I do not care if they are in there plotting the murder of the bloody pope! For now they stay, and they can stay as long as they need to!"

The woman, one of those whom Rayna had found out was gossiping about her years ago, shook her finger at Kevin.

"I am leaving this church, then!" she shouted. "These people attack us every chance they get, and now you are giving them food and shelter. Did you think to wonder if God brought this down on them because they deserved it?"

Kevin shook his head at her and walked off. The woman began to walk away but spotted Rayna and walked up to her.

"I will never set foot in this church again!" she shouted at her.

"Congratulations," Rayna said, and the woman froze, stuttering.

"I am going to go help people," Rayna said, walking toward the church and watching, in the window's reflection, the woman stare at her.

Inside, the church looked more like a hospital now than a

place of worship. More doctors had arrived, and government bureaucrats were scurrying around, carrying clipboards and mumbling the same questions to victims as they sat on cots and mattresses and chairs drawn around their belongings like forts.

She stopped and watched. Kevin was sitting with a family, making them laugh with some crazy line or other that he always seemed to come up with. She held his clothes tightly, and as she walked closer to him, she started to laugh, too.

"Ah, and here's Rayna!" Kevin said, the exhaustion on his face making the strength in his voice sound as if someone else behind him had spoken.

Rayna handed the clothes to him.

"You like that chicken soup?" he asked the family.

They all nodded and smiled. Rayna looked at them, realizing the father ran the little Pentecostal church down the hill that most of the evangelicals down there attended.

"Well, it wasn't Catholic soup," Kevin said, pausing for effect. "It was Rayna's soup, and she's making some more right now!"

Rayna blushed, looked at the family seated arm in arm, and nodded to them.

"I will make it even better today," she said. "Even tastier. Yesterday we were a bit rushed. Vegetable soup today, Padre Kevin," she said.

"Ah, my favorite," he said back, winking at the young son of the Pentecostal preacher. "My favorite from Chef Rayna!"

They stayed, old men and babies, Baptists and Witnesses, inside Corpus Christi for two weeks; Rayna kept cooking night and day for two weeks; at the end, when the last and least person had gone and the church was empty, Rayna realized she had never felt so happy in her life. She had forgotten about time, about her increasingly irritable stomach, about her children's struggles and her own, about the violence in Juarez. This was work. This was great work. This was what Kevin liked to call God's work.

That evening, as Father Kevin and Leo were helping her clean, Rayna stopped and watched Leo disassembling the cots. She wondered if he had slept at all in two weeks. He just kept stutter-stepping around, half smiling, helping anyone who asked him for it, then stutter-stepping his gentle path toward the next task.

He looked up and caught her watching; then he pointed mischievously at Kevin, seated in a chair with his head flopping up and down, sleep at last gripping him.

Leo started laughing.

"No sleep, Padre!" Leo half-shouted, in poorly accented English, to Kevin. Kevin, slowly lifting his head, permitted a grin, and Rayna could tell this man she knew so well now wanted to lift his arm and make whatever obscene gesture they make in Australia to his mischievous buddy over in the corner breaking down the beds.

◈ ◈ ◈

HER COOKING WAS PLEASING HIM AND JOHN, SHE COULD TELL, BECAUSE SHE HAD NOTICED THAT SHE WAS BUYING MORE AT THE STORE and she had had to ask Kevin for a larger stipend for her trips downtown to the market. There was no decent food market in Anapra, of course, and she knew that Kevin's Western stomach, despite having survived three years of dysentery in Bolivia, could not tolerate the meats or fowl from the local bodegas. So Leo would drive her down to a mercado downtown each Monday morning, and they would load up Kevin's pickup truck with the food for the week. She made her lists by menu and by day, so she would walk in with a list that said "Martes chicken enchilidas" or "Friday sopa de maíz" and would send Leo, ever dutiful, off having to remember her instructions for ingredients while she wandered the aisles.

They rarely spoke, and she deep down suspected that Leo wasn't a typical male pig but was at least a little bit machista, for he would never shut up if he were sitting having a rum with Kevin. But the way to draw him out, she also knew, was with a bit of gossip. Leo loved his gossip, she could tell, and she had witnessed an encounter between Kevin and Billy and John the night before that she was sure would make Leo slow down or take a detour just so he could get every last detail.

So she told him, slowly, with vivid detail, just like she had heard Kevin tell stories so many times in a way that left everyone entranced: Billy had arrived in a rage after a court ruling in Mexico City siding with Zaragoza; the thugs had burned a house not knowing a man was in it—he died and there was no police action taken; the water and electricity to the houses in Lomas had been cut off; Billy was going to take the fight to the Mexican Supreme Court. And then, talking him down, calming him, Father John suddenly stopped, his face reddening, and said, calming but strongly: "Billy, we are not in America! We are not in America!" Billy grew quiet, shook his head, and looked at her in a way that told her it was time for her to leave, so she did.

"¿Te fuiste?" Leo asked. You left?

"Sí," Rayna said. "I was very uncomfortable."

"You didn't stay by the window to hear how it ended?"

"No, Leo, that is something a gossip would do," she said. "I am not a gossip."

She knew that got him, but as she began to toy with Leo, she also began to grasp the gravity of what she was telling. Leo wasn't interested in the story in a gossipy sort of way, she could tell. Instead of slowing down the car, prying details from her, he was speeding up, his face and hands tightening as he drove.

And he stopped talking, stopped asking anything at all. They pulled up in front of Kevin's house, and Leo silently helped her unload all the groceries and put them away.

But as he turned to go, he stopped in front of her and looked her straight in the eye.

"The bishop of Juarez wants Billy out," he said. "Zaragoza has won, he was always going to win, that is what Kevin realized. But if Billy has to leave soon, well, soon…"

"¿Qué?" Rayna asked, angrily.

"We have to take more care of them than ever, these Yanquis," he said. "They don't know what they're getting themselves into. They are about to see a Mexico they had never imagined."

His demeanor had eased, and she swore she could almost see his goodness coming out of his pores.

"Bien," she said. Okay. She didn't know what she was saying okay to. She knew nothing was going to be okay. But Leo made her feel like it would at least be survivable, tolerable, so long as they all remained together. That was what they had to do. If they lost Billy, Lomas was lost for good. But what would it take for them to kick Kevin out, too? One more public flare of his temper? That was what Leo was really trying to say. They had to make sure nothing jeopardized what they were building, make sure nothing jeopardized the lives they were finally building. She suddenly realized these men had bosses, that they were here because someone wanted them here and that they could just as easily be ordered to some other poor place anywhere else on earth tomorrow simply because their boss wanted them to be elsewhere.

CHAPTER SEVEN

Kevin

AS HE OPENED THE DOOR TO THE HOUSE, THE **SMELL THROTTLED HIM.** It was coming from the kitchen; it wasn't food. So perhaps she was spraying one of those cans of artificially exotic scents that she had begun to put next to the toilets in each of the bathrooms.

But as he walked in, he suddenly felt like he was walking into a greenhouse back in Brisbane. There were flowers of all colors on the kitchen table, on the kitchen counter, on the shelf against the back wall. Flowers of all colors and odors and shapes such that his first thought was: here, here is proof of God.

Then his next thought countered that one, for he knew no flowers like this grew here. He supposed that she had purchased them, and he was certain that she had spent the house's monthly budget on them in one fell swoop.

"This is how you will get even more people to come to your

church," she said to him as she cut at the stems of a batch of big
purple monsters with gusto.

He regularly took pleasure in her arrogance, her self-certainty. But who the hell was she to know how to attract churchgoers
to a struggling parish?

"Estas, y música," she said. "Beautiful flowers and even better
music."

This time she looked up and smiled sheepishly.

"Where did you get these?" he asked.

"Un secreto, Father Kevin, un secreto," she said.

"Well, a secret needs one person to be told to make it a secret,
so you can tell me."

She only smiled.

"Rayna, at least tell me how much they cost. We are going to
be accused of excess. The Catholic Church is always vulnerable
to that, and if word gets out that we are spending too much
money on miscellaneous things, these evangelicals around here
will have even more grounds to attack us."

She laughed a comfortable laugh, one that showed, to him, how
much her self-confidence had grown over the years. He poured a
glass of water from the sterilizer and sat down at the table.

"There are some amazing children in this year's confirmation class, Rayna," he said. "One of them, Mario, came up to me
the other day and said he wants to join us on the street prayer
drive-about this weekend. I really think the young people are
now starting to like it here. They are starting to encourage their
parents to come."

She looked at him and smiled. That was what he usually hoped
to see—her world-repairing smile—whenever he sat down and
began talking with her. It never came easily, but when he was
finally able to provoke it, he had realized, she had a hard time
turning it off. That's all most of us poor, solitary priests want,
really, he thought often. The pedophiles make the world think

we're as genitally preoccupied as the world at large. But here I am needing an occasional hug from my cook and her heart-warming children, and even a bloody smile from this woman is sometimes enough. That's the brutality of celibacy for you.

"At the end of class another boy, Jose, he was leaving with his mother and he turned and hugged me," Kevin said.

Rayna smiled.

"Bien," she said, and she smiled again, almost sympathetically, as if she knew deep down how he craved hugs from watching his reaction whenever her grandchildren hugged him.

"Across the border a kid does that and his mother would scold him the whole way home and withdraw him from the class out of fear of an old priest."

"Seguro, pero estamos en México," Rayna said. "No es lo mismo." Yes, but we are in Mexico. It is not the same.

He smiled. It's not the same. Sure as hell isn't, he thought. People hugging and kissing all over the bloody place, keeping viruses in business with promiscuous affection. He looked up at her as she shifted from one cutting board to another. He almost said, might I cop a hug from you now? But he held his tongue and fell into his armchair.

The flood had brutalized him both physically and emotionally, and he felt, at moments like this just after sitting in his chair, like gravity was pulling harder on him since the flood. But the weeks of caregiving had also restored part of him. He had always thrived during crises, dating back to his days during the Pinochet protests in Chile, and knew by now that these moments energized him, gave him his reason to be.

Indeed, he realized another difference between him and Billy was the difference between a practical and impractical priest. Billy had fought against the injustice in Lomas like a lawyer would; Kevin, ever impractical, had turned to group prayer and vigils. Now Billy had been thrown out of Mexico, and part of

Kevin believed it would free him up. His approach hadn't been vindicated—his prayers hadn't stopped the floods, for example. But now I'm going to double down, he determined. I'm going to make this church stronger than ever, and that spiritual strength will uncannily become practical strength. The floods showed that. Where did all the victims go? To the hospital? To the evangelicals' buildings? To the government downtown? No, they came to me. And we served. We healed them and helped rebuild their homes and prayed with them, and now guess who keeps coming to Mass? And what with these stinking flowers filling the air with their chemical odors, Good God, we won't lose.

◈ ◈ ◈

CORPUS CHRISTI NOW HAD OVER 350 FULL-FLEDGED PARISHIONERS IN 2008, AND THE MUSIC, KEVIN HUMBLY ADMITTED, WAS ROLLING STONES QUALITY. The band, with teenage musicians now competing to join it, had accompanied Kevin and the prayer vigil leaders one Saturday on a big steel stage that Leo and Juan Pablo had built for just that purpose. They hitched it onto the back of Kevin's pickup truck, and as Kevin said, "a traveling preacher man now had his portable stage."

But its purpose was far more practical, even critical. The Lomas war had been lost, the floods had wrecked the place, and now the real war, the one Kevin had been sensing for a couple of years as the violence kept mounting—the battle between the Sinaloa and Juarez drug cartels—had suddenly begun, seemingly overnight in the eyes of the press but with stunning gradualness to anyone who lived among the people. The press had only now made it official, and Kevin began reading about the killings almost every day in the paper. He had long heard about the legendary escapes and startling massacres orchestrated by the infamous El Chapo, the head of the Sinaloa cartel. Indeed, he had seen graffiti honoring him downtown. But he realized he had one thing in common with the press: they had had no premonition that El Chapo would now have identified the drug corridors of the Juarez gang as his next target. It was so obvious—Juarez, with its proximity and easy passage to America—any fool should have known that El Chapo would want to control the city. Kevin chastised himself for not suspecting El Chapo when the violence seemed to be spiking. The Juarez cartel controlled the lucrative drug channels from Mexico across the border, and El Chapo wanted them. And already Leo was whispering that indeed the government and the police had known it was coming. Indeed, Leo had suggested during their last rum session that the government was encouraging it, this civil war between the two cartels. They wanted El Chapo to control the whole country; they wanted an identifiable, controlled drug economy; they wanted the clarity that one gang's dominance would possibly bring.

One night he walked home after confirmation class, still marveling at this amazing boy Mario and how he moved so kindly through the world. He reminded him so much of Saul down at the tire shop—such an easy smile, such lack of guile, such self-possession. He walked into the compound, spent a few minutes petting his new dog Willie, and had his nightly rum inside. He hadn't been in bed for ten minutes before the gunshots broke out right in front of the house. He swore bullets were ricocheting off the compound wall, so he got up and ran into the windowless bathroom. And there he sat for thirty minutes. It's bloody Gallipoli out there, he thought.

He decided he best make good use of the time, so he picked up a copy of his beloved *Economist* magazine and read while the gunfight raged. He sat there for thirty minutes afterward just to be sure.

The next morning, he walked outside and expected to see police ropes, yellow tape, and used ammunition all over the street. Instead, people were walking about as if it were any other morning, carrying their water, chatting on a cell phone, pulling a cart full of groceries. Leo would help him realize that these people were accustomed to violence already, most of them having come from parts of the interior where it had already been raging. The most terrible thing then, to Kevin, wasn't its swift arrival or its pervasiveness but its terrible normalcy. In Chile during the Pinochet violence, you could almost touch the fear and dread, Kevin had told Leo. Here, where the murders are even more atrocious and public, it seems like life has not changed in the least. This is going to be a long one, Kevin thought, using a line seminarians used to whisper to one another whenever a particularly loquacious old-guard priest was saying Mass. This is going to be a long one, he found himself thinking throughout the day.

❖ ❖ ❖

BUT THE TROUBLES SEEMED TO TRIGGER EVEN MORE ENTHUSIASM FOR HIS CHURCH AMONG ANAPRANS. He remembered a Columban in Chile who loved to repeat the truism, "Love is born of our poverty." And the real boom was occurring in the confirmation classes that Rayna was coordinating. People had been filling the pews for a couple of years now; couples were getting married; but now—and this, to Kevin, was the real sign of full blood flow, of a living, breathing Corpus Christi—the children were coming, wanting to come, having fun while there. Corpus Christi was attracting them—teenagers—the hardest group to enchant for any church anywhere, not just here in Anapra.

And Mario was reminding Kevin of Rayna and Leo. As he sat down with Leo and Kevin one afternoon in the church courtyard, Leo jokingly said, "Mario, you should become a Columban."

"Let me think about it," Mario said, blushing.

◈ ◈ ◈

**THE FINAL CONFIRMATION CLASSES HAD JUST ENDED, AND
RAYNA HAD BEEN THE SPEAKER.** Kevin was as entranced as the
kids who were listening to her tell how she didn't take the sacrament
seriously when she was their age, but now, having lived and had
children of her own and come back to the church, now she thought
it was perhaps more important than even First Communion. The
only interruption in his attention to her was when he would check
and check and check again for Mario. He had never missed a class,
and here we are three days before his confirmation and he doesn't
show up. His inseparable buddy Jose was missing, too.

But Rayna would grab his attention again, dancing slightly as
she spoke. Delegation, he realized, was the key to his success. He
hadn't read any leadership books in his lifetime, and he would
be the first to admit that he had lunged for Rayna and Leo out
of necessity, not methodical strategizing. But, as he watched her
today, and watched the kids seemingly start to orbit around her,
he felt proud of his intuition.

Rayna's daughters were now following in her footsteps—
singing in the choir, training dancers, organizing the ushers,
helping her clean. He had made his bet on her, and on Leo, and
was coming up aces on both counts.

As Rayna started to sing and clap, the children followed suit,
clapping and soon standing on their own and swaying with her.
And she teases me about my charisma, he thought to himself.
How dare she!

After the last of the parents had arrived to pick up their children, Kevin walked over to Rayna.

"My boy Mario picked a great class to miss, Rayna," he said.
"You were wonderful."

But she didn't smile. She looked at the floor, then back up at
him, and stepped closer.

"Leo and I were debating telling you," she said. "Leo is working on him. He is in with the wrong crowd, Padre Kevin. Mario
and his friend Jose, too. They are coyotes. Lots of boys are here.
You know that. But Leo thinks they are smuggling drugs, too.
They have a problem with their boss. He is accusing them of
stealing some drugs. It is not true. They are good boys. But Leo
is working on it."

He had learned a few years ago that a coyote is a smuggler,
then of people and now, in more dangerous days, of people and
drugs, or just drugs on a day when there were no people wanting
to cross. I have never been so fooled in my life, Kevin thought
as he lay awake at home that night. But that implies Mario was
trying to hide something from me. I wasn't fooled. I just didn't
see the full circle, see him as a boy growing up where he is growing up and doing what he needs to do. I was a hell-raiser, and I
would have been doing the same thing had I been born here now.
Trying to make a buck, probably giving the money to his mother.
He is still innocent; doing this to earn money does not take that
innocence away. I will speak with him but still confirm him. That
is not grounds to keep him from the sacrament, Kevin thought.
It is grounds to give him a good belt like my father used to do,
but I'll leave it at a tongue-lashing, the bugger. How can he not
realize the slipperiness of that slope, how every young coyote
who goes up and down those mountains ends up lost among
them eventually, or ends up dead in the streets here.

◈ ◈ ◈

HE WOULD NEVER SEE MARIO AGAIN. A few nights later Mario's employer executed him in the valley between the
mountains just behind Corpus Christi. Mario's Auntie, whom
Kevin knew to be the boy's de facto mother, had knocked on
his door that morning to tell him that his favorite confirmation

student's body was lying up there in the dust, waiting for Kevin's final blessing.

They left the cars where the roads ended and started up the mountain to the place where the police had said the bodies had been found. Mario's Auntie walked beside him behind the men in her family. She didn't look up, and Kevin couldn't help but think biblically, a mother climbing a dusty hill to behold her dead son. At one point during the ascent she wobbled, and he reached out and steadied her.

She looked up at him, again he thought, with a biblical face— resigned, reflective, yet surely, he thought, with her insides ripped up. He knew, though, that her saintly guise would falter once they got there, for there was no value placed in Mexico on stoicizing grief. He knew she was simply doing what she had to do to try to get up the hill, and that he was imposing his own narratives on her. Here the women wailed, and she would wail.

Near the summit of the climb he looked up and saw the men standing there shaking their heads and wringing their hands. He knew they had spotted the scene. But before he could take his last steps and look down, the stench slammed into him. The catechist at church had told him, as he was grabbing his vestments, that the police had abruptly taken the bodies to the morgue. But, with this odor, she must have been wrong. Kevin knew well the smell of death from all the hospitals he had worked at, and this was it.

He reached over to Mario's Auntie but stopped when he saw the look on her face. Horror. The best actress in Hollywood could not impersonate this woman right now, he thought, as she smelled her boy's death. He reached into his pocket for a handkerchief, started to hand it to her, and then stopped. Good God, he thought, you fool. You want to hide her from this? You really think she is offended? Sickened?

One of the men in front of them turned and looked at Auntie as she looked down. Kevin dared not look but kept watching her out of the corner of his eye to see if he would have to catch her. He had grown used to that, too: the wailing and weeping of female Mexican grief often ended in collapse. It was the expectation, the culmination of the ritual.

But his almost prideful clerical cool collapsed when he looked down and felt himself stagger before he could even focus his eyes. Dead dogs were strewn all around the point in the valley where the police had left their markings. But it was their stench, and not the sight of them, that hit him first. He forced his knees to lock in place and, seeing Auntie do it, he, too, covered his nose with his arm. The men stopped shaking their heads and covered their faces with scarves.

They slowly descended, in a straight line, Kevin last behind Auntie. Everyone kept looking at the dogs. Were they here when the police were? Did the killers come back after the police left and spread them around the site of the boys' murder? Kevin wouldn't put it past the police to not even mention the dogs, to forget to mention them, and they surely were not the sorts of lads, in general, to clean them up out of respect to the family.

As they walked closer, he spotted a pair of torn jeans on the ground; near it a shirt. There was blood everywhere, rotting blood he thought, for blood, like bodies, has the substance and texture to decay. But the dogs' blood and the boys' blood had bled together. Everyone stopped by the clothes, and then Auntie began. Kevin followed her line of sight and saw the brain matter spread across a bunch of big rocks. The rocks themselves, pointy ones, had been the murder weapons, he realized immediately. Why hadn't the police taken those with them?

"Cabrones," one of the men said. Bastards.

Indeed, Kevin thought. At the hospital in Chicago, the wise old Lutheran minister who was his mentor had said he only had one word of advice for him. "Never say it was God's will," the fellow said. The Lutheran minister had ended up marrying a Catholic nun, so it would be fair to claim God's will in that, Kevin had teased him. But the advice came to him here now, as the sun was shining down on the blood and brains like a cruel surgeon's light.

Then, and he could never explain where the impulse came from, he walked over and started to pick up the brains of Mario and his friend Jose. There were chunks, some of which he had thought were rocks, and he lay them on the shirt and wrapped them up. Auntie walked over to him suddenly, and he handed the shirt to her. He then stepped over to the jeans, folded them neatly, and handed them to her, too.

She was calm, cradling the clothes as if it were Mario himself not many years ago. She even rocked them for a few seconds.

"Cabrones, cabrones," the man kept saying.

Kevin stood up in the middle of them, in the middle of the scene.

"Let us pray," he said.

They all bowed their heads, but just before he finished making the sign of the cross, Kevin lost focus on his breathing and breathed through his nose again and not through his mouth.

He gagged, staggered again, and a man put his hand on his back to steady him. He cleared the stench from his nostrils, breathed deeply through his mouth, and stood taller.

"Otra vez," he said. "Let us pray."

He finished the sign of the cross slowly, wondering what the hell he was going to pray for and whom he was going to pray to.

He looked each of them in the eyes and then simply bowed his head. The blood, surely the boys' blood and not the dogs', had dried on the desert below him all around his feet.

He lifted up his head, and they did in turn.

"Amen," he said, joylessly, almost dubiously, he realized.

They all made the sign of the cross, paused for one last moment, and then turned and trudged back up the mountain. As he walked, the silence was so striking that the sound of the dirt crunching under everyone's shoes began to torture him. When I first came here, we only had to deal with drug addicts, he thought. Now we are burying children employed by drug gangs. How did I miss the transition? How did I not see it coming, this shift in Anapra from victimhood to viciousness? How did we all miss Satan's encroaching? Were we too preoccupied with Lomas de Poleo? Were we too proud of our success?

He felt Leo walking beside him now, and, though he didn't look up at him, Kevin felt something different emanating from his friend. Leo was slamming his feet into the desert with each step, his anger almost shuddering the earth between them.

"Ha llegado Satanás," Leo said. "Ha hecho su casa aquí." The devil has arrived. He has built his house here.

And Kevin realized that Leo's old time religion was the first thing to make sense today. The devil has arrived. He used to dance in and out, otherwise preoccupied with myriad people and places in Mexico. But now we have his full attention. All the sociological and socioeconomic explanations in the world cannot explain with such satisfactory precision what is happening here. Before, Satan had merely sent his envoys—the rich men, the women killers, hunger and dust. Now he himself has swooped in, and he is bashing our boys' brains in.

◈ ◈ ◈

AND THEN *SATANÁS* BROUGHT THE COLD, THE COLDEST COLD KEVIN HAD YET FELT. He knew the name of the band Three Dog Night, and early on in Chile he had heard the phrase "Noche de Perros." But he thought it referred to nights so bad— cold or rainy, windy or, here, dusty—that only dogs would dare linger outside.

But as Rayna looked at Kevin's dog Willie and said, "Es una

noche de perros," she nodded at the dog and motioned, with her head and hand, for Kevin to take Willie inside with him. And then it clicked. Take him to bed with him. The true, practical meaning of the phrase suddenly clicked. Rayna walked off, and as he looked down at Willie, a white ruffian of indeterminable mix, the dog started for the door. He had never done that. Indeed, Kevin could not remember Willie ever even trying to enter the house. He knew his place; he seemed to luxuriate in having a courtyard that he could call his own. He pooped in one corner, reclined in two others depending on the sun, and reserved the fourth corner for his nighttime correspondence with the other canines up and down the streets of Anapra.

Kevin put his foot in front of Willie. The dog stopped and didn't raise his eyes off the foot. Kevin realized he had not given Willie a bath all winter; he began his calculus with that hard fact. But Willie cleaned himself like a cat and did not sleep on the dust per se but on rugs that he himself had dragged from the tiny deck into each of his sleeping corners.

But tonight it would be zero degrees in the street, and, with the heaters broken for two days now, it would be not much warmer than that inside. Maybe, he thought, tonight there will be no murders in Juarez. Maybe God has brought this cold upon us to save our lives.

He remembered the homes in Chile—the living area and bedrooms built on the second floor above an interior yard housing the cattle and pigs. Their heat would rise, and animal heat, as a peasant once said to him, was better than a woman's.

But Willie, sweet Jesus, the good dog stunk and loved to lick human flesh. Perhaps on top of the bed, not under the sheets? But that wouldn't be fair to him, would it? His coat was thinning now as he aged. Kevin looked down at Willie, and the dog had yet to lift his eyes off his foot.

Willie would warm him, surely, but, looking at it from his

perspective, would the poor creature even survive outside? Perhaps they needed each other.

A one-dog night, just this once?

"Come on, Willie," he said.

He swore Willie nodded, a nod that said, I agree, just this once. Or until this passes.

Willie walked inside in front of Kevin and didn't look left but headed right, straight to his bedroom.

How the hell did he know my room is in that direction? Kevin wondered.

He turned one last time. These poor Juarenses, he said to himself. May they not freeze to death tonight. He realized he heard no dogs barking. Were they all inside, in bed?

John had said that afternoon that he had never felt cold this cold, even in the Andes. As Kevin looked out at the lights of El Paso, he longed for Chile for the first time in a long time. He longed for it only because there the cold rarely killed. Here it was a killer, joining the long killing list.

Maybe, he began to think, that old Columban who called this place godforsaken was right. Maybe there are places on earth where evil is not worth fighting, where it is so inexorable and total that the enemies of evil forsake the battle, forsake the place and choose, out of practicality, a place like El Paso, just a few feet away, where the playing field is more flat. Maybe I am becoming Billy, he thought. Maybe I have more in common with him than I realized. Maybe I am a dreamer, an idealist, just of a slightly different strain. Maybe a church, a single, thriving church, is insufficient here. Maybe it is a fantasy.

◈ ◈ ◈

HE HAD BOUGHT THE HAT ON A TRIP TO LONDON MANY YEARS PRIOR, a big, Russian, wrap-around, fur hat that made his already girthy head look the size of a bear's. He wore it all the time during the Chilean winter and fit right in—a Russian Jew in Santiago had started a mail-order hat store, and it felt like every tenth guy in South America was wearing a Russian hat.

So he did not know that the only man in Mexico who wore such a hat was supposedly El Chapo, the boss of the Sinaloa drug cartel. Nor did he know that there were rumors that El Chapo was in Juarez. All he knew was that Leo and Juan Pablo deserved a good meal after all the cold they had suffered, and, his ever-reliable brother-in-law had wired him some money to treat them. He loved being with Rayna but cherished the company of these chaps in a way that reminded him of his buddies with whom he would go camping in the Outback when he was a teenager. The camaraderie energized him just as it did then.

They drove to the best steak house in Juarez that night, and even with the heat on full blast in the truck, Kevin could feel the cold under his skin.

"Leo, I slept with Willie last night," Kevin said dryly, expecting a chuckle.

"We slept with all three of ours, and I considered bringing in some strays," Leo said, even more matter-of-factly.

"I have slept in huts in Chile with the wind blowing up my nostrils, gentlemen, and even that cold was not so bitter as this," Kevin said. "I think we should all have soup before our steaks to warm the belly a bit."

"Father, you said we could order whatever we wish, no?"

"Of course, Leo," Kevin said. "I didn't say it, my brother-in-law did."

"Good, then no soup for me," Leo said. "Two steaks."

And he and Juan Pablo laughed all the way into the parking lot.

As they walked into the restaurant, the bouncer looked startled by Kevin's big Russian hat. When the hostess slinked over, she, too, could not take her eyes off it.

"I'm going to wear this to the table," Kevin said to Leo. "I may have discovered the key to keeping the parish's attention, Leo, during my homilies."

"Lo dudo," Leo said, following the hostess. I doubt it. But as they walked to a table in the center of the room, every diner at all the tables stopped speaking or eating and looked up at him.

They sat, and Kevin looked at Leo.

"I'm keeping it on, Leo," he said.

Leo laughed.

"I always thought you should have gone to Hollywood instead of the priesthood, Padre," he said.

Leo and Juan Pablo each ordered two steaks, and Kevin ordered his soup and a bottle of wine from Australia.

The waitress seemed nervous, and as she walked away, Kevin noticed the people at the tables on either side of them getting up and leaving, their plates and glasses each half-full.

Kevin admitted that he was starting to get hot under the hat, so he took it off and placed it on the empty chair at their table.

"I knew you couldn't last," Leo said. "Imagine wearing that thing on the altar. All the little kids at Mass would go running off."

"Leo, you Westerners are so materialistic," Kevin said. "I guarantee you that you are going to have a cold tomorrow, wearing what you are wearing, and my hat, amigo, is going to keep me as healthy as always."

The waitress came with his onion soup and their first steaks, and Kevin noticed her arms were trembling as she placed them in front of them. Then he looked up, and even more tables had vacated.

"Leo," Kevin said. "Before we say grace, I'd like to point something out to you. Everyone is leaving."

Leo and Juan Pablo looked around and grew curious when the noticed that, indeed, Kevin was right. The place was emptying out.

They all returned their eyes to their plates.

"You say grace, Leo," Kevin said, not least because he knew it would be quick.

Leo made the sign of the cross, and as he did Kevin spotted their waitress standing with the hostess and doorman talking animatedly and motioning toward their table. Other diners passed them and walked toward the exit.

"Something is about to happen here, Padre Kevin," Leo said. "I will be right back."

Leo got up and walked toward the bathroom. Juan Pablo began cutting his steak as if he were angry at it, which was the same way he sawed a board or hammered a nail.

"Disfruta, Juan Pablo, disfruta," Kevin said. Slow down and enjoy.

But Juan Pablo did not even look up at him.

Kevin had taken a few spoonfuls of soup, feeling the warmth run down his belly, when Leo came back laughing.

Leo sat down and began to carve his steak into fifteen or so pieces without eating, laughing all the while.

"¿Leo, qué pasa," Kevin said.

This time Juan Pablo looked up.

"They think you are a Russian Mafioso, a partner here with El Chapo," Leo said, this time laughing out loud. Kevin looked up at the nearly empty restaurant.

He had pondered the Russian metaphor more than once. A few rich guys, pilfering the state-owned companies at the favor of the ruling political party. Crony capitalismo, and the added willingness to be vicious, to crush an entire society, an entire people, if it meant increasing the size of one's assets.

But now, here, he suddenly felt sick to his stomach. I have ruined these people's meals, he thought.

But then Juan Pablo started laughing, quietly at first and then uncontrollably. The waitress came with his second steak, and he stabbed at it with equal aggression but laughed all the while he ate.

"This is their restaurant, Padre," Leo said. "The ricos of Juarez. Don't worry. It is good to disrupt one of their evenings. Just pretend it is vengeance for all the nights our power goes out. For the times the police never come when we call them. It is okay. You can put the hat back on if you want to."

Kevin started to laugh along with them and turned to his steak. The restaurant was virtually empty now, and even some of the help was leaving.

Vengeance. He liked it, at least on a small, blundering scale. He felt no need to apologize for it, no need to confess to nor pray to God for forgiveness. As he ate, the steak tasted better and better with each bite, the meat's subtle sweetness reminding him of the steaks in Buenos Aires.

The waitress came over with the check.

"Where do you get your meat from?" Kevin asked. Leo and Juan Pablo looked at him like he had asked the girl an intimate question.

"No sé, Señor, I can ask the jefe," the waitress said as Kevin stuck his brother-in-law's pesos into the little case.

"No, no es necesario," Kevin said, realizing now that Leo was dissuading him with his eyes from further conversation.

They got up, and Kevin gleefully put on his hat. He waved to the remaining workers as they exited, and they waved nervously back.

Suddenly, the waitress came darting at him, holding a wad of pesos toward him.

"No, no, es tuyo," Kevin said.

Leo turned to her.

"No es un ruso," Leo said. "He is not who you think he is. He is a priest."

The girl dropped her arm to her waist, and her face seemingly drooped not with relief but with disappointment.

As they drove home through the menace of Juarez's night, he felt wickedly good. Each of them would chuckle to himself, and then they all would chuckle for a few seconds. It's come to this, Kevin thought. It's come to this. We are in a hell of a spot here in Juarez when the help thinks I'm a drug lord.

"Esto es grave," he said to his friends, and they started laughing again, laughing, he knew, because that was the only option. Laughing, he knew, because they were scared not of the night but of how fearful the whole city had become, one massive assembly of people all looking over their shoulders at who was coming up from behind.

Kevin pulled up in front of Leo's house, and the steady, cold wind felt like it was blowing right through the truck.

"Adelante," Kevin said. Forward. Leo, nodding, got out, and Kevin watched him look around as he opened his gate. Juan Pablo moved into the front seat, his house the next stop.

And as Kevin pulled out and turned down toward Juan Pablo's house next to Corpus Christi, he wondered when he would have another such dinner with these men, or if he ever would. There is no way we can win this one, he thought. We were winning when the enemy was hunger and drugs and shady evangelicals. But now I'm out of my league, in over my head, and I pray we will dine again, the three of us. I will pray we get out of this bloody mess alive.

◈ ◈ ◈

THE CARTELS WERE NOW TARGETING THE FUNERALS OF THEIR VICTIMS, as if slaughtering and carving the victim himself to pieces were not enough. They had to get his buddies, his brothers, his mother and sister, too. Funerals and viewings here often took place in the home of the deceased, and just last week in the next barrio over, a car pulled up and machine-gunned the house during the viewing.

Kevin woke up this morning out of sorts, as he liked to say, knowing he was going to be saying a funeral in a house of a boy who had been butchered for some cartel-related reason or other.

"You can't go," Rayna said as she put a plate loaded with beans and rice on the table in front of him.

"Rayna," he said, "I appreciate your concern, but this isn't a case of free will. It is my job, I have to go."

"No one in that home ever went to church, and now they want you to say a funeral for a murderer?"

Indeed, the funerals were becoming deadly gatherings. Twice in the past two months there had been drive-by shootings at funerals in neighboring barrios. Each time the priest escaped unharmed, he knew, but one only saved himself by diving behind the coffin. Bullets riddled it, killing the dead guy again.

"Rayna, I promise you I don't want to die a hero. I assure you I don't even want to die just yet."

He walked into the home, and a group of young men didn't even look at him. They were standing on either side of the only window in the shack, looking out at the guys he had passed on his way in.

This mother had already lost three sons to the drug wars; her lone remaining one, five or six years old, clung to her legs.

Other than the young men at the window, the mother, and her clinging son, no one else dared come. That, or else cared to. He would never know.

He walked up to the body, and the first thing he noticed was how only the young man's right hand was sticking out of the sleeve of the brown suit they had stuffed him into.

The other hand, Kevin knew, was missing.

He genuflected, blessed the body, and turned to the mother, extending his hands toward her even as he was suddenly self-conscious of having them attached to his wrists.

She took his hands in hers and gripped the tips of his fingers. "¿Por qué, Padre?" she said. "¿Por qué?"

She kept saying it over and over, pausing between each word. ¿Por qué?

His Spanish was funny-sounding, as Rayna regularly reminded him, but fluent and rich. This was the one question that was so much easier to answer in Spanish than in English. They both meant "Why?" in each language, but, more literal-minded in his second tongue, he knew the Spanish strictly translated was "For what?" not "Why?"

¿Por qué? For what?

And the literalness of the translation made him want to give a literal answer. For what? For the money he was earning as a smuggler so that he could support you and that poor boy clinging to your legs.

He had decided the Mexicans, at moments like this, almost wanted the practicality of such an answer, as they weren't prone to the philosophical grief of the Anglo-Saxons. The big, causal "Why?" wasn't a preoccupation of theirs. God was a rote fact of life, and he saw little motivation in them to question God's ways, let alone the ways of the world. The question this woman was asking was simultaneously more profound and simplistic. For what? For me? For what? Perhaps she wasn't asking for what did he die, but for what did he live? For what did she live? There had to be a reason here, and as she kept repeating it, her eyes kept seeking a response from him.

As he walked down the hill with Leo from the funeral back to his house, an evangelical accosted him and made the sign of the cross with his fingers to ward off the devil. Kevin scowled at him.

"You are nothing more than a fanatic," Kevin said, turning abruptly. He normally toyed with these sorts, hearing them out often to try to illustrate the proper way for a Christian to

conduct himself. But this time, as the guy trailed him, continuing to spout about Satanás and hell, he realized that there was
something in this place and current cohort of Mexican people that bred fanatics. Some fanatics joined gangs, slaughtered
guys from other gangs, and wrote cryptic messages on their
dead bodies. Some got hung up on the devil and made their
hatred of the Catholic Church, the pope, his priests, and the
Virgin Mary their reason for existing. Was a common anxiety
at root? A basic fear of death, of not being, the eternal anxiety
that his philosophy books provided as the explanation for fa-
naticism?

"God, if I weren't a priest, the things I'd say to that fellow!"
Kevin said, making Leo burst out in laughter.

The evangelical stopped and stood speechless. He had obviously caught the irony but seemed flabbergasted at its originality.

The evangelical laughed, slightly, halfheartedly, but clearly.

Kevin winked at him, nodded, and continued down the hill,
tasting with every step the glass of rum he was about to pour
for himself.

"How about that one, Leo?" he asked.

"Muy bueno," Leo said. "Muy bueno." Very good.

They walked inside and sat down, Kevin with his rum in hand.

"How do we get out of this, Leo?" he asked.

"No lo sé, Padre Kevin," Leo said, shaking his head. "No lo sé."

"And you know what, Leo?" Kevin said. "I don't think God
knows either."

Leo looked at him, unblinking, and Kevin felt ashamed. I
have to keep my guard up, he thought, even in front of Leo.
Despair and gallows humor are one thing. But if he thinks I'm
giving up on God, if anyone thinks that, then I deserve a death
worse than crucifixion.

He sucked the rum off his ice cubes and turned to Leo.

"I'm just joking, Leo," he said. "Una broma mala." A bad joke.

"We'll fix this mess, faith will still win out," he said, knowing it sounded halfhearted to his faithful friend, knowing none of his Australian irony could undo the accuracy of the statement.

CHAPTER EIGHT

◇

Rayna

HER NEW HOUSE WAS COLD, AND SMALL, AND HAD NO RUNNING WATER. But she loved it. She loved paying her micro-mortgage on it to the builder every month; she loved walking out to the outhouse on a cold night to go to the bathroom; she loved being free once and for all from the attacks the women at church had made on her all during her years living at the church. She loved the walk to Kevin's house, knowing her detractors knew she was gainfully employed and living alone.

One afternoon she was in the kitchen at Kevin's house preparing lunch when the house phone rang. So many times Kevin had talked about getting rid of the landline to save money, but then, inevitably, a call would come in the middle of the night from someone seeking his comforts, and the idea would fade for a few months.

Sometimes she ignored the phone, for she knew her old enemies loved to say she was living with Kevin, picking up the phone as if she were his wife.

But, given the hell that was breaking loose outside lately, she had started to pick up with more regularity. The house phone ringing was almost now like a fire truck or police siren sounding—trouble there was.

"Rayna?" a woman asked.

"Sí," she said, matter-of-factly, only seconds later, during the odd pause in the woman's retort, realizing this woman's voice was hushed, almost muffled.

"¿Estás con tu hija, no?" the woman said.

"Sí," Rayna responded, looking over at Clara. Then instantly she knew. They—whoever they were—had been pulling this trick on poor people all over Juarez. The police didn't care; the banks may have been in on it, she figured; and some of them really followed through with their threats.

"I know who you are," Rayna said. She didn't specifically, and they obviously knew who she was, and she said it more to eliminate some of the menace, the teasing leading up to the blackmail.

"Bien, Rayna, bien," the woman said. "Now do you have a pen?"

"Eh, no, un momento," Rayna said, putting her hand up to the phone and about to put it down on the table.

"Rayna!"

She pulled the phone back up to her ear.

"You know the rules," the woman said. "If you hang up, if you tell me the phone fell and hung itself up, bad things, very bad things, will happen."

"Sí, lo sé," Rayna said, shocked at her own matter-of-factness.

She set the phone down gently, facing up, and walked over to get a pen and paper from the counter. Clara looked up at her.

"¿Quién es?" Clara asked.

Rayna picked up the pen and pad and turned and looked at her.

"It is the extorsionistas," she said calmly. "In a moment they are going to tell me to pass the phone to you and send me to wire them money. They will tell you over and over that if you hang up, they will kill me. They will tell me right now that they will be watching me and if I don't comply, they will kill you or me or both of us."

She looked at the phone as she spoke, talking louder so the woman could hear her clearly.

"They may be copycats, fakes, or they may not be," she said, walking slowly back and picking up the phone while willing Clara with her eyes not to panic.

Clara stood up and, though flushed in the face, was steady. Rayna knew Clara was responding to her own strength and calm.

"We are real," the woman said. "You obviously understand what to do. But I promise you we are not fakes."

"Congratulations," Rayna said.

"Are you ready for the account number?"

"Sí," Rayna said, clicking the pen next to the phone so the woman could hear her.

She wrote down the bank account number and stood there silently.

"One thousand pesos, Rayna. One thousand. Now give the phone to Clara," the woman said. "We will be watching you from all sides, even from above. And we are tracing your cell phone. If you make one call the deal is off. One call and we bring hell to you and your family."

"Sólo Dios watches me from above, and he will be watching you, too," Rayna said.

She held the phone by her side and motioned to Clara to come over. She went to hand the phone to Clara, then stopped, and held it back up to her ear.

She set the phone down hard on the table to hurt the woman's ear.

"Do not hang up," she said to Clara. "I will be back in two hours."

Then she motioned to her to step away. She cupped her hands and whispered.

"Lock all the doors and windows," she said to her daughter. "I will find Kevin and he will come home before I do and you will be safe."

Clara nodded, and Rayna stopped for a moment to admire her. She has seen so much more than I had at her age, Rayna thought. I am ready for this, ready for anything here now. But it took me fifteen years to steel myself. My daughter already treats evil like an angry dog or rabid cat passing in the street.

She nodded to her, kissed her, and turned.

As she walked out into the courtyard, Willie stumbled up to her and began licking her. She gave him a treat from her pocket, walked over to the gate, and opened it. As she walked out, she wondered if she would feel like someone was watching her. She had seen it in the movies, that sixth sense, and she waited for it as she turned down the street toward her home.

She wanted to call Kevin but decided to keep her cell phone in her pocket until she got to her home, just in case they were watching.

The world, the planet, felt smaller. She felt like everyone was watching her; for a moment she imagined a little airplane in the sky tracking her and sending her coordinates to a cartel leader in Culiacan or Mazatlan.

But I'm not that important, she reminded herself. This is just a prank. One of those nasty women at the parish who is always trying to undermine me. Or maybe one of them gave Kevin's number to one of their sons, or maybe one of their sons stole it. Or maybe one of the gang members who still went to church was doing this and would show up and sit across from her at church next Sunday and she would never know.

She walked through her courtyard door and looked around. No one in the street, not even a car passing. She walked inside and took out her cell phone. She knew Kevin was downtown for meetings at the bishop's offices today. She raised her thumb to dial but then paused. Who knows what is the truth in Juarez? This could be a gimmick, or it could be real, or it could be both.

She put the phone back into her pocket and bent down to look for the money she had hidden under the sink in a can of detergent. She stuck her fingers in the can, took out the bills, and shook out the coins. Six hundred pesos. She took her wallet out of her purse. Forty pesos. She looked at her watch. One hour and forty minutes left.

This is a hoax, this has to be a hoax, she thought. They had been killing mothers and children but still no priests, and, even though the bishop had sent out warnings, Kevin had yet to hear of an instance when they were extorting priests. Doing this to her was akin to doing it to Kevin. She knew and cherished that he was a sort of shield for her family, not from the nasty stuff of jealous women but from the brutal stuff of bad men.

How can I borrow money if I can't use my phone? she wondered. She stuffed the pesos into her wallet and the coins into her pocket. She walked out of the house, looked around, and this time saw two men, twenty years old or so, whom she had never seen in Anapra. They were walking on the street across from her, and one, the furthest one, looked at her. She could swear he snickered at her. She stopped, waited to watch them, but compulsively looked at her watch. One hour thirty minutes left. She thought she heard one of the young men laughing. She turned to look, but they were now twenty feet past her and not looking back, not even peering.

I will wire what I have. This is all that I have. I will tell them that I will wire the rest in two days. I will wait until the very last minute, for Kevin will be home by then, and they cannot kidnap

Clara if he is there. They are not so smart. They are not as smart as they think they are. They are only plotting a hoax anyway. Why am I going along with this?

But she went along. She caught the bus downtown, went to a bank, wired the money that she had, and rushed home, telling the bus driver she would pay him her fare the next day.

She rushed inside and saw Clara there asleep with the baby on her breast. The phone was still off the hook, and Rayna walked over to it, picked it up, and listened.

"Hola," she said. But it was dead. It had been a hoax, she thought. The devil is playing games with all of us now, torturing the whole city. She never mentioned the event to Kevin until years later, for she knew it would incite his Aussie rage in an instant. She knew he would have called their bluff. And she didn't want him to know that she didn't have the courage to do the same.

◈ ◈ ◈

FATHER KEVIN HAD SPENT A MONTH ORGANIZING THE PEACE MARCH, and Leo and he had agreed to convene in the roundabout and head downtown instead of marching over to San Marcos where the violence was just as bad as in Anapra. Rayna woke up earlier than usual and walked outside. At 6 AM, at least, Juarez felt safe. She sometimes laughed to herself that the good ones should try to live by an alternate clock to avoid the bad men who did the killing. She even feared for the march today. One day soon they were going to murder the innocents en masse, too, just to make a point. One day, too, they would behead a priest, or crucify him, or take him for ransom, and then there would be no priests left save the ones seeking martyrdom.

The sun was up and the trucks were starting to rumble on the main street. She looked up at the sky and wondered how many people would be murdered today.

Claudia was awake and ready. Rayna knew she wanted to walk not just as part of the protest. She wanted to walk to show how well she was walking with her new prosthetic; she wanted to walk because, as her city was going to hell, she was starting to thrive at school, with her friends, and in the parish. Rayna kissed her and felt better.

They dressed, ate breakfast, put on their coats, and walked outside together. We only live here for work, all these people, and yet now we are fighting for the place we don't even call home.

As they turned the corner, she could see people clustering in the roundabout. People were coming out of side streets and coming down the hill from Lomas de Poleo. Soon she spotted Kevin in the middle of the group with a few other priests from the nearby parishes. She started watching him as they drew closer and realized he was not his usual laughing self. He wasn't smiling; he was grim, as was everyone. Then she realized no one was speaking.

They arrived at the circle, and the group now spilled over it out onto the street. It kept getting larger, and she wondered why they couldn't just walk around like this all day every day and police the city themselves if the police wouldn't do it for them.

Then the prayer began. Dios te salve María. Hail Mary full of grace. At the same time, someone somewhere took a step forward, probably Kevin, she thought, and everyone else simultaneously began to move, step by step all the way downtown to the cathedral.

She took peeks at Claudia as they walked and took peeks at Kevin, too. His gray hair was gleaming in the sun, and she marveled at how stunning he looked. And yet even he, with the church growing and growing, could not stop the violence from growing, too. Satanás, she said to herself. No one talks about him anymore. But Satan is winning, Satan is stronger than even barrel-chested, brawling Father Kevin. Most people would think me a fool for believing in the devil, she thought. She would never say it out loud, but that was what the devil wanted, to keep her silent.

But she knew she had to help Kevin help Corpus Christi adjust to the devil's ways. The devil was suddenly winning even at Corpus Christi—fewer people were coming to the parish for events at night; Masses were more glum; all the deaths were gnawing at the people's faith. Kevin needed a Mexican response. He needed to make things even crazier to respond to the craziness. She knew, finally, it was time for her to tell him she wanted to start a charismatic group at the church. Desperate times called for desperate measures, he always joked, saying it in English first and then translating it. Well, here we are, she thought. He won't like it; he'll go along grudgingly; but it is what these people need now as their sons and daughters are being murdered all around them. We need to bring God down to us, convince him to come down to us to stop all this. We need to talk to him and hear him talk back. That is not their way, I know, that is not the way of these white men, she said to herself. But that is the only way left to fix this catastrophe we are living, that is the only way to fix these people.

◈ ◈ ◈

THOUGH THEY SEEMED TO BE KILLING FEWER WOMEN, THEY REALLY WEREN'T, she knew—it was just that the drug killings were getting all the press. They were just killing more men and boys along with the women. And whenever she read about a woman's body being found, she thought of Viktor, Clara's boyfriend. She liked him, never saw a moment of anger or a flash of rage—the sort of glimpse every Mexican man she had been with had revealed within a couple of days of their courtship. But who was to say that Viktor wasn't just a bit smarter, smart enough to conceal that inner Mexican male in him in front of her?

She wanted to ask Clara if he had ever raised a hand toward her. She wanted to ask her, bluntly, if he ever grew rough in bed, like they always did the second or third time, or even the first after a few minutes of sexual formality. But she knew Clara would turn on her, just like she would have done on her own mother, and act as if some violation more holy and outrageous than rape had just been perpetrated.

We comply, we perpetuate, she thought to herself. We do. These girls thrown into the desert up the hill, they were taught it early, as ten-year-olds, taught to accept being looked at, to walk and bend as the controlling male eyes directed them, to not necessarily like it but see in it the only tiny bit of power possibly attained in a country where power, the tiniest bit of it over the smallest, weakest creature, was still life-affirming when felt.

But Kevin, deep down in Kevin, she knew this did not exist. Why? His parenting? More specifically, his father? Australia? Because, as she had now found out, his mother had put him up for adoption when she was merely a teenager? Something in the English language? Some difference between the English and Irish who, he explained, had settled there and the Spanish who arrived here?

She had learned to think more deeply after so many years watching him think deeply, she realized. She realized she hadn't ever really thought at all, intentionally keeping her mind empty, perhaps just never realizing it was there up in her head. But his was always racing, jumping from topic to topic like he jumped from place to place. He was never still, she realized, because his brain never stilled.

How could she expect from her daughters what she had not done herself at their age? It outraged her when Kevin said this to her, and yet he would say it again each time he saw her lamenting the straits of her grandmotherhood. Clara had already had one child and was living with Viktor in unión libre, the term for the relationship between the scores of couples whom Kevin, every chance he could get, kept urging to get married. The term was deceptive, she thought, too appealing to young people for them to embrace any more formal status. Who at that age would not want to live that way, in free union, as he told her it was translated, at that age? Nothing in a relationship is free.

And she liked Viktor, as much as a mother who knew the mistake her daughter was making could like the boy she was making it with. He worked hard; he lit up when he held his child; and, for all she could tell, he never raised a hand at her daughter.

Nor did he travel with a bad crowd; no, his biggest flaw of that sort was that he seemed too loyal to certain mongrels from his past who needed a bed for a night, or two, or twenty. Or for a meal, or two, or fifty. He was generous but, as Father Kevin said, not discerning with his generosity.

Lately an old friend of his was sleeping on their floor, eating with them at every meal Rayna walked in on. She had stopped asking Clara what the issue was with this fellow or that but had warned her that anyone involved in drugs should not be welcomed. Clara had promised.

Perhaps this time she didn't know; perhaps even Viktor didn't know.

The boy had left but had left behind trouble. The evening before, the police had arrived at the house, barged in, and searched the house for Viktor. His parents were staying with Clara and him, and the old man thought he was having a heart attack.

"Your son is stealing cars," the cops had said.

But Rayna knew it was his friend who had been stealing cars, and she knew the second Clara told her the story that Viktor's supposed friend was spreading word that Viktor was the thief.

Rayna rushed over as soon as Clara called to tell her the story, and she scurried the two blocks from her house to theirs trying to dissuade herself from insisting on spending the night there. The cops had come; the cops would be back. Nothing was more certain in Juarez.

When she walked in, they were all sitting at the dinner table eating.

No one spoke; no one even looked at her. They knew she was angry. They knew she thought the cops would come back. What no one knew was that the mongrel friend had blamed a series of crimes—the cars, store thefts, drug trafficking—on Viktor.

"I am going to stay here tonight," Rayna announced.

Clara looked up with that face of protestation that Rayna had been seeing since she was born.

"Mamá, qué no, estamos bien," Clara said.

Rayna shook her head and sat down with finality. She was not going to move. Still no one spoke, even while they cleaned the dishes and got the baby ready for bed.

"Buenas noches," Viktor's parents each said in unison, and Rayna nodded but did not speak back.

Clara walked out one last time, looked at Rayna, and shook her head. It was eleven o'clock, and Clara shut off the last light, leaving Rayna sitting there staring at the fish tank.

"Vete a casa, Mamá," Clara said. Go home. "They come at dinner time. They won't come tonight. Viktor said they won't come back; he promised."

Rayna went, and the cops came soon after. Clara called her at midnight—the cops had just stormed in and carried Viktor off. Rayna jumped from her new bed in her new shack and didn't notice the chill, didn't notice for the first time that she had no electricity or heat yet. She ran out the door and up the street toward Clara's house like she hadn't run in years. A car was waiting in front of it, with people getting in, and she jumped into the passenger seat.

"They went up toward Lomas, up toward the desert!" Viktor's mother shouted, and whoever was driving floored it in that direction.

No one spoke, intent only on trying to see car lights on an adjacent road or up the hill. The driver, an aunt or cousin, Rayna thought but didn't ponder, saw a dog right in front of her and didn't even try to dodge it. Rayna didn't hear a thump but didn't care for the first time in her life about an animal's fate.

But there was no one out driving. A random house light but no car visible anywhere.

"They are already in the desert," Rayna said. The woman drove up the hill that led to Lomas and then out toward the dirt road that connected with the main road toward Santa Teresa. And then, up in the distance, she saw the lights of a parked car and pointed to it. At the same time, Rayna realized they were all women in the car—Clara, the driver, Viktor's mom, and her. What are the cops going to say to a bunch of women?

As they came within a hundred feet of the cop car, she saw that there was no one standing around it. As soon as the driver slammed their car to a stop, dust from the dirt road rising all around them, Rayna jumped out and ran into the desert.

"¡Os veo, os veo, cabrones!" she shouted, even though she didn't see anyone and was choking on dust. "I see you, bastards! Don't touch him!"

And then she came upon them, one pushing Viktor's head into the ground, and another with his pistol pointed at Viktor's head.

"You will have to kill me, too," Rayna said, calmly. "You will have to kill me, too."

The other women had come up alongside her now and stood staring through the darkness at the figures of the cops. The cop with the gun looked at the other, shook his head, and smiled slightly. He extended his arm even more stiffly at Viktor's head, held it there, and then dropped his arm to his side.

"Vamos," the cop said. The other cop then grabbed Viktor by his handcuffed arms and pushed him toward the cop car.

"Where are you taking him?" Rayna shouted.

"A la estación. I am sure we will see you there, and, for the record, that will be the first place we have seen you."

They got in the cop car, turned around, and headed back toward Juarez.

"Vamos," Rayna said, not realizing she was the leader, not grasping that, without her, Viktor's mother would have been weeping over a dead son.

As they drove back, she realized the best guarantor of Viktor's safety wasn't them, even though the cops had already pulled back from executing him, but Father Kevin.

"Take me to Padre Kevin's house first," she said.

The woman didn't even look up or question, and Rayna felt how unanimously she was in charge. If they only knew, these people depending on her so, how much she depended on Kevin.

They pulled up, she jumped out and opened the courtyard door with her key, and as she opened the house door, she already saw him pulling up his trousers.

"The police have taken Viktor," Rayna said.

"Lo sé," Kevin said. I know. And she didn't ask how he knew, and didn't care.

They squeezed into the front seat together and bounced into each other as the car slammed into every pothole on the way to the station. Kevin ran out ahead of her once they pulled up to the station. She realized as she jumped out of the car that it was still moving.

"No digas nada," Kevin said as they raced through the door of the station. "We just sit and don't speak."

"Sí, sí," Rayna said. "Like a vigil."

"Eso es," Kevin said. "A vigil."

They sat, taking turns coming in shifts, for three days, until the cops released Viktor. It was Kevin's shift when Viktor wandered out, dazed and bruised, and Kevin dropped him off for Clara and his parents to begin to treat him.

Rayna was standing in the little courtyard when Kevin pulled up in his big pickup truck.

"They beat him," he said. "They beat the hell out of him. And they said they may not be done with him."

And all she could do was attack herself once again, just as she had done when Gabino had gone off to die. She had doubted Viktor; she had wondered if he would ever raise a hand to Clara. And now here he was the one who had been beaten.

"He is a good boy, Padre Kevin," she said, fighting back tears.

"I know," he said. "But there is a wave now, a big wave, and it's trying to carry away all the men his age here. It's trying to kill them all. We should think about getting him, getting him and Clara, out of here. Get them somewhere else for a while. Somewhere safe."

She walked over to the couch and sat down. If they go, I will go, she thought, and bit her tongue as she was about to say the same words to him. If they go, I will go and take all my children with me if that is what we have to do.

She looked up at him, standing there, a man flummoxed, overwhelmed, fighting the force of the wave himself.

But what will he do if we leave him here? she asked herself. What will this man do without his grandchildren and his cook?

❖ ❖ ❖

SHE KNEW WHEN THE PHONE RANG, SHE KNEW BY THE WAY HE LOOKED AT HER AS HE JUMPED FROM THE TABLE AND SCURRIED TO HIS ROOM TO TALK, THAT THEY WERE CALLING HIM IN. There had been several murders in Anapra in the past week, bloodletting across the city, and two parish priests downtown had to go into hiding after refusing extortions. She knew they had tried to extort Kevin, even though he would never tell her and neither Leo nor Juan Pablo would admit it when she confronted them.

And now she knew the bishop or his superior or whoever was his boss was calling to tell him to prepare to evacuate. He had taught her the word, making jokes about it referring to a bowel movement, saying it was an appropriate word choice because it usually took place when assholes conquered the bowels of the world. She could hear his voice behind his closed door; even here in the kitchen she could hear the word. It was the only word she could hear distinctly. Perhaps he said it louder than the others, for she could tell when he said it that he disdained the word.

Would he do it? Would he leave us? He knows, she thought, he knows we will crumble just as he would crumble. And here I thought it was us who might be forced to leave him? He says every man is replaceable, but she knows he says it to control expectations, says it with false humility, says it with pride in his role here. She knows he knows that not only for her and her brood but for dozens of others in the parish, his departure would mean, if not physical death, then certainly the slow spiritual and moral death that eventually leads to physical death anyway.

But Kevin would dare not heed his boss, she thought. He just pays false courtesy; he loathes anyone telling him what to do. He would leave the priesthood first. He would find a way to stay. She had always been unclear on who his boss was anyway. The American Columban from Omaha he talked about? The big guy in Hong Kong? A priest back in Australia?

He won't leave us. He knows what would happen, how everything we've managed to build in spite of it all would all come crumbling down.

She heard the silence and knew, since he didn't come right out, that he was pacing in his room, red-faced, tight-fisted.

Or maybe we all go, at last, our separate ways? We go back to Mexico City; Kevin back to wherever in the world they will send him next. Maybe that was the way it was always going to be. No, I mean, yes, that is the way it was always going to be. I just blocked it out of my mind. I just thought we would live this way, here together, here somehow content despite it all, forever.

CHAPTER NINE

Kevin

THE MURDERS OF MARIO AND JOSE, HE THOUGHT, WERE GOING TO BREAK HIM. Now, when Leo woke him and told him one hot summer morning two years later that little Saul had been murdered, Kevin felt like he wanted to walk out into the sun and just let it burn him to oblivion. Little Saul—they had even corralled *him* into smuggling drugs over the mountain? A local hood nicknamed The Centipede who was somehow connected to the Sinaloa gang was the main suspect in the murder. The Centipede lived just a few blocks from Kevin; he came to Corpus Christi for Mass once a month or so, turning Kevin's stomach each time. Kevin sat with Leo in the darkness of the curtained kitchen until lunchtime when Rayna walked in. They didn't speak; even Leo could not console him.

For two more weeks he went through all his duties halfheartedly, and Leo and Rayna, he could tell, were sleepwalking, too.

They didn't even attempt to shake him out of it, he knew, because they could not shake out of it themselves. Then the final Sunday of the month came, and Leo had already calculated for himself a few days prior that The Centipede always came to Mass on each month's final Sunday. So here we are, Kevin said that morning as he got up and made a coffee. It feels like the devil is putting me to his most perfect test. Will I walk down in front of all my parishioners and strangle him?

He didn't even let himself look at The Centipede until the first reading from the Old Testament. The sun was always so shocking on his way into the church that he didn't even try to discern faces. The sun was his excuse for not making eye contact. He wore his sunglasses until he reached the altar, and they eased the adjustment for both his eyes and his nerves, particularly now that the crowds on Sundays had grown so large that he felt obligated to, as he liked to say, bring some real Mexican to bear. None of that Anglo solemnity, he realized. Instead, here you have to mount a jamboree, and he was getting good at it. He had grown comfortable with his cultural obligations. Learn to sway your hips a bit, Padre, one of his seminarians had said.

But a deacon had whispered to him before Mass that The Centipede was in attendance this Sunday, and all that Mexican mojo Kevin had cultivated evaporated in a moment. He felt blocky and rigid. He felt as if his whole body had clenched up. How could he not try to strangle, for all his parish to see, the man whom they said had killed lovely little Saul? This bastard who decides to show up and rub it in my face?

He sat listening to his parish recite the responsorial psalm, and suddenly he looked up directly at The Centipede because something—he later would not be able to decide if it was fear or curiosity—forced him to. The Centipede did not look back. In fact, his eyes were closed tightly, as if in tortured or grief-filled prayer. Father Kevin couldn't decide later if it were torture or grief, or if he was simply positing that explanation for the man's twisted face.

Maybe his eyes were just closed. Father Kevin was always catching himself when he applied explanations to behaviors here. The erratic nature of life in Juarez, he believed, undermined the explanations for excessive reactions. A woman wails, and her goat may have run out of milk. A child giggles uncontrollably, tickle-type laughter, and his friends stand around a mouse whose legs they have pulled off.

A schoolboy had first educated Father Kevin about the nickname—no one had dubbed The Centipede for the arthropod like Kevin had assumed but rather for the video game from the 1980s. The Centipede kept coming at you in the video game; it never stopped its deadly, robotic march. The recycled Centipede game consoles—booths, really—got sent here from America in the '90s. Kids still played them a decade later, and so a murderer got his nickname.

As Kevin pondered the killer in his pews, he let himself believe that the expression on The Centipede's face became the primary excuse to give communion to The Centipede: he has come here to apologize to God. Father Kevin looked at him again, and the face was still twisted up in anguish. That's it, Kevin thought, and what's more, we know he didn't murder Saul himself. We know his gnats or ants or bees did it. So without blood on his hands, I must give him the sacrament.

Kevin got up and coughed along with half the parish, who had breathed in that day's polluted air. He didn't use a lectern during his homilies, preferring to walk back and forth across the altar. His Spanish was fluid but flat, monotone, and he had realized that his pacing gave more variety to his voice. As he spoke, he saw The Centipede out of the corner of his eye. No change in his tense face. He did indeed look a bit bug-like: tiny head, pointy eyes, a pointy forehead, and a miniatureness that belied his power and the fear people had for him. And with those eyes shut so violently tight, he looked oddly weak, fearful, as banal as all the killers become at the end of the day here.

The children's choir got up to sing the second song, and Father Kevin felt sweat dripping down his back. He suddenly felt like he was giving himself a body bath when he realized what would come once the children now assembling in the back of the church brought up the bread and wine. Saul's killer would be sticking his tongue out right in front of him, waiting to receive the host from his hand.

Kevin thought back to the murderer who had confessed to him early on here, nearly a decade ago. It had happened to many priests he knew in Juarez, and he had heard all sorts of justifications for maintaining the secrecy of the confessional. From the new age one about priests as psychiatrists maintaining absolute confidentiality to the old school one about the confessional being truth's tomb.

The Australian solution would be to hear his confession, meet him outside the confessional, and rough the bad guy up a bit, spiritually at least. But communion was such a more public sacrament here that such a self-satisfying act could undo the years of progress he had made in building up this burgeoning congregation.

Kevin motioned for the children to commence the bearing of the gifts, and as he did he felt The Centipede's eyes open and stare straight at him. Kevin stood in front of the altar and wondered for a moment if he should stare right back, but while he was wondering, he began to see Saul again, scampering on the ground from tire to tire, the ultimate whistle-while-you-work worker. Saul, fixing a tire for him every other week in this city with the worst roads in the world. Saul, proof of God crawling around in the dirt. And this man here in front of me who took that proof of God from me!

Then his adoptive mother's voice came hurtling into his ears: You are in the House of God!

He had been fiddling with an insert into the hymnal. He was about seven years old, they were in the cathedral in Brisbane, and it was the only time he ever felt the threat of violence from her. She didn't raise her hand or contort her face but simply transmitted an anger that he had never felt from her before with that stern sound from her vocal chords. From that day forward a church would be a place apart for him, insistently so.

But The Centipede kept looking at him, and Kevin finally couldn't resist looking back. It may be the devil making me look, he thought. Even as he blessed the Eucharist, he kept one eye on The Centipede.

Then the two young eucharistic ministers walked up beside him, took their trays of hosts, and walked to either end of the altar.

And now the holy showdown, Father Kevin thought, as the first pew of parishioners made its way up to the altar in single file. They all came toward him; The Centipede was four rows back, directly behind them. Father Kevin barely made eye contact as he mouthed the words "El Cuerpo de Cristo" to each communicant. He kept watching The Centipede with one eye.

The Centipede had destroyed Christ's body by murdering Saul, he thought as he mechanically lifted hosts and mouthed the words. But here I am holding a hundred bodies of Christ in my hand, and I am defiling Christ with my violent thoughts. That is what Juarez does to you; the devil pulls at you even in the holiest moments in this town. The devil is always tugging at your shirttail.

He saw The Centipede's row rise and fall into line in the center file. But there was a slight commotion at the end of the pew, and he realized The Centipede was squeezing past people back to his place in the pew. He was skipping communion. He sat back down in his spot after everyone had filed out. He would be the only person in the church to not receive communion.

As Kevin made the concluding remarks, there were bugs, big, buzzing zappers, darting around up in the beams, and he could not help but imagine that video game and one of those big zappers targeting The Centipede's head and shooting straight down at him from the rafters.

He made the final sign of the cross and led the recession out of the church. Beside The Centipede's pew he paused and looked him dead in the eye. But The Centipede's eyes were shut tightly again.

Father Kevin moved forward, determined to wait for The Centipede out front, not to speak to him but to take off his sunglasses and stare unblinking at him out there where the desert sun made everything crystal clear. But The Centipede never appeared. Kevin scanned every face in the courtyard. After everyone had dispersed, Kevin stepped back inside and scanned the church for him. But the only souls there were the bugs up above, still shooting and diving from the rafters.

Kevin scoffed. Keep this noble head on these noble shoulders, he often said to himself when he felt hot-blooded. The advice had come, in jest, from an old Irish priest who had served in Nicaragua for thirty years. The saying stuck with Father Kevin but as much as a challenge as warning. He felt tempted to defy it, called to be arrogant, to sin and act—go hunt down The Centipede and avenge Saul's death in God's daylight. But he knew he had learned—from affable Leo and steady Rayna—to tone it down, to rebel less against what he could not change. If he comes back a month from today, I will even give him communion, Kevin said to himself. Who am I to turn away a murderer? Who am I to judge the bastard who killed our little saint? And part of him, the part he resisted every day, said: I am just that man, more that man every damn day.

◈ ◈ ◈

"IF I STICK AROUND LONG ENOUGH, YOU WILL TURN ME INTO A CATHOLIC, RAYNA," he said as he walked into the kitchen before dawn a few weeks later. He kept marveling at the effect Leo and she were having on his very personality, softening his edges even as the stress of life in Juarez was giving him every reason to blow up the way he used to do as a young man.

He stood and took in the precision of her choreography—the utensils and pots all hanging in studious order behind the sink, the countertop polished shiny as tile, and the settings, even for breakfast, as tidy as in any fine restaurant. He sat down at the table. She placed eggs with green sauce in front of him. It was dark outside, just like it had been the night before when she had said the words that he kept repeating to himself like a rosary.

And then he repeated her own words, the words she had said to him at Corpus Christi one afternoon after there had been God knows how many murders the night before.

"They will scream and tremble and fall on the ground, but tomorrow they will stand upright and almost forget."

"Almost forget?" he asked her as she stood in front of the coffee machine chugging with its morning brew. "How can a parent even come close to forgetting?"

"Because it is the only way to survive," she said, as if they were picking up the conversation right where they had left off days before. "Maybe because we are Mexican."

She picked up the pliers she had used the day before to make the flower arrangements for him to take to the funerals. And then she had turned around suddenly and stared straight at him as he ate the eggs halfheartedly.

"You want me to tell you because God wills us to," she said. "But I cannot. It is our strength. It is because we will ourselves simply for the sake of our other children."

He shook his head dubiously.

In the neighboring barrio, the massacre two nights ago would surely test that uncanny ability of Mexican parents to stand back up, he thought. What had been planned as a friendly soccer game organized by a youth group ended up pitting two drug gangs, two young, aspiring branches of the Juarez cartel and the Sinaloa cartel, he assumed, against each other. The losers lost poorly on the field, kicking and swinging and spitting. A few hours later, one group executed seven members of the other group outside a roadside restaurant. Thirteen more boys from a neighboring parish died simultaneously in another ambush at a party.

In Juarez, drug gangs usually overlapped with youth group teams, which typically coincided with parishes. So after the massacres, a single priest usually bore the brunt of a massacre's funerals. Father Kevin had driven over to the ill-fated parish to offer to say some of the funerals. The poor Mexican priest, so weary he barely seemed able to make it through a wedding, shed a tear at the offer.

After breakfast, Kevin put on his vestments and prepared to leave. As a sort of public protest and show of solidarity, he had decided to walk to the church wearing his vestments instead of donning them there. He wanted to stand up for God even as God was fading away, losing the battle with Satan, in this hell. He and Leo and some volunteers had already carried Rayna's flowers over the afternoon prior and laid them on the altar.

He felt weak this morning. As he walked to the door, he looked to Rayna for her usual consoling gaze. But she was crying. She knew none of these boys, and yet there she was, as weak as the whole city.

Was she finally breaking? "This is the worst day yet, Rayna?" he had half stated and half asked.

She shook her head yes. He had expected her to say no, the

same way she would never admit she had suffered in her personal life.

"Why?" he had asked the night before. ¿Por qué? He knew she wouldn't answer, couldn't, but he said it out loud, he realized, to show solidarity. He, the priest, the man with all the answers, couldn't get his head around this one either. He had realized clearly that he looked to her as much as she looked to him. He had realized a while ago that he had been doing this for years. The dynamic of their relationship had gone from one-sided to total equilibrium. The mutual need hung steady right in the middle of the high wire they were living on. But now, these days, perhaps I need her more than she needs me, he had said to himself with a chuckle. How about that? And now this morning, at that balancing point between darkness and dawn, he held the door open, surveyed the kitchen again, and, under his breath, blessed the place and her sitting there, this woman who had gotten up early to prepare him a special breakfast.

When he turned down the street from the parish, the sun was about to rise over the El Paso mountains. People were trickling out as usual at this hour, but he felt the collective sluggishness. The violence could still penetrate the hardest of hearts, he realized. It took great numbers, mass murders rather than one-offs. But the capacity for collective tragedy still existed.

Normally no one looked at him when he walked about in his priestly vestments—even though it was a rare occurrence. But today, the people nodded and touched his arm and walked closer to him. Even the Jehovah's Witnesses nodded and gestured. Pity that this is what it takes, Kevin thought. Pity this is what it takes for me to get out of my street clothes and wear the formal, priestly attire.

When he arrived at the parish at last, the hearses were backed up on the bumpy street in front of the afflicted church. As he passed, Kevin saw a coffin in each waiting for the subsequent Mass.

He said four funerals that morning. At each one, family and friends trembled and screamed and fell to the concrete floor. And by the third Mass, he kept saying Rayna's words to himself every time someone acted up. He even paused on the altar, collected himself, whispered her words such that the families, had they not been distraught, would have thought him a madman.

After the third service, he retreated to the sacristy. He normally hugged those in need out front after a funeral, but today it was too much for him.

The only thing that got him through the fourth funeral was looking at Rayna's flowers.

Halfway through it, he touched the rosary in his pocket and decided to go for broke on the homily instead of repeating the same one again. He had felt the load of death and grief slightly ease suddenly with the permission he had given himself to stray from his remarks. He got up and talked about flowers and Mexico and hope and survival. He didn't even know what the hell he was saying, where it was coming from. But his Spanish was less clunky, his accent as fluid as if after two glasses of wine but not a third to tip fluency into slurring. When he had finished, he sat down and marveled. He regretted not having given such a good homily at the first three funerals, for he noticed the effect this time—the first calm out of the four Masses that poured down over the people in the pews.

He had to urinate the whole time, a nagging sensation that he was feeling more and more these days. He thought it was nerves, the stress of all the violence. But he even forgot about his bladder this time

As he gave the final blessing, he knew this was one of the best funerals he had ever celebrated. The people were wailing and beating themselves again, but he felt their attention fixed on him despite their grief. He felt like he had performed well finally, like he had spit in the devil's face at last.

At dinner that night, her chiles in front of him like a child's reward, he felt an even stronger sense of absurd contentment.

"You don't get your cheese for the chiles at the usual places," he said. "It is real cheese, not processed."

She smiled.

"Queso de cabra," she said. Goat's cheese.

So that was the secret. He was no connoisseur, having eaten food cooked by someone else since he entered the seminary at age 17. But every once in a while he would end up dining in the home of an incredibly wealthy person who would put such exquisite plates on the table that there would be no option but to marvel at what they did to one's tongue. And here he was essentially living with a woman who cooked like that, like the cooks cook for the wealthy up in the hills across the border, and he felt not the guilt he would once have felt but simple joy at the taste and the blessing of the good fortune.

He took a forkful of a chile, chewed scrupulously, and then took another.

She sat next to him and wiped silverware that she had already washed.

He knew this was the time to ask her the question he had wanted to ask her for ten years. Amazing, he thought, how that one curiosity becomes an obsession. He did not know why he needed to know; he had spells where he was resigned to never knowing, telling himself that it didn't matter and chastising his sordid curiosity.

He had come close to asking her but beat back his curiosity every time for fear of offending her. But tonight, with life seeming both more absurd and more fundamental than ever, he didn't ask her, he simply decided to tell her he knew.

"Rayna, I know your second husband tortured you; Father Morton told me many years ago when I first met you."

She did not move or even change the direction in which she was polishing a spoon.

"And today in Mass I saw tortured people, mothers and brothers and sisters with their backs and knees broken by grief."

She brushed her long gray hair off her forehead. She must do this a thousand times a day, he thought. It wasn't a tic even but seemingly a reminder to herself that she was still herself, alive, physical.

"You have suffered at many points in your life, too," she said back. He didn't expect her response. He had hoped she would continue down the road of self-revelation, for, even though he technically left the First World and its self-centered spirituality behind thirty years before, he still could never quite shake its hold on him. Faith was about me, my life, my spirituality, my advancement over there in the rich lands, he often said now. Here, in places like this, it is about survival, about community, about supporting each other with spiritual glue to bind our hearts and brains and guts and souls against all the evil.

Her response immediately upheld and exemplified this different model, this Third World one. "Faith is about us, not me. I go to church to share with you, to sing and dance and pray with you; we support one another, and we strive for faith together so we can survive together."

He decided to stop, let her be. His mind, as it always did, imagined a man tying Rayna up, beating and burning her with cigarette butts, slapping her. He had heard the rumors. But why pursue that story, now or ever? Why not learn from her once and for all?

"I talked about your flowers in my final homily today," he said. "It helped me. It helped them."

She smiled slightly, pushed his plate closer to him, and then lifted her right hand and pushed her hair up off her forehead.

◇ ◇ ◇

HE STUFFED A PACK OF MARLBOROS INTO THE POCKET
OF HIS BROWN LEATHER JACKET AS HE WALKED OUT THE
DOOR INTO THE JUAREZ NIGHT. He rarely went out after dark
since all the killing began. No one did. During the day the streets
were still zigzags of cars and carts and mules. At night now, with
the war between the Sinaloa and Juarez gangs at full tilt, people
were getting their heads cut off.

He knew people were cringing and looking with worry at one
another from their rows of beds inside their shacks as they heard
him crunch past on the dirt road. He cowered now, too, when he
heard footsteps or cars or voices at this hour.

But for several months now he prided himself on what he
called his cigarette courage. As much as he smoked, he still
couldn't stand the smell of it inside the house. So in the middle
of the night his unruly prostate would insist on a piss, and then
his unruly brain would insist on a cigarette. And he would step
outside, light up, and think about nothing except the cigarette.
That was, he noticed, the rare peace in this place. Aussie medi-
tation. And the bloody cigarette corporations up north sending
us all their cartons, he chuckled. They must know it is the one
respite in hell.

As he walked toward the belly of Anapra, he wondered if
he would ever stop noticing the same thing at night—the white
lights of El Paso. Every night it was the first thing to grab his
attention. In Juarez, most of the street lights were a stark yellow,
some even Christmas tree green. But across the highway and
river, the thousands of lights of El Paso were so white that they
seemed to blend in with the stars and moon. Another priest
told him the discrepancy in color was the perfect symbol for
the economic disparity between the two countries, purity and
pollution. He thought the priest was overthinking things a bit.

El Paso is a dump, too, he thought, but at least the lights beckon toward something better.

The air was so much clearer at night without all the trucks and pedestrians and carts and animals kicking up dust. He laughed that he needed a smoke to restore the air to its proper polluted state.

He stopped at an intersection, four dirt roads curvily crossing with no lights or signs. He fumbled for his lighter, and as he lit up he saw the graffiti on the corner of a wall: Festival Santa Muerte, in perfect chicken scratch. There was no date or time, and he wasn't sure if it referred to a specific event or to the idea that a life devoted to this saint, to Saint Death, could be one long festival in itself. Saint Death, just a notch below God now here in Juarez, the holiest of the saints, the most accessible, and growing in popularity every day. Rebellious boys, old women who had lost too many sons, middle-aged women who had lost too many daughters: the cult was booming and shrines to Saint Death were popping up everywhere. Here he was trying to preach hope, and all around him people were fetishizing hopelessness with this cult of Saint Death, worshipping it now. He decided to try to find the shrine that Leo had told him had been built here up the hill. He knew it was deep in the bowels of Anapra, up by a vacant lot that had become a makeshift dump. One day he told the kids in confirmation class about Lourdes and Fatima, and how people from all over the world go there every day to pray and be healed. How people wept with joy there and left flowers instead of tequila and switchblades and water pistols like they do here now in front of the Santa Muerte statues. How, and here he lost his cool, he was ashamed that this powerful people, this people of the great Mexican backbone and tradition, was giving in to death and the devil. It's one thing to celebrate the dead, a glorious thing. But not Death; please, he said, half-shouting, do not let Death be sanctified and almighty. Go home and go to your internet bodega and look up Lourdes, please. Look up Fatima. See the real glory, the real hope that they offer people. See the real shrines. Go learn about the real saints, the hundreds of them whose statues we should be building on every block to get us through this darkness.

He didn't wear a watch, but he supposed it was now 3 AM. Up here the smoke from the homes' chimneys seemed to get trapped by some sort of invisible lid over Anapra. He started to cough but tried to stifle the sound so no one half-sleeping in their shack would be startled. He lit another cigarette and kept smoking as he walked.

A truck suddenly roared, and as it turned the corner, its lights shone straight on him, and he realized he was in the middle of the road. But it wasn't slowing down, either, and he froze as it nearly brushed up against him. Soldiers sat in the open back. He stood there staring, and the whites of their eyes showed that they had disregarded him completely. The patrols never stopped, but they almost never got out of the trucks, save to cover a corpse with a sheet or buy lunch at a taco stand. They just kept driving around, as if their presence were the total fulfillment of their duty.

He turned and walked to the top of the street. It dead-ended in a desert mound, and the shiny trash that was building up on it reflected the moonlight, making the area brighter.

Then a powerful green light on a pole cast the area in front of him in a laughably putrid light. This is the local shrine, he realized, and they sure have a sense of style. The scythe stood about a foot above the head of the statue's skull, and the whole thing felt like Halloween. The scent from all the flowers irritated his nose, so he lit another cigarette. The match's light showed tequila bottles at the foot of the statue. The gnarled little globe in the saint's left hand looked like a preserved brain. He smoked and scoffed at the same time. All this hype, all this devotion, and this is the best they can come up with. Clownish.

He lit another cigarette, and the match light illuminated the face of the statue. And there, pointing out at him, was a cigarette someone had stuck in the statue's toothy mouth. This is where you will end up if you keep smoking like you do, he thought; they'll make a goofy statue out of you.

He lit another match and reached across the flowers. He held it in front of the statue's cigarette until it caught fire on its own. And then he turned and walked back down the hill, a bit faster. And then faster still, Catholic guilt pushing him like it always had since he was a kid. He didn't look back. He assumed the cigarette had extinguished itself. But he hoped the whole thing caught fire, spreading to the dry flowers below and maybe fueled by the tequila on the ground.

And then he stopped. He had an irritating conscience; as a boy he had started to measure his deeds—their goodness or cheapness—by how his adoptive mother would have viewed them, and that habit, like many, only got worse with age. He lit another cigarette insistently, for this was the one thing he would defy her on always, his cigarettes. Then he turned and walked back to the shrine. He made certain there was no fire, studying the cigarette to be sure it had died out. Then he laughed, shook his head, and yanked the cigarette from the statue's mouth.

"The stuff will kill you," he said out loud.

He threw the cigarette to the ground and stomped it into the dust. And then, suddenly and from out of nowhere, he made the sign of the cross in front of Santa Muerte.

He found his way home, smoking the whole walk back, and fell into his bed at 5:30. He got up at 6, his usual hour, and did his morning sit-ups and said his morning prayers, sluggish but more defiant than ever.

CHAPTER TEN

---◇---

Rayna

"I DIDN'T PERFORM MIRACLES WHEN THOSE PEO-
PLE GOT OVER THEIR ILLNESSES, LEO, it was..."
Kevin said, words failing him, as they always did at
this point in the conversation about incorporating
charismatic elements into the services at Corpus Christi. Rayna,
for over a year now, had been trying to convince Kevin that the
people were craving charismatic prayer services, that this was
the way to not only defeat the evangelicals once and for all but
also to bolster the soul of his parish just as the violence was
weakening it. But Kevin, not conservative but still somehow old-
school, had kept sidestepping her, not resisting but surely not
embracing her idea.

Rayna walked over to the sofa and sat down with them.

"Father Kevin," Leo continued, "if you don't believe, how can
we believe?"

She wanted to kick Leo now, for he was rubbing it in. She
had coached Leo about how to make the case to Father Kevin
but knew he would stray from the script the first chance he got.

"Padre Kevin," Rayna said, "you know what a neighbor said
to me the other day? She was looking at the newspaper, a body
with messages scribbled in magic marker all over it in a photo
on the first page, and she looked at me and said, 'It is November,
and God is very far away!'"

Rayna leaned closer to Kevin, who nodded.

"It is November, and God is very far away, Padre Kevin," she
repeated.

"Rayna, I have utmost respect for this culture, for this people,"
Kevin said. "For me, the presence of God during Mass, during
the Eucharist, is enough. But I understand what you need. I just
can't, I don't know, I..."

She loathed this line of thought of his more than any other,
the condescending Anglo knowing our needs, the needs of these
poor Mexicans which, if fulfilled, might just make their pain
slightly more tolerable, make their world slightly more bearable.
She felt anger, the kind of anger only he could arouse, welling up,
and she got up and walked over to the kitchen again.

"Why are you here?" she asked, fully aware of the brutality
of her question. She could tell he knew he had offended them,
Leo now realizing he should be offended just like her. Leo leaned
forward on the sofa and looked at her. These men, she thought.
At the end of the day it is about men and women. People still
think I am here at the whim of these two men, prostituting myself still. But I know I am half-running this place now, and I know
these two men in front of me know it. I did not seek this out; the
vacuum needed to be filled by a woman.

Kevin muttered.

"You are here to help us, but we are helping you, too, correct?" she said, her voice calmer now.

"Well, surely," Kevin said. "Grace is a two way..."

"Déjalo, let's not talk about grace and all that fancy stuff," she said. "We are trying to build a parish, correct? A place filled with God's light? A place to hide from the killers and the killings? Well, the way to do that is to let the light in. Open all the windows. He wants in, Padre Kevin, he wants in."

"I already said OK, Rayna," Kevin said. "I already said it. Go ahead. Maybe you will convert me."

She snapped, turning and walking back over to him.

"Convert?" she half-shouted. "The last three popes have recognized the charismatic movement. One of its leaders is from Brisbane. Brisbane, Australia, Kevin! Your home! This is not some Protestant loco group getting its money from Dallas! If you want God to be with us here and now, you need to let yourself see that he *is* here and now. Even *here!* Even *now!*"

"Rayna, you are officially our charismatic coordinator! I will announce it on Sunday! God bless!"

He got up and walked quickly into his room.

Leo looked at her with astonishment.

"You were a little hard," Leo said. Un poco duro.

"Cállate, Leo," Rayna said. She got up and put on her coat, Leo sitting there watching her with astonishment.

"Adios," she said, walking past him.

She paused in the hallway, listening for sounds from Kevin's room.

"Adios, Padre Kevin," she shouted.

Through his thin door she could hear papers ruffle.

"Adios, Rayna, gracias por la comida tan rica," he shouted. Thank you for the fine meal. His go-to line.

She chuckled to herself as she walked out the door.

Outside, the November sun barely warmed her despite there

not being a cloud in the sky. She walked down the street, debating for a moment whether to go home or go to the church and do something, what she was not sure, but something to start organizing the charismatic program. If he really is going to announce it on Sunday, I better be ready, she thought. God is going to be coming closer soon, and I am going to be ready. This is the only way to save us now, this is the only response to what is happening all around us. It is time to speak with God directly.

SHE KNEW THAT THEY WOULD COME HARD FOR THE PRIESTS, FOR THEY WERE ALL THAT WAS LEFT. The crime bosses, the big ones, made a show of their faith, just like the oligarchs. Money for schools, money for the homeless, money for the hungry: at the end of the day they were all capitalists, be it drugs or gasoline, but at the end of the day their sole boundaries, their untouchables, were only their children and mothers, not their brothers or fathers or wives, nor their priests.

While hiding Father Alfredo, the parish priest from San Marcos who had to come live with Kevin for two weeks and could never leave the house because of the threat against his life, she saw, for the first time, her own world cracking. Father Kevin is far more controversial, a much bigger statement for them. To kill Kevin would be to exhibit absolute mastery over not just the state but the people, the soul of the people. All priests, yes, but here in Anapra, a bullet to the head of our smiling Kevin wouldn't incite us, it would break our spirits.

And why the priests, why not the evangelicals? It shows, she thought, how little this new stuff from the North really means down here. She had heard Kevin speak enough about social justice to know why the priests were the threat. They were the only ones really sticking their necks out into the crossfire, she knew.

The others were bean counters, fanatics, at best more focused on heaven and God's opinion than this hell here and how to get us out of it.

"How much is an offering really worth to them?" she had asked Kevin one day at lunch.

She had helped him count the offerings after Mass for years and knew that, on a good day, a holiday perhaps, it would be enough to buy a good gun for a murder at most. So she knew they were extorting the priests not for the financial benefit but to simply intimidate, to show their absolute control even over the final refuges from them here.

She was tucking in the corners of the burritos when his phone rang. He looked at the incoming number, reacted, and she knew that face. How often he would look at the number, say that funny "hallo, hallo," and start to twitch and pace while the other party spoke. He was not a phone man, Father Kevin.

"Hello, Father," he said as he got up from the chair. She knew it was his superior back in Omaha.

He didn't look at her as he walked past the table and towards his room. The door rarely made a sound when he closed it, as if he were trying to politely retreat to his privacy. But once in a while, like this time, he closed it hard and fast.

She finished preparing the burritos stuffed with chicken and corn, one of his favorite dishes, and stood there.

He was being called out this time, not merely warned. She didn't even need to eavesdrop.

But she did anyway, just to determine when he would be gone. Leo walked in, and she raised her finger to her mouth. The interior doors were so thin that they served no acoustical purpose, only visual, and when he raised his voice, as he was doing now, she could practically maintain a conversation with him from the kitchen.

Nor did she know why she had shushed Leo. The poor man

stood there looking bewildered, surely realizing Kevin was speaking in English and knowing she understood about twenty words of it.

"¿Qué?" Leo asked, shrugging his shoulders. She raised her finger to her mouth again and then averted her eyes. Now there was only silence.

"They are taking him out," she said.

"Nah, impossible," Leo said, shrugging, and walked around the counter to look more closely at the burritos.

"He'll never leave," Leo said, plucking a slice of cucumber from the salad bowl like he always did.

"They'll have to take him out of here dead," he said, crunching on the cucumber.

Still silence. She imagined him sitting in his chair, or sitting on the edge of his bed, with his head in his hands. No, that wasn't right. He was pacing, saying the Rosary, wondering how to tell us.

"If his boss tells him to go, he has to go, Leo," she said, perturbed at his lack of anxiety.

"No tiene jefe," Leo said. He doesn't have a boss. She slapped his hand as he reached for another piece of cucumber.

Then she heard the door hinges squeak as Kevin opened it. He walked back in and sat at his place. She carried the plates over and set them down. He said a quick grace, and they began to eat.

"Va a hacer frío mañana," Leo said. It is going to be cold tomorrow.

Oh, how she loathed Leo at moments like this, his obliviousness—such a male characteristic. Kevin had it, too. They couldn't see an emotion if it spit on their noses.

But the silence was right there in front of them, and Kevin kept shifting positions in his seat.

She decided to speak, to cut right to it at least to see how these idiotas eating alongside her reacted. The Maryknolls had pulled their priests out, and she began to try to formulate a vague question comparing the Columbans with them. But suddenly she thought of one better.

"They are afraid you'll become another Frank Douglas, Father Kevin?"

He jumped.

Frank Douglas was the Columban martyr from New Zealand whom the Japanese had tortured for two days to try to get information on the confessions Filipino guerrillas had made to him during the Japanese occupation during World War II. Kevin had spoken of him a dozen times over the past year as the violence grew and grew. Frank Douglas was a martyr; Frank Douglas was a saint. Frank Douglas was, she sometimes thought, the man Kevin tried to model himself after.

He looked up at her. She felt the tears fill her eyes, then looked at Leo, and, ese cabrón, that sob, she thought, now he decides to tear up, too.

"I told him I'm leaving only as a corpse, Rayna," Kevin said.

"I told him I would temporarily join the Juarez diocese and leave the Columban order, seek incardination as they say," he said.

The tears started to trickle down her face, and Leo got up and walked over to the kitchen.

Kevin cleared his throat.

"I thanked him for his concern," he said. "I'm not leaving. The shame of it! And that you'd even think me capable!"

Suddenly Leo started laughing, filled a glass with water, and came back and sat down.

"¿Ves, qué te dije?" he said, leaning on his elbows toward Rayna. You see, I told you so!

Kevin started to belly laugh, and Rayna did, too.

That lasted more than a minute, and then there was silence again as they all wiped their tears.

"Good on ya, mate," Leo said. "Bonzer!" Rayna understood what he had said, imitating the Aussisms they heard over and over from Kevin, but she could tell he didn't pull off the Aussie accent sufficiently for Kevin to understand.

"¿Qué?" Kevin demanded, staring at Leo.

This time, Leo wet his lips, contorted them for a second, and turned right to Kevin.

"Good on ya, mate," he said. "Bonzer!"

She could tell Kevin was about to crumble. But suddenly he threw his head back and roared his devil-may-care laugh as loudly as she had ever heard it.

AND HOW THEY DANCED DURING THE MEETING OF THE NEW CHARISMATIC GROUP OF CORPUS CHRISTI! She had promised him this was how it would be, but the riotousness of it had surprised even her. She had led prayer meetings for over two months now, and this was the first he had attended. He sat in the back row of the circle of chairs she had come to assemble around her and the guitarist at the center.

As she began to pray, raising her arms to the sky, closing her eyes, she could feel the people, about fifty of them now, imitate her and begin to pray and start to sway, too. She could feel the strength of the group, of the circle, and that strength made her feel even stronger herself.

She motioned for the guitar player and drummer to get ready but realized they didn't even need them. The music was in the lyricism of their prayers, the guitar following their words and her movements.

She decided to say it in Latin for him; she had memorized the Hail Mary in Latin each night over the past week and now raised her hand to pause the music.

"Ave Maria," she sang. "Ave Maria."

She motioned to the drummer to imitate the beats of her words.

"A-ve Ma-ri-a, A-ve-Ma-ri-a."

She motioned for the rest of the prayer group to repeat her rhythm, then for the guitar player to accompany, and then the whole church was swaying, shouting the phrase over and over and over, feeling the words coming through their bodies.

"A-ve-Ma-ri-a!"

"You are so full of charisma," she had said to him soon after he had given her permission to start the charismatic group, "and this movement is called charismatic, so it all makes perfect sense."

She knew she had him, had him by that vanity she once loathed but now adored.

As she turned, she opened one eye and saw him watching her, then saw him turn his head and watch his flock. He was startled and amazed and apart and yet a part of it all, too. She could tell he was fundamentally pleased that his parish for a while could shed the outside world, could forget about what was colliding with Juarez every night, and be here, now, together inside his Corpus Christi. The devil couldn't get in here even if he brought all his assistants to try to break down the door, she wanted to tell him. The devil is scared of this. And this is the way back, she wanted to tell him, this is how we will fix our city, by shaking and shouting and crying and jumping up and down. I know you don't understand, but this is the only way.

PART III

Confirmation

2012-2014

CHAPTER ELEVEN

Kevin

AS THEY WALKED THEIR FIRST ASCENT UP THE HILL, KEVIN AND LEO USUALLY SPOKE HEARTI-LY. The second time up they spoke less; then, by the third climb, when they were so winded that their breathing matched each other's rhythm, they didn't speak at all. The third ascent, the culmination of this daily exercise regimen that Rayna had at first encouraged and then demanded that her two rotundish charges undertake, was always Kevin's favorite. And he loved this pause now, this rest they always took before com-mencing the third climb. He loved looking out over an Anapra that suddenly seemed to be calming. Leo had told him that the Sinaloa cartel had defeated the Juarez cartel in their battle for control of the city. Leo had told him this was what had been necessary all along to restore order. Leo had told him it would last, this peace. This relative peace, Kevin wanted to correct him. This lull, as he was still dubious when Leo gave his opinion on politics.

But he had grown to love Leo for his good nature and his loyalty as much as for his handiness and work ethic, love him as deeply as he loved Rayna and her children. And as he walked this hot summer afternoon next to his fine companion, he looked down on the bowl, the dent in the desert that Anapra really was, and marveled at the brutal beauty of the place. There was no natural beauty to speak of, save for a few mountaintops in the desert expanse. But all the people trudging up and down the hilly dirt roads, the people that Leo embodied—that was what made the place so breathtaking.

He felt more out of breath this day than usual, felt his heart racing such that he wondered if its quickening was a sort of total weakening within his body, a comprehensive capitulation. After six months of pissing blood and telling no one, he had finally gone to El Paso to get himself checked out. The blood test was off the charts; now he was awaiting definitive word from radiology, but he could have told the doctors himself even before any of their tests that it was cancerous. And though prior to the doctor's visit he had no fear and virtually no heed for his health, after the appointment he suddenly questioned his own sanity for waiting so long. The violence, the exhaustion, the funerals— scores of urgent matters kept him from taking care of himself. That and an Australian disdain for weakness, for decline, he decided. And a distaste for doctors' offices.

They stood looking down over Anapra from the perch on the hill where they had parked the truck.

"What a place," Kevin said.

Ever since he had begun to formally employ Leo and Rayna, he felt ashamed every time he paid them for their work. It was their company he needed more than their work. It was their companionship and their reliability. Deep down, *that* was what he was paying for. He realized while he was serving back in Chile that he had the missionary's knack for identifying the bulwarks of a parish, the trusty ones who, while not necessarily the most holy, were surely the most trustworthy in a jam and simultaneously the most pleasant to be around.

That was the most striking thing about Leo, his ease.

He noticed Leo had turned slightly to look northward toward the Rio Grande.

"I still have the raft I used to cross on," Leo said. "There was a time, not all that long ago, when it really was a river. Sometimes, when it was windy and the raft was full, it even got dangerous. A few people drowned."

"You know how to swim, Leo?"

"¡Sí!" Leo said proudly. "¡Un poco!" A little bit. Enough to save your life, Kevin thought.

Kevin felt his heart rate slowing and realized that it had not been the exercise that had accelerated it in the first place but what he had been thinking. He had been thinking melancholically, wistfully, and he loathed himself when his brain took that direction. He had been thinking about this place without him, and the opposite, too: himself still in this place without Leo and Rayna. Being with them made the ugliest dent in the earth stunning. Despite the dust and poverty and brutality, this place, with them, could, on a day like this, be heavenly. That was what the journalists and Yanquis failed to understand. We love this place; we, I like they, came solely for the work, but we stay because of one another; we now say we are from here, because of having been together here. Even I say I am from here. He would never dare voice such dewy thoughts, not even in a homily. It would blow his tough guy Aussie reputation out of the water. But God, did he feel those thoughts—not in his brain but in his bones, in his quickening heart.

"Leo, would you ever leave here?" Kevin asked.

"¿Por qué?" Leo asked back, looking up at Kevin suddenly. Why?

"I mean, you have extended family here now, friends; is this your home? They've been murdering thousands of people a year for years now. Don't you think about leaving?"

"I guess I would leave if you left, Padre Kevin," Leo said, looking back out over the town.

It was a delightful answer for Kevin but also a chilling one. The one Kevin did not want to hear. On a day as hot as hell, Leo had given him the chills. He knew the obligation of every missionary priest was transience—build, help, but don't fall in love, and, most of all, don't let them adore you. Embrace the spirit, not the heart. But they both ended up being the same thing, someone's spirit and someone's heart. And he knew he had broken that rule running both ways. He knew they were embracing his heart, and he had grown to cling to their hearts, too. Their spirits, well, that love was off the charts. He didn't ever want to leave. He had thought the other day, in passing and from out of nowhere, that he wanted to die here. And now, he thought, I just might.

Imagine saying that to my superior when he tells me it is time for me to go work with the aborigines in the Outback, he had thought as he lay awake one night recently, pondering a future transfer, the inevitable transfer. Or worse: I am riddled with cancer, Father Superior, but I wish to forego that useless chemotherapy and stay here to die.

He looked at Leo, smiled, and took his first step back up the hill. Leo took his first step before Kevin's foot had even hit the ground. Their heavy breathing resumed, synched, and Kevin's heart stayed fast.

At the top, the sun was so hot and close that he felt he could reach out and touch it.

"Wouldn't be a bad time for a raft ride now, would it, Leo?"

Leo laughed.

"Imagine what that could do for the economy, freeing up the

old Rio Grande so tourists could steamboat along the border, look across here at us, and pity us as they gawk!"

The Amtrak train from the west tooted in the distance, and both men turned to watch it. It always slowed as it tracked the border, and Kevin wondered if its passengers could see him and Leo staring at them.

"What a different world," Kevin said through his breathing.

"¿Qué?"

"Nada, Leo, nada," Kevin said. "I was just thinking how this place grows on you, its beauty, the desert and everything. Someone passing by in a train can't possibly grasp that."

They turned and began their third descent, Kevin's mind slowly going blank, focusing on their matching steps and matching breathing, his heartbeat slowing to its normal exertion given the exercise, not the momentary lapse into sentiment.

❖ ❖ ❖

HE WOKE UP EARLY ONE MORNING THINKING OF BILLY'S PLACE IN THE TRADITION OF CHRISTIAN SOLDIERS. That afternoon, he was going to celebrate a Mass up the hill in Lomas de Poleo for the residents who had moved, been evicted, or been killed during the crisis in Lomas over five years ago. It seemed like decades ago when Billy was leading the charge against Zaragoza and the thugs were forcing the evictions of the Lomas residents. The intervening years, with all the murders and fear and suffering, had made the Lomas conflict recede in the consciousness of most Anaprans. The enemy then—intimidating a few hundred Lomas residents so they could rob them of their once worthless parcel of desert—seemed almost comical compared to the enemy now. The crisis then compared to now? Kevin laughed to himself. Those were the days, he thought, the days before the terrible flood a few years ago that, though they

had recovered from it, had seemed to herald a sea change in life
in Anapra. Thousands of murders tend to clarify our priorities
as human beings, he thought. He faded back into sleep for a
few seconds, then caught himself, and forced himself to wake
up. He had been having a dream lately in which the floods of a
few years past didn't fill the streets with rain but with blood. He
didn't want to dream that one again.

He got up, drank his coffee, and kept thinking about progress and about Billy. Foxconn had opened its big plant, the first
and still only one, out in the desert by the border crossing.
Zaragoza had built a gleaming high school up the hill on the
edge of Lomas. But between the high school and the Foxconn
plant, there was still one vast, uninterrupted expanse of desert with a dirt road running through it. Kevin's supposition—
that a new mass of plants out there would improve the lives
of Anaprans, albeit incrementally and according to the screw-
the-worker rules of border capitalism—depended on that desert being developed. Had he made the wrong bet, now that no
other plants seemed to even be in the planning stages? Would
Foxconn, way out there in the distance by the Santa Teresa border crossing, be it? Did his own build-it-and-they-will-come
approach to churches not apply to factories? All these questions
still dredged up the eternal question in his head—had Billy been
right? Were the truth and its companion, justice, more important than jobs and an improved standard of living, especially if
those jobs, those new factories, had only been a real estate de-
veloper's fantasy?

Billy was indeed a Christian soldier, Kevin thought, but this
isn't a very Christian world, despite the more or less official ongoing reign of the Catholic Church alongside the political elite
in Mexico. Maybe I was wrong to assume even oligarchs would
have built their shining factory city by now.

Billy would have stayed true to the fight, and Kevin could sense he had been willing to die for it before he got recalled. Kevin could sense Billy had been willing to be martyred. But Kevin wasn't. Kevin had rationalized it by saying he did more good alive here than dead. He rationalized it by saying the collateral damage of continuing the fight would have meant more death and suffering for Anaprans. But part of the answer, the part that wasn't a rationalization, was that he didn't want to jeopardize a good thing. He didn't want to risk what he had built; this community—Leo, Rayna, the burgeoning Corpus Christi—would have come tumbling down if they had pulled the Lomas linchpin.

Kevin wondered for a moment if he should call Billy to tell him the Lomas folks who had stopped talking to one another— the ones who took the buyout offers for the lands and the ones who resisted until the bitter end—were coming together this afternoon to at least try to talk to each other indirectly, at least pray together at a Mass of Reconciliation. He wanted to tell Billy there were going to pray for him, for the spirit he embodied and the fight he always brought.

But he didn't call. Instead, he prayed for a couple of minutes. For Billy, and for jobs and homes and all that he thought would have arrived out there by now.

Leo picked him up five minutes early. That alone threw everything off. Leo was always late, his tardiness so reliable that Kevin had grown to depend on it as one of the steady things here in chaos. And while it was reliable tardiness, it was tardiness with flair, for one day's five minutes were another day's thirty. No apologies, no face showing shame, just the nod, then the rough pedal to the metal acceleration once Kevin had jumped in but before he had closed the door.

So Leo had unnerved him before they even set out up the hill. On his way up the hill, he turned to Leo and laughed. "Conquer and divide," he said. Leo looked confused.

"If Julius Caesar were a Mexican."

Leo squinted his eyes. Kevin knew he had no interest in his frequent historical allusions. That's why Kevin kept making them at odd times.

Kevin didn't elaborate; he knew Leo would tune him out faster than even Rayna did when he started off on some tangent from the history books. But there it was: here the rich men conquered, rather easily, and left behind Anaprans more taken up with squabbling than their own suffering. Those who left begrudgingly but of their own will would today sit alongside those who were willing to die before leaving, and they would pray together—if there were no fisticuffs or shouting matches. Meanwhile, wherever the real estate developers were drinking their fresh-squeezed orange juice this morning, they surely had no sense of the division, the petty fallout they had wrought apart from the practical victory they had won.

Indeed, as they drove past the white fence posts—now weather-beaten and, the wire between them long since dismantled, looking like a poor man's Stonehenge type of sculpture— Kevin thought that they looked like the tombstones in a military cemetery. And he was suddenly struck by the inanity of what he was about to undertake. This was a Mass for which he had little patience. Part of him wanted to stand up during the homily and say, look at yourselves; they got you and they're going to get you again, the old conquistadors somewhere in their mansions drinking their fresh-squeezed orange juice.

Then, for about the ten thousandth time during his life here, he marveled at the absurdity of the street names. Trucha. Salmón. Cangrejo. Bacalao. Trout. Salmon. Crab. Cod. Had they been mocking the utter illiquidity of this place, that is, until the rich men realized how valuable the land up the hill in Lomas really was and built some modern water tanks? Had the naming of the streets been a sincere but misguided effort to uplift, to encourage these parched people to dream of salt air and sea breezes as they lugged their containers of purified water from the water station up the hard hill to their shack?

"Leo, remind me once again why the hell they picked these street names?" he asked.

Leo laughed a little but didn't respond.

They stopped to let some parishioners hop in the back of the pickup.

"Satanás picked the names," Leo suddenly said as he accelerated.

Nowadays Leo, like Rayna, blamed just about everything on Satan, Kevin thought, because he has heard me doing it so much over the past few years. But he takes me literally, and I suppose I should have stopped to explain the metaphor sometime or other. But perhaps he is right. Why go mad looking for specific culprits when, at the end of the day, they all emanate from the same source? Particularly here in Mexico, with pantalla over pantalla, as the locals say, screen over screen, shielding the true bad guy, Leo and Rayna had seemingly ceased to be curious. Ill fortune, violence, and deception had beaten the curiosity out of them. Satan picked the street names. Fine.

Leo put the truck into second gear for the final ascent up to Lomas Arriba, literally, "Lomas Up Above." As they crested the hill, he saw two groups of people, already distinctly standing apart on either side of the tent set up in the desert adjacent to what was once their neighborhood.

"Mírales, Leo," Kevin said. "They've segregated themselves already."

"Es Satanás," Leo said.

Again, yes, you are right, Leo, Kevin thought. Why hurt our brains digging any deeper to rationalize why these people who were once neighbors now can't even stomach looking at one another?

"Satanás, Satanás," Kevin said, imitating Leo.

They laughed together as Leo pulled up and stopped the truck. Kevin sat for a moment, looking out at them. Zaragoza's community center stood clean and shining just beyond them. His new high school shined even cleaner further up the road toward the highway, toward the someday land of the someday maquilas.

"Vamos," Kevin said, but as he got out of the car, he felt foolish; he felt like he was a puppet strung up and jerked left and right by the oligarchs he had never met and never would meet.

Then he stopped, looked at Leo, and laughed one last time before putting on his game face.

As he walked into the desert field, he caught the pink crosses out of the corner of his eye. Seven of them, seven bodies of murdered women found here in this same field where they were about to celebrate this Mass. How foolish we seem now, bickering over desert land while the city was being slaughtered!

He stood there for a moment and made the sign of the cross, demonstratively.

He continued walking, motioned to all of them to be seated, and set his case and Bible down on a stand behind the big wood altar that Leo had lugged up here that morning.

"Please, sit!" he half requested and half insisted. "Be seated!"

The opposing groups slowly sat, but a line of chairs remained empty in the middle.

Kevin pointed at the line of chairs and then brought his hands together as he nodded at the people seated on either side of it. No one moved. He extended his arms again, just wide enough to match the expanse of the empty seats, and brought his arms together. No one moved. He walked down to the front row, extending his arms wide until his hands rested on the inside shoulder of each person on either side of the empty row, and pulled gently.

"Por favor, show me an act of courage," he said to a man seated there. "Please," he said, motioning with his head for the man to move.

The man folded his arms over his chest, breathed in, and held his breath so long that his cheeks puffed up. Then he blew out and relented, sliding over while looking at the ground.

Kevin smiled. He patted the man on the shoulder. Then he nodded to the woman seated by his side. She followed his eyes and moved into the empty seat.

Then Kevin pointed—you! and you! and you! and you!—and at last the gulf had been filled with frowning former residents of Lomas de Poleo.

Then, just as he was making the sign of the cross to begin Mass, he noticed everyone looking up with a keenness that he instantly knew was out of proportion to the moment. Some moved closer to the front of their seats; a few seated in the rear stood up, sat back down halfway, and then stood up again.

Behind him he suddenly heard the truck. In fact, he had forgotten about it. He had learned early from the evangelicals the power of the connection between the belly and the soul. Indeed, he reckoned that someday, as technology kept improving, the anatomists would posit the soul somewhere near the stomach, perhaps even wrapping the soul around it in a way only visible to the particle detector in the mountains of Switzerland that he had read about. He had ordered a truck full of chickens as a gesture of goodwill—but had ordered it to arrive an hour from this moment, at the end of the Mass. He had even built in a little wiggle room for Mexican time. And here, behind him down the hill, for the first time in his twelve years here, someone was arriving exorbitantly early.

He finished the opening blessing and decided to call the clerical version of a time-out. But before he could, everyone seemingly stood up at once and ran toward the truck. They ran in such unison, in such communion, he thought, that perhaps he had already achieved what he had come up here for.

He turned and watched. As the truck driver climbed up the truck bed and began snagging chicken after chicken by the throat and passing the birds to the grabbing hands below, Kevin looked across the border to El Paso and wondered what Billy was doing right now. Good God, would he love this mayhem!

He had arranged for toys to be delivered, too, and, oddly, he noticed the women clutching the chickens and the men the toys as another man handed them from the truck. The delivery was complete in a few minutes, and Kevin knew he now faced his real test.

Would they come back, linger in the back rows, and then drift back to their homes, bounty in hands? Or would they sit, clinging to the gifts? Or would some of them just matter-of-fact-ly make a beeline for their shacks immediately? Had Satan intervened once again, cleverly instead of violently?

He prepared himself for the latter and rationalized it by telling himself this was the first step of many. They had come together, at least for a few minutes.

He kept watching. And it was lovely. He knew who had sat on which side of the invisible line initially; now, as they returned, some combination of the unwieldiness of the live chickens and toys and the cold was affecting their old grudges. They all sat where it was easiest to sit. And so, as everyone returned but for a couple of sinvergüenzas, a couple of clowns who went racing home, Kevin began to marvel at the uncanny ways of the Lord. Here we are now, chickens squawking and people squirming, but we are all suddenly sitting here together. I'll make it fast, Lord, for their sake, as a further sign that your grace is at work!

He began to feel so cold that when communion rolled around, he tried giving it with his gloves on. But after dropping a couple of hosts and turning red at the obvious affront to the sacred, he took off the glove on his left hand and resumed. The Mass-goers showed stunning dexterity as they managed to keep subduing their chickens and receive communion simultaneously.

As he stood to give the final blessing, Kevin nodded to Leo, who began pouring cups of hot chocolate on a table behind the chairs. He had intentionally not once said the word "reconciliation" the whole Mass long. He did not allude to the differences, the disagreements, or even the Zaragoza thugs.

But now, as he gave the final blessing, he wavered. He wanted to point out how marvelous it was to forgive, how delicious it was, how it tasted as good as the hot chocolate they were about to drink together or the fresh chickens they would later cook. How that chocolate and chicken were such beautiful symbols. He looked at them, their reddening but calm faces suddenly fully attentive, oblivious, and even peaceful. He decided to stay rote and blessed them as he would at any church at the end of any Mass on any given Sunday. Then he pointed to Leo, the hot chocolate steaming slightly up from the cups laid out in front of him. One by one people started to smile. One by one people stood, went to the back, and nodded as Leo handed out cup after cup. A couple of people toasted. No one spoke much. As he took his first sip himself, feeling the warmth of the chocolate slide down his innards, he winked at Leo. Leo winked back, took a cup, and raised it, winked at Kevin again, and giggled.

THE TORRENT OF BABY KEVINS BEING BAPTIZED KEPT COMING. It was beginning to unnerve him, he had admitted to Rayna one night at dinner. But he hesitated when she told him she would push one of her children to follow suit and name a grandson in his honor.

"You are joking, right?" he had said, realizing Rayna had begun to tease him as deftly as he teased her these days. "That would be horrific, Rayna," he had said. "If you think people are talking about us now..."

Then she had started laughing, and he realized she was teasing him. But his own vulnerability to the joke was what sat in the air between them for a few seconds. He knew she could tell how unsettling the whole thing felt, people naming the baby you were baptizing after you.

This baby he was about to drip water on this morning was the third Kevin to be baptized in the parish this year and the eighth since the first one he had baptized during the floods, and he had now mastered his gag line to get a few laughs from his colleagues when he told them what was happening.

"Don't worry, Father. None of them to date have blue eyes!"

He knew his detractors across the border—the priests who considered him a wild card, an ego, a strutter—saw vanity even in the joke. And he was glad they did, for he didn't want them to see what satisfaction lay deep down.

As he looked at the baby in his hands, he paused for a moment and smiled. I joke about it, but there will be no confusion. This baby is as brown-eyed and brown-skinned as can be. But he bears my name. He is named after me, for God's sake!

"Kevin," he said, looking deep into the brownness of the baby's eyes. He looked up at the parents and smiled at them.

You know what you have given me? Kevin wanted to say to the baby, to the parents, to everyone gathered.

Ten years or so ago I would have been dripping with vanity right now. I would have thought myself a rock star, George Harrison here to change your lives. And now I feel only gratitude to you. I could not feel more honored. I am embarrassed with honor that Kevin is becoming a Spanish proper noun.

He baptized this baby Kevin, but as he wiped the baby's forehead, he buckled for a moment. The doctor had told him his prostate was riddled with cancer, though there looked to be no metastasis despite the severity of the cancer. But for the first time he felt a sense of transience inside, a feeling at moments like this that this moment may never be replicated for him here again. He had never felt such a sensation during all the years of violence, oddly, when mortality had become an hourly reflection not just for him but for everyone living here. But now, all because of a silly organ, he thought, an organ a damn priest doesn't even use, now I am wondering how many more Kevins I will hold?

You've got to be kidding me, you self-indulgent fool, he said to himself.

He handed baby Kevin back to his parents and smiled at them again, cursing silently to himself his pressing, outrageous, absurd, and cursed need to urinate again, the adjectives he used to describe the urge always the same albeit in different order.

◈ ◈ ◈

HE SAW HIS OLD ANTAGONIST, THE RABBLE-ROUSING EVAN-GELICAL MINISTER, AFTER A SATURDAY EVENING MASS. He had been seeing the man less and less, wondering lately if he had moved on to another border town to try to set up shop. The sun was setting softly, and even Anapra's dogs were momentarily quiet at this hour. This was his favorite time of the week, reflecting on his best line from the homily and tasting the first sip of rum that he would swirl around in his mouth within the hour. The stillness of the desert asserted itself such that he felt for a brief moment what the place had been not too long ago—just this, just desert.

As the minister came toward him, Kevin stopped in the middle of the field behind the church where he envisioned base-ball fields and even a swimming pool someday if he could raise enough money. Scores of plastic bags lay limp on the brush. He laughed.

"Las bragas de las brujas," he said to himself. The underwear of the witches. He had heard the phrase for the first time early after his arrival and loved it so much he used it as his punch line in the homily at least once a year. He had used it a few weeks ago. When he heard the laughter, the children's laughter, he stopped. He repeated the phrase, sucking his lips and jaw inward to devour the delicious b's. Las bragas de las brujas. The kids laughed again, even harder. They giggled. Las bragas de las brujas. Again. The kids roared, their parents shushing them.

Now, as he stood in the field of bags waiting for the minister, he felt suddenly victorious. The war, without anyone really realizing it, suddenly did indeed look like it was over. Leo, he of the half-baked theories and superstitions, he of the political hearsay and faulty logic, had been right. It was as if one day word had spread that the Sinaloa cartel had defeated the Juarez cartel, El Chapo, Sinaloa's head, had installed his emissary, and the violence stopped on a dime.

I can now return to the friendly rivalry with this curious Pan de Vida pastor, Kevin thought. Indeed, there had been 2,754 murders in Juarez in 2009; 3,602 in 2010; 2,086 in 2011; but over last year, as Leo kept pointing it out to him, Kevin had begun to sense the uncanny lack of violence almost every day. The grand tally at the end of 2012—only 797.

He had memorized the statistics to be able to match wits with Leo whenever they discussed the politics of the drug wars. So as he watched the plastic bags blow, he recited them to himself in case they would come in handy as a conversation piece with the approaching minister. We can now return to our old ways, the evangelicals and I. The violence at least had achieved that, a truce in our silly jousting. As the pastor came up to him, Kevin thought he looked haggard, ten years older. Kevin had always been friendly toward the fellow despite all the hassles he gave him, even letting him borrow some chairs recently when the pastor asked for them. Kevin did not believe he really needed them but was making a show of the request out of chagrin at his own dwindling numbers in the face of Kevin's flourishing parish.

"Kevin, Kevin," the pastor said, never calling him Father. "Are you ready yet? Are you ever going to be ready?"

"Ready for what, Pastor?" Kevin asked patiently, having been through the same routine a couple of dozen times over the years. He had never learned the man's name, preferring the distance of a title, however sarcastic it felt when it came out of his mouth.

"Well, we are ready for you!" the pastor said. "We are ready for you! You are welcome with us! Whenever you are ready to leave the devil's church, we will welcome you with all our open arms!"

Then the pastor turned and walked off, just as he always did, leaving Kevin in the middle of the field with the plastic bragas starting to swirl around him as the evening wind set in.

He laughed. Even this fellow, what fine company he has been. Where else, where else on earth, might so many heartwarming people exist as in this place everyone used to call godforsaken? Even this fellow, despite his quackery and grumpiness, what a joy it has been to joust with him all these years.

◈ ◈ ◈

SOME DAYS, TO ENJOY THE NEWFOUND PEACE, TO BE ABLE TO ALMOST TOUCH IT, TO TRY TO PINCH IT TO CONFIRM ITS TRUTH, HE HAD TAKEN TO WALKING DOWN TO THE MAIN STREET TO GET A COFFEE AT A NEW LITTLE SHOP THERE. He liked a cup in the afternoon to give him a boost through the rest of the day, and, on Tuesdays and Thursdays when Rayna wasn't in the kitchen, he liked to have a chat with the shop owner or whoever else was hanging around.

Lately he had been bumping into two police officers, or coppers as Kevin called them, outside the shop, and he had enjoyed their easy smiles and seeming innocence. Indeed, he also hoped that their chats might serve as an exemplary public display of sorts, for he had begun to lament the profound distrust Anaprans had for the army and, even more so, the police. It was, in Kevin's view, an impediment to any lasting peace that Juarez might try to build. No authoritarian by any means, Kevin still argued with Leo and Rayna that the rule of law was critical to building a civil society, that there had to be some good apples alongside the bad ones, and that forgiveness, and then reconciliation, were their Christian duties. He had had difficulty accepting the disdain Rayna and Leo held for law enforcement, and one day he had chastised Leo for scowling at the police they passed on the highway.

"They can't all be bad, Leo," Kevin had said, receiving only a grunt in response.

"They can't all be crooked, Leo," Kevin had kept on. "I bet you eighty percent of them are just regular guys looking to keep a job and feed their families. Just like you."

"En el ejército, quizás, pero en la policía, no," Leo had responded, gruffly. In the army, maybe, but in the police force, no way.

Kevin had let it drop, but Leo's differentiation stuck with him, so one day a few weeks later he brought up the subject with Rayna.

"Tiene razón Leo," she said, almost angrily. "La policía está cien por cien corupta." Leo is right, the police are one hundred percent corrupt.

"And the army?" Kevin asked.

"Un poco menos," Rayna said, pensively. A little less.

He tried to pursue the topic more with her, but she shut him down just like Leo did. Either because of their own experiences, or exhaustion, with the men who were supposedly supposed to protect them, neither wanted to discuss it.

So Kevin, having nodded and small-talked with the two coppers over the course of a couple of months, decided today to go straight to the source. He knew the army was supposed to be in cahoots with the cartels, in particular the invading Sinaloa group run by El Chapo; he knew the police had tried to kill Viktor; but he couldn't believe, in his heart of hearts, that these two men, and all of their colleagues, were evil.

As he turned the corner to the deli, he spotted the two coppers on the corner out front. He waved first, and they waved back, and as he approached, he made the gesture for drinking and asked if they each wanted a coffee.

They nodded and smiled, and when he walked out balancing three cups, they rushed over to assist him by taking theirs.

He decided to come right out with it.

"How is it that you seem like such fine young fellows and everybody around here despises you?" he asked, laughing slightly as he did.

The men smiled back.

"I mean, I know there are a few bad apples, as we say, but how do you gentlemen feel about it?"

"Hay muchos buenos," one of them said, "muchos buenos." There are a lot of good ones, a lot of good ones.

Kevin nodded at them, looked at the ground, and nodded again.

"There have to be, but the people don't believe it..."

The men stopped smiling, and both looked into the distance at the same time. They are shutting me down just like Leo and Rayna, he realized.

So be it, he thought. There are some things here I do not want to penetrate, do not want to think harder about. There are some things I will never be able to understand.

A few days later, Leo came running up the street and started banging on the gate for Kevin to come out.

"¡Tus coppers!" Leo shouted. "¡Tus coppers! They've shot them!"

As he raced behind Leo toward the corner where the shop was, he kept chastising himself for getting complacent, for thinking it was over, the chaos, for thinking he had helped put it all to rest.

When he came upon them, their two bodies were already covered with plastic. Kevin pushed his way past some fellow police who were guarding the bodies and knelt down beside them. I thought I was done with this, he thought. I thought we were going back forever to funerals for old men and premature babies.

He lifted the plastic off the one copper and saw his brains smeared across his face. He anointed his forehead, nudging the brain matter aside as he had now learned to do to make a spot on what remained of a person's forehead to receive his final blessing.

He dabbed oil onto the man's head and then looked up at Leo scowling at the sight of it all.

He blessed the second copper, whose brains he had to nudge aside to clear space on his forehead, too. As he stood up, he nodded at several of the coppers standing around them. They looked unmoved, cold. They looked like they wanted him to leave, so he did.

As he walked back up the hill with Leo, he felt like he was going to start retching. He stopped for a moment and felt Leo pause beside him and look the other way.

Once he had gathered himself, he looked at Leo looking away from him.

"Who did it?" he said, struggling to speak.

Leo shook his head.

"No lo sé," he said. I don't know. "The other police don't seem to want to know. It may have been an inside job."

Kevin scowled.

"Better but not good," Kevin said. "This is not peace. There is not peace here yet. I let myself think we suddenly had achieved it overnight. But no. Nothing comes overnight."

Leo didn't look at Kevin, keeping his gaze locked on the street below where police cars kept slowly assembling at the murder site. Cops meandered, but no one was doing anything with the bodies.

And then Kevin became angry with himself. He wanted to stay here with Leo, have the people see him, have the people know he had not grown overconfident in Anapra's newfound peace, have the people chatter about how he had given the sacrament to the coppers even though he knew they would say so with distaste. But his disgust got the better of him. He turned up the hill and walked into his home's courtyard. I'm tired of seeing brains, he thought. Forgive me, God, but today is not the day. It's better for me to show my outrage now. This should be over. This was supposed to be over. I am going to demand that it be over.

CHAPTER TWELVE

—◇—

Rayna

"**N**O ENTIENDO. I DON'T UNDERSTAND WHY YOU MAKE A FUNNY FACE WHEN I BRING UP MIRACLES?" SHE SAID.

Kevin had sat down on the sofa after his lunch. Leo was sitting there, too, just like he had been when she had won Kevin's permission to form the charismatic prayer group, and, although she had not conspired with Leo to put Kevin on the spot this time, she knew Leo would provide ample support. She knew he believed in this stuff. She knew Leo understood miracles. And she wasn't going to let Kevin get away with it. She would pepper him monthly on the topic, frustrated by his agile ducking and weaving to this side and that of a straight answer.

"And you are the priest, we are not," she said. "If you don't believe in healing, well, what kind of church is that? We believe but you don't?"

She had come to realize over the years that she could admonish Kevin, exert a power, maternal, feminine, some mix of both, and quite quickly assume the strong end of a conversation, send him backing up right there in his seat.

Leo piped up right away, as she knew he would.

"Padre Kevin," Leo said, "that baby you baptized last year, the girl with the bad heart who they said would die, she is fine now. Todo bien. No tiene ningún problema. Not a single problem. How do you explain that? You have to believe. And the last rites you gave to that father of three children—he never died, he got well the day after you blessed him. The sacrament brought him back to life. If people find out you don't believe in miracles, you will lose them. Es así. Somos así." We are this way.

Rayna saw Kevin's face reddening, which she knew was a good sign.

"It's not that I don't believe," Kevin said. "I said the same thing with the charismatic prayer group. It's not that I don't believe!"

She knew this would be his first line, like always. It's not that I don't believe. Whoever taught him, taught him well. He was a great dodger when he wanted to be; he could wiggle his way out of an argument like this and leave her wondering for days how he did it. But now, with Leo here, and with the parish having enthusiastically embraced the charismatic prayer groups right under his approving nose, she knew he would sooner or later have to come to terms not just with the desires and stubbornness of his flock but with their very convictions, with their, as he liked to say, intellectual differences.

"I respect your convictions, I do," he said, more calmly but still agitated. She knew that would be next, his predictability allowing him time to assemble a respectful response that would once again leave them with no progress, answer, or agreement.

But then she decided to speak his language.

"You said it the other day," she said. "This year Juarez is on track to have a murder rate lower than most American cities. You said it. I know you were joking, but you said it when they finished the S Mart down the street. 'If you had told me they were going to build an S Mart in Anapra, I would have told you it would have been a miracle back when I first came here.' That is what you said."

Rayna had started buying food and supplies at the S Mart, a sort of mini Walmart, and noticed how much Kevin had enjoyed the steak she had cooked for him a few nights ago.

"A steak this good, from a market just down the street," he had marveled.

He laughed knowingly at her line of logic. She knew he admired how, over the years, she had come to match wits with him, to debate him like he said the priests used to do when he was studying in the seminary.

"But you misunderstand miracles," Kevin said. "God worked through you. God didn't transform Anapra; you did. He let you. He wanted you to, but he let you, everyone here, change the place. Do you remember how much everyone laughed a couple of years ago when the government changed the name of the city?"

She remembered the moment well and thought back to it with fondness. Kevin had walked in with the newspaper opened wide. He dropped it on the table ceremoniously and looked at Rayna with pride.

"We've made it, Rayna; look here, we've made it!"

Rayna had looked at the newspaper but didn't recognize the politicians in the photograph.

"¿Qué?" she had asked, frustrated, for she knew Kevin was up to his old tricks whenever he walked in with such aplomb.

"The headline! Read the headline!"

Following his finger as he pointed at it, she read the headline and then the first few paragraphs of the article.

"¿Qué están diciendo? ¿Heroica?" she had asked.

"It's simple, Rayna; they've finally recognized all the brave Anaprans, living out here without water in this dustbowl, earning four dollars a day! They are calling you at last heroic!"

She had been appalled, shaking her head as she read the first few paragraphs over and over. With no irony seemingly intended, the fathers of Chihuahua State had changed the name of the city from Juarez to Heroica Ciudad Juarez—in honor of the role the city had played in the defeat of dictator Porfirio Diaz in 1911, not in honor of the thousands of murdered men and women the past few years.

The irony had been similar to her feelings during the floods, when the streets named after fish mocked her for days afterward. But now, looking back, looking at it through today's eyes, she felt like as if God, through some government officials downtown—if Kevin had to have God work through a person—had challenged them to live up to what they could be.

"The heroism was always here, Rayna," he said. "It has been here for centuries. The miraculous was always here."

She found herself getting angry, exasperated at his changes of direction and refusal to use the word, to agree with her.

"No, it was a miracle," she said. "The miracle is that we have come through; the miracle is that we are alive and this church is thriving. We didn't do it, God did it. God healed Juarez. Just like you healed that baby girl."

Leo had grown silent, seemingly confused by their points, but at last nodded.

But Kevin nodded, too.

"We are saying the same thing," Kevin said, smiling.

She loathed him right now. He stood up, nodded to them both, and smiled again as he walked to his room. She thought she saw him wink at Leo.

She turned to Leo, who sat wide-eyed.

"Sometimes I want to strangle him," she said.

Leo nodded.

"Leo, don't just shake your head," she said. "Say something. Don't just sit there next time."

Leo rubbed his hands like he always did when he was thinking hard.

"I think you both are right," he said.

She exhaled.

"Get out of here," she said. "Go do something useful."

These men, she thought. I have worked my way into this parish, and I will continue to do so. They will see. I didn't see it ten years ago. But I see the hand of God everywhere now. Look at Claudia, I should have said. That child studying to be a nurse. That child whom a doctor told me would have no life. Claudia going to be a nurse! But then Kevin and Leo would just have said that is just Claudia being heroic, heroic Claudia overcoming.

◈ ◈ ◈

THE TOPIC, AND HER SENSE OF REJECTION, PREOCCUPIED HER FOR DAYS. This morning, as she cooked Claudia breakfast before she went off to nursing school, she stopped and looked at her and saw her, nineteen now, with the face of the young girl whom she used to have to help put her prosthetic leg on. Her girlhood face kept appearing and reappearing as Rayna watched her this morning, so much so that Rayna thought she was getting ill.

Once Claudia had kissed her goodbye and went off to school, Rayna sat down and tried to collect herself. She had been feeling ill lately, shooting stomach pains forcing her to eat less and, some days, not eat at all. Yesterday had been one of those foodless days, so perhaps that was it, she thought. But then she saw her Claudia's face again as a young girl, not just as if in a vision, but right there in front of her on top of a little limping girl's body as she hopped about the house. She was smiling and wearing a white dress, and Rayna realized that it was her communion dress, that it was Claudia on the morning of her First Communion right in front of her.

It was the first time that Claudia had really dressed like a pretty girl was supposed to dress. The communion outfit, which Rayna had laid out on the couch the night before, had been handed down in her family for two generations now. Each of her own daughters had worn it, and now Claudia, this girl Rayna feared no man would ever consider pretty, was going to put on this white costume and limp up to the altar alongside all of Anapra's other seven-year-old girls shining in their whiteness.

"¿Estás nerviosa?" Rayna saw herself asking.

"No, Mamá," Claudia said, but Rayna could tell that she was, could tell she felt awkward and out of place. This girl had been through so much already—the poking and tugging of examinations by doctors and nurses since the day she was born, the operations, the teasing by the wicked boys—that nothing seemed to bother her.

"Yo sí," Rayna said to her. "I am."

Claudia looked up at her, then at the dress she was wearing, and frowned.

"No quiero ponerme este vestido," she said. I don't want to wear this dress. Rayna looked over at it again. She didn't want her to have to wear it either. She didn't want her to have to walk in procession with all the other boys and girls into the church and have all the parents and family members turn and stare at her. She didn't want to have to subject her to the competition, the comparisons, the making of a simple sacrament into a village spectacle.

"If you don't want to go, you don't have to," Rayna saw herself saying suddenly. Then she instantly regretted saying it. She knew she had been using her daughter, her whole family, to compensate Kevin and Billy for their help; she knew they didn't ask for anything in return, but the shelter Kevin was now providing her, she realized, had forced her to keep pretending, keep making displays of faith that she otherwise would not have made. She had gone to confession that day because she had been told Billy might help her find Cristina; now she was putting Claudia in a dress and subjecting her to a drama that a girl who had already suffered so much should not have to suffer through.

She watched herself notice that Claudia was about to cry. She watched herself straighten up, look determined, get up, and, without saying another word, help Claudia into the dress. And then she saw herself standing there and looking at her daughter. Her leg, usually covered in pants or a long skirt, even in summer, would surely draw the stares Rayna had feared. She tried to think of a way to cover it. Should she wear pants underneath? Would that look worse? Not wear it at all, just wear pants?

"¿Está bien?" Rayna saw herself asking.

Claudia looked up at her and smiled. She looked down at her leg for a moment, lifted her head again, and smiled thinly.

"Sí, Mamá, está bien," she said. "Está bien."

Rayna closed her eyes and grew more relaxed as she remembered the day. Kevin was beaming as the Mass began, so much so that Rayna started to feel guilty. He is acting like a proud father up there, she thought.

When it had come time for his homily, he walked down from the altar and stood close to the children in the front, boys on one side and girls on the other.

As she looked at Claudia, she realized her daughter was the only child smiling, the most carefree one of all. Claudia was staring at Kevin, who was laughing at his own story about his own childhood—she wasn't paying attention, so she wasn't really sure what he was talking about. But she was sure she had never seen her daughter look so carefree, so joyful.

The girls, their white dresses blurring together so their heads looked like they were all poking through a white blanket, followed Kevin back to their side of the seating, and suddenly they all laughed at once at whatever it was Kevin said. She is acting just like one of them, Rayna thought. But wait until they all stand up and walk to the altar. Then we will see the stares.

As Kevin finished speaking, he bowed to the children, and a couple of boys giggled. He shot them a glance and then laughed along with them. Then all the children started laughing.

Kevin walked back up to the altar and motioned for the children to rise. Rayna felt her stomach turn. The first row of boys and girls walked out and up, and now the second row, Claudia's row, turned and slowly began to walk. Maybe they would go so slowly that her limp wouldn't call attention to itself, Rayna thought. But she noticed the first boys and girls coming back down from the altar, people taking pictures of them and applauding and shouting, the kids beaming, and realized that this would be the moment of disgrace.

The kids were sauntering up the aisle, and as Claudia turned, Rayna could barely tell that she was walking differently than the others. But, as Claudia inched closer and closer to Kevin, the returning children were now bounding down the altar as the atmosphere grew more celebratory, child by child.

Then Claudia reached Kevin, and Rayna felt a sudden stabbing in her lower back. She sat up straighter, but the pain rose up her spine so that she was wincing as she watched Kevin slowly lower the host to Claudia's mouth. The pain wrapped around her sides, into her belly and chest. It was so intense she had to close her eyes, and when she opened them again, Claudia was following the other girls along their row of seats. Claudia looked at Rayna and smiled proudly; in that instant the pain disappeared as quickly as it had arrived upon her. She smiled back at her daughter, looked up at Kevin, the last handful of children in line in front of him, and felt this time not pain but her whole body shiver.

She closed her eyes gently this time and felt warmth now, like an envelope of warm air was enclosing her gently, almost lovingly.

She opened her eyes again. Everyone else was standing, clapping, beginning to sing and sway as the choir began the Mass' final song. She could hear the children clapping, singing above everyone else, and she stood. My God, she thought, my daughter is there dancing, jumping around just like all the other lovely girls, their white dresses twirling all around them.

Rayna released her reverie, opened her eyes, and felt the tears dripping down her cheeks. If Claudia is not a miracle, she thought, then there has never been one in all of the time of man. I will say that to him next time. He won't be able to wiggle out of that one.

◈ ◈ ◈

BUT THE DAY SHE WENT TO TELL HIM HER DREAMLIKE MEMORY, tell him that this girl was the proof, she found him sitting in the dark on the sofa with his head resting in his hands.

She had noticed his sluggishness for weeks, perhaps months, now and had attributed it not only to the wear of the years but also to the relief that everyone was feeling as Juarez slowly settled down. She had felt it herself; all the stress had surely caused her stomach problems, and now, with murder and madness no longer hourly experiences, she had felt her energy level drop, too.

"¿Qué haces, Padre Kevin?" she asked, quietly. What are you doing, Father Kevin?

He was slow to respond, and she wondered for a moment if he were taking a siesta.

"I feel like we can all take a breather now and then, don't you?" he asked back.

"Sí, sí," she said, realizing he felt the same way as her. "Un descanso." A rest.

She turned on the kitchen light and lifted a few bags from the S Mart onto the countertop.

She had bought several boxes of cereal, as she always did, the big, bulk size, and took them out of the plastic bags.

She walked to the back of the kitchen and poured herself a glass of water from the tall filter.

As she turned back, she stopped and looked at him through the cereal boxes.

"Esto es más que un descanso," she said to herself. This is more than a rest.

She walked over to the counter, around it, and turned on the living room light.

"¿Qué te está pasando, Padre Kevin?" she asked, emphatically. What is happening to you?

He looked up at her with a face she had never seen before, part shame and part fear. And he told her all, the tests and the results and the date for the surgery, and she instantly felt the same sensation she had felt when the extortionists had called her that day and sent her down to the bank to wire them money. She felt like someone was playing a trick on her; she felt like Satanás was back, and she looked over her shoulder and all around to see where he was sneaking.

CHAPTER THIRTEEN

Kevin

AS HE LISTENED FROM THE DESK IN HIS BED-
ROOM TO THE FOOTSTEPS COME THROUGH THE
COURTYARD, he easily identified what he liked to
call the tranquility in Leo's gait. He heard the front
door open and waited for the sounds of Leo preparing coffee.

But instead, Leo knocked on his bedroom door and then
stuck his head in.

"Our good man, Leo!" Kevin called out.

"Se ha dimitido el Papa," Leo said. The pope has resigned.

"Good God, Leo, after all these years I finally know what it
takes to get you out of bed early!" Kevin said.

Kevin stood up and followed Leo into the living room. Leo
turned on the BBC, knowing well now it was the only news
channel in the Western world that Kevin could stomach watching, and there was St. Peter's in all its glory.

"¿Por qué?" Leo asked. Why?

"Only God knows," Kevin said. "Or, you'll pardon me, Leo, perhaps even God doesn't know."

They watched the coverage for the rest of the day, and Kevin knew Leo and Rayna wanted an explanation from him. They expected him to provide some sort of insider insight for them to understand what was going on. And for the first time in his life, he felt regret that he didn't have better proximity to Rome, a better grasp of power and how it works.

That Saturday, the first bus of Jehovah's Witnesses stopped in front of the parish. Kevin had arrived before the Saturday evening service, so he decided to stand in the courtyard and greet his parishioners as they arrived. He assumed that they, too, would be as bewildered as Leo and Rayna.

He stood watching as very serious-looking men and women, the "true believers" as he sarcastically called them, stepped off the bus and fell into line in front of the church. For a moment, he thought they were preparing a World War I sort of phalanx to charge this sinful Catholic structure and send the place to the hell where they believed it belonged.

But then another bus pulled up, and a third and a fourth. As the true believers got out, they started to form a double line, the women in front and the men behind them.

The ringleader, a middle-aged blonde fellow who looked straight out of a Munich beerhouse, stood in front of them and shouted instructions in a Spanish that made Kevin feel, for the first time in his life, proud of his dreadful Aussie accent.

And then they dispersed, in groups of three or four, marching up the street, then out into the arterial streets, and then into the shacks that lined them.

Kevin had long ago decided, with both frustration and admiration, that Mexicans never turn a visitor away. That was why the Mormons and Jehovah's Witnesses and every other door-knocking religion thrived here. No one ever slammed the damn door.

He walked out into the street and up toward the houses. He knew the family in the first one across the main street, so he walked into their courtyard and listened.

"The Catholic Church has ended, imploded," he heard the Jehovah's Witness say. "The pope himself said it in his resignation speech: the Catholic Church has come to an end. He apologized to you and urged you to take your faith elsewhere. That is why we are here. We want to welcome you into our church."

Now what have I done wrong? Kevin wondered. My people should know by now to throw these rascals out on the seat of their pants, and yet I don't even hear a whimper. He stuck his head out of the gate and looked up the empty street. All up and down the roads of Anapra, it looked like this same conversation was taking place on the threshold of almost each and every house.

He walked back in through the courtyard and knocked on the door, and a little girl opened it. His parishioners stared at him, at least guiltily, he thought.

"¿Cómo estamos, amigos?" he asked, looking at the three Witnesses standing there defiantly.

"Father, your pope has resigned and dissolved the church," the oldest of them said. "We want to invite you to praise God with us, to join us in the true church."

Good God, they do have nerve, Kevin thought. You have to admire them for that.

"Well, my friend, I do appreciate your offer," he said. He looked at his parishioners sternly.

"We do appreciate the offer of these good people, don't we?"

His parishioners nodded nervously, not taking their eyes off Kevin.

Then Kevin turned abruptly to the Witnesses.

"Now get the hell out of this house, get your friends the hell out of this neighborhood, and go and study church history a little bit. The church is not the pope any more than I am the church. We serve the church, the pope serves the church, and the next one will serve the church even better!" Kevin stepped toward the Witnesses, and they seemed confused.

"Now, out!" he shouted.

He had clarified things for them. They turned and filed out one by one. Kevin nodded at his parishioners.

"See you at Mass in thirty minutes!" he barked, and they nodded.

Then he went out into the street and began walking up the hill, passing the Witnesses whom he had evicted without looking at them and shouting the names of each parishioner as he passed their house.

Suddenly he saw Leo coming running down the hill.

"Go ring the church bell, Leo!" he shouted. "Ring it and ring it loud!"

Leo nodded and continued running down the hill.

Kevin stopped in front of the house of a family that had recently come to the church. They had been Jehovahs for years but told him they had grown enchanted with how joyful everyone at Corpus Christi seemed.

He stood there and heard the bell starting to ring, then ring louder and with greater and greater frequency.

Leo is swinging the hell out of that thing, he thought.

He entered the courtyard of the house and spotted two Jehovahs in the doorway.

"Out! Out!" he said. "You are making these good people late for Mass!"

The two Jehovahs looked up, startled, and Kevin recognized one of them. He lived up the hill, so he must have joined up with the busloads once they arrived.

Kevin had long admired the guy's perseverance. He rode a bicycle everywhere, even when he went to the store a few blocks from his house.

"Et tu, Brute!" Kevin bellowed, laughing.

The guy looked at him blankly, failing to catch Kevin's sarcasm.

"The Catholic Church has died!" the guy said, walking toward Kevin. "I have long told the people of Anapra they should not call you 'Father'! There is only one Father, the Father Almighty, and we are all his sons and daughters. We are all brothers and sisters!"

"Thank you for your lecture on the appropriate family structure," Kevin retorted.

Kevin seethed the whole Mass long. As they approached the point in the Mass where they prayed for the church leaders, he began to formulate phrases in his head that might be fitting for the situation. Let us pray for our future pope, another Germanic strict constructionist who has never spent the night in a one-room shack without heat? For an orthodox Nigerian, fed and educated by the Catholic Church but who went astray once the Curia got its tentacles on him and who now out-Europeans the Europeans? For a dignified American, sullied by the sexual abuse scandals but noble nonetheless?

Or should he just come out and say it, say it straight to these people: Let us pray that the College of Cardinals sends up the white smoke to signal the election of a Mexican who grew up in the dirt and dust like you, or at least a Chilean who knows what it is like when your stomach cramps with hunger and your insides, your organs, shiver with the cold?

Instead, he bit his tongue yet again, for the thousandth time in his clerical career.

The weeks passed and he and Leo and Rayna followed the speculation each night, Kevin knowing Leo and Rayna were amused by his running sarcasm but ultimately still befuddled by what was happening to their church.

"Maybe they will pick an Australian," Leo said, his acquired Aussie accent sounding worse, Kevin often told him, than Kevin sounded in Spanish.

"Good God, Leo," Kevin said. "There's not enough beer in Italy for an Aussie to take over the Vatican. Teetotalers only, I'm afraid. The Curia members only drink alone."

Leo made a face of exaggerated shock.

"Leo, I've noticed something about you over the years," Kevin said to try to distract their attention even further from any serious query for which he had no answer. "You are losing your Aussie accent when you try to speak English," Kevin said. "You're watching the BBC so much you're starting to sound like a well-dignified Englishman."

"Bugger off, Father," Leo said, and they both burst out laughing at Leo's imitation of Kevin, Rayna shaking her head at them.

Kevin got up to go to the bathroom for the tenth time in two hours but stopped in his tracks as the BBC reporter began to talk about the deliberations among the College of Cardinals.

And for the first time he heard the name Bergoglio. The reporter said he was emerging as a possible and surprising front-runner, but his role, or lack of one, during the civil war in Argentina might prove controversial.

Bloody hell, Kevin thought. He thought back to the height of the troubles in Chile when he was living in Santiago.

Unless this poor fellow was Jesus Christ himself, how could he have stayed clean during those years?

"¿Qué está pasando?" Rayna asked.

"They're saying there are rumors an Argentinian might be the surprise front-runner for pope," Kevin said. "Close enough to Mexico for you, Rayna?"

Rayna thought it over.

"Quizás," she said. Perhaps.

"I bet you a dinner at Garufa they nominate an Italian," Kevin said.

He realized that his jokes might be getting these people's hopes up for a Third World pope. He was cutting too close to the bone, he realized.

"Good night," Kevin said, getting up and pouring himself the glass of water that always remained full on the nightstand beside his bed. And he left them there watching the BBC together while he made a beeline for the bathroom yet again.

◈ ◈ ◈

KEVIN HAD GONE DOWN TO THE CHURCH TO TALK TO A COUPLE ABOUT THEIR WEDDING PLANS. On his way back up the hill he found himself wondering how each person he passed would react if dropped onto the streets of Rome. Why the hell were they taking so long over there, he wondered? Don't they realize the work they are undoing here? Don't they realize the power in Mexico of all this gossip about the pope? He hadn't once given his mind to the speculation about why Benedict had resigned, only to the practical effects of the event on the street. But picturing that woman with her three kids in tow, or that old man with two canes, seeing them walk into the giant piazza in front of St. Peter's, that was something worth speculating. How different each Catholic is around the Catholic world! How different are our preoccupations and our needs!

He opened the gate and patted Willie for a few moments.

"What would your life have been like, Willie, if you had been a Roman stray and not a Juarense?"

The dog looked up at him, he thought, not unlike the way Leo had been looking at him recently whenever the topic of the pope came up.

He could smell Rayna's cooking through the window.

As he walked in, Leo and she were standing in front of the television.

"The food is burning, Rayna dear!" Kevin said, only half-joking. Then he looked at the television and saw the crowd massed in front of St. Peter's.

"Ya lo han dicho," Leo said. They have already announced him.

"Who is it?" Kevin asked impatiently.

"Una sorpresa," Leo said, shaking his head. "No es un mexicano." A surprise, but it is not a Mexican.

Kevin sat down, noticing but not caring that Rayna had not heeded his warning about the food. He knew she had adopted his preoccupation with the election, and he appreciated it. He desperately wanted them to have a pope they could call their own.

"It's like the blacks in America praying for Obama to be elected," he had said to Leo a few days prior. "It will uplift a continent."

Leo, as if he could understand a hundredth of what they were saying, kept switching the channel between the BBC and CNN to see who would break the news first.

After a commercial break on CNN, the reporter came back on and said it was the Argentine.

Kevin looked in bafflement at Leo. Rayna moved closer.

"¿El argentino?" she asked. "¿El argentino?"

Kevin was not a man for jaw dropping, but he felt it happening as he watched. He looked over at Leo, who was staring back at him. He looked up at Rayna, who was looking at him to calibrate her reaction, too, he knew.

"Dios mío," Kevin said. "It looks like you might have one of your own, almost your own, at last in there."

She jumped at the smell of food burning and ran to the stove to turn it off; then she came racing back over. And the three of them sat and watched with increasing glee.

"Look at him there on that balcony, a humble fellow, and he asked you to pray for him, Leo," Kevin said. "Imagine that, someone in power realizing he needs our prayers." But what Kevin didn't say was that he couldn't believe it. You want to see your miracle, Rayna? There it is right there. There it is right there. A bloody miracle right in front of your eyes. A Latin American in charge. You'll never understand what this means, just because you're not an Australian missionary who never believed he would see this day.

But he didn't say it because he had to go rushing to the bathroom. His doctor's appointment was the next day.

IT WAS THE DOCTOR'S FACIAL EXPRESSION MORE THAN THE DIAGNOSIS THAT SHOOK HIM. The prostate is riddled with cancer, shot; he understood that loudly and clearly. But it was the doctor's delivery, that grim jawline and those wincing eyebrows, that told the worst of it.

All he could see for a few seconds was Corpus Christi, the building standing there in that gorgeous late sunset light that he had come to crave, that he had come to realize was a light unlike light anywhere else in the world. But there was no one around the church in the scene; it stood empty and quiet.

Egomaniac, he said to himself. You didn't receive a death sentence. He didn't say your vital organs are riddled with cancer, just your damn prostate. You don't even use the damn thing. It's like taking your bloody appendix out. And the church will thrive without you anyway whenever you go. The church is them, not you.

He turned to the doctor.

"Well, Doc, I guess you'll have to tell your patients celibacy is not a preventative measure!" Kevin said, his mouth seemingly coming out with it while his brain still flagellated him for his melancholic, self-involved imagining.

The doctor laughed halfheartedly, began with his description of the imminent surgery, patted him on the shoulder, and, without the hard face but still with an unnerving seriousness, warned him that a cancer this pervasive risked reappearing in neighboring organs.

Kevin heard something about testing every six months, but his mind had already shifted from self-indulgence to perplexed: Leo will be fine with the news, but how in God's name will I break the news to Rayna?

And the days turned into weeks as he tried to find the moment and manner. He rehearsed delivering the news to her when he lay awake at night.

He opened his mouth and found himself speechless several times.

At last, at lunch one day with Clara nursing her new baby, Jenny Violeta, on the sofa and Rayna warming formula in the tiny microwave, he told her.

"Rayna, me van a operar, me van a quitar la próstata," he said. They are going to operate, they are going to take out my prostate.

But before he could get out his joke about the pandemic of prostate cancer among old priests, she looked up and smiled sheepishly at him.

"Lo sé, me contó Leo," she said. I know. Leo told me.

"Ese cabrón," Kevin spit out. That bastard.

"Todo va a estar bien," she said. Everything is going to be okay.

She has become a master at deflating dramatic moments, Kevin thought. A bloody master. She is officially the most drama-free woman I have ever met. She is less capable of drama than even I, an old Aussie hard-ass.

And with that, they would never discuss his surgery again

until the morning he was packing his bag to head over to the hospital in El Paso.

◈ ◈ ◈

HE FELT LIKE A SOLDIER GOING OFF TO WAR. She had come early to prepare him a good breakfast, speaking little, even less than usual.

But he did not want to eat, and, by forcing himself to swallow the eggs and sausage, he was making himself even sicker, making his nerves even worse.

Why can't she talk about things? he wondered to himself. Why does she so perfectly imitate me and avoid all sentiment?

And then: who the hell are you, you pea in a pod with her, to wonder such things? You haven't made an emotion-filled statement toward another human being in your lifetime, you tight-jawed, tongue-tied, cancer-ridden old fart.

He sat up straighter, ate the last of the eggs, and took his final mouthful of coffee.

"Okay, I'll be back in a few days, my friend," he said. "I hear Leo waiting for me out front."

She nodded, picked up his plates, and turned her back to him as she walked to the kitchen sink to clean them.

Perfecto, he thought. Absolutely damn perfecto.

He walked outside and nodded at Leo sitting in the truck. Surely more of the same here, he knew.

"Buenos días, Don Leo," he said zestfully as he hopped into the passenger seat of the truck.

"Buenos días, Padre Kevin," Leo said.

And that was all they said until they said the exact same thing to one another as Kevin hopped out of the truck downtown at the bridge to El Paso.

◇ ◇ ◇

AS THEY WHEELED HIM DOWN THE HALLWAY TO THE OR,
he felt absurdly like a family man haunted by anxiety over his
last will and testament should he not emerge from sleep. Clara?
Did she have enough of the healthy cereal to put in her formula
and not that sugary junk? Jenny Violeta, were her mocos, her
boogers, receding so that she could sleep at night?

As the anesthesiologist was preparing him for sleep, Kevin
caught his surgeon out of the corner of his eye and raised his
thumb to him.

"How we doing, Father?"

"Remember, Doc, we priests don't need to do anything more than piss well, so just make sure you get it all,"
Kevin said. "No erectile dysfunction to worry about here."
He heard a nurse laugh just as the anesthesiologist put the mask
over him. And while he quickly found himself fading, her laughter kept echoing in his head.

When he awoke, another nurse was checking his blood pressure and smiling at him. Her face reminded him of his mother,
and his first thought was the irony that a boy who had been
born near Brisbane had now, as an aging fart, had his prostate
removed in El Paso.

And then he thought of Rayna. And Claudia. And Clara. And
Jenny Violeta. Were they all sitting by the phone? Were they
praying the Rosary together? The damn border, he thought. Not
even an exception for them to be here with me today, more for
them than for me. No, no, he forced himself to admit. You know
well it's more for you than for them.

The nurse was speaking to him now, but he couldn't focus on
her words yet. But her smile haunted him like the Holy Spirit.
He kept seeing it flash in his brain as he drifted in and out of
sleep. At one point, he thanked God for her smile.

A few hours later, after his first ice chips, the doctor came and reviewed the surgery with him.

When he finished, Kevin reached up his index finger just as the doctor was walking away.

"What about all my girlfriends over there, Doc, they're gonna want to know when I can get back in the saddle?"

The doctor shook his head and laughed.

"A few months, seven or eight," he said. "Then you'll be the envy of Mexico again!"

When the nurse came back, Kevin asked for his phone.

"Your belongings are all waiting for you in your room," she said.

When they wheeled him there, the first thing he did was reach in his bag for the phone. He expected a few dozen missed calls, but he had to look twice to be sure: three. Good God, he thought, I need God to love me because it looks like no one else does.

He dialed home.

"¿Síííííí?" Clara answered, her long, slow Spanish not a function of her age but of her gentleness, her pace through the world.

"Soy Kevin. ¿Cómo estamos?" he asked.

"Padre Kevin, ¿todo bien?" Clara asked. "¡Te paso a Mamá!" Father Kevin, everything OK? I'll pass you to Mom!

He heard silverware clang.

"Kevin," Rayna said. "¿Todo bien?"

"Well, Rayna, I weigh about a pound less with that thing out, pero todo parece bien!"

It was just like her to realize any more conversation than that would be a struggle, so she told him to get some rest and call back first thing in the morning. And he obeyed.

AS HE LAY IN BED IN MORPHINE HAZE THAT NIGHT, HE
HELD A ROSARY IN ONE HAND, THE MORPHINE PUMP IN THE
OTHER. He stared at the little photo of Jenny Violeta that he
had brought with him and asked to be placed on the tray table
beside his bed.

When the nurse asked who the baby in the photo was, he
had replied, "My granddaughter." He had called her such often
enough at home—when they first passed the baby to him to hold
her, whenever he asked Rayna or Clara how she was, whenever
he babysat for her when Rayna and Clara went out for a walk.

But even in his stupor he realized he had surprised the nurse
with his answer. "Not really my granddaughter," he said, "but I
consider her one."

She looked even more confused, and he couldn't think
straight, so he squeezed the morphine pump and forgot about
the whole encounter for a few minutes.

When the nurse came back later, he was still having trouble
saying the Rosary, but just the feel of it made him relax, just as
it had done, he remembered, twelve years ago when he had first
arrived in Juarez.

Oh, how I couldn't wait to get the hell out of that place, he
thought. And now I just want to get the hell out of here and get
back there.

In and out of sleep he caught himself dreaming not about
Jenny Violeta but rather about Claudia. Claudia was now
studying nursing, and during another visit he tried to tell his
nurse about her, his adopted daughter, the soon-to-be nurse,
but the words still didn't come out right, and he realized this
woman might start thinking him crazier than he was. And all
night he kept waking and checking the time to see if he could
call yet, and, counting backward from the forty-eight hours he
had been told he would have to remain there, he kept counting
until he could go home.

◈ ◈ ◈

LEO PICKED HIM UP IN THE BIG WHITE PICKUP, and as they drove away from downtown, Kevin realized that riding with Leo now felt exactly like it had felt a few days prior on the way downtown. The streets were full of life, people walking on them, squeezing the cars into the middle as if a moving car, after all that these people had been through, were a mere nuisance and not a life threat. Kevin still moved poorly and felt weak and woozy, and and the bumps that Leo was forgetting to avoid caused pain to go shooting up his pelvis.

"Leo, acaban de operarme, amigo, un poco más despacio," he said. Leo, they just operated on me. A little more slowly, please.

Leo laughed and smiled at him and honored his request for all of about two minutes before slamming into another pothole that made Kevin wince.

As they approached Anapra, he could see all the traffic pouring in and out of the S Mart store. As they turned up the street for home, he felt not expectation or joy but rather a plummeting, a gnawing anxiety inside.

I am coming back here to recuperate for six weeks, he thought. All the turmoil of the past few years surely took its toll, but good God, were we doing things! Now I'm going to be nothing more than a patient in my own home. I could be going home to any suburb in the world right now. I've become a regular old parish priest, and I'm not sure how much I like how that feels! And then he chastised himself. You used to dream about being a parish priest in a place like this! You need the Hollywood stuff to thrive, do you?

They stood in the doorway waiting for him, Clara and the baby and Rayna behind them.

He slowly got out of the truck, the step down agony, and stood there, with his shades on, about five feet from them. The baby was crying, and Clara and Rayna seemed more worried about Jenny Violeta than about him. The shades, he had learned, come in handy at times like this, too.

He reached out for the baby and started to lift her up in the air but then caught himself just before the pain froze him.

"Qué guapa," he said, Jenny Violeta's cries instantly turning to a smile.

He handed the baby back to Clara, and she hugged him with the baby in between them. Rayna looked over Clara's shoulders into his eyes, but he had made sure to keep his sunglasses on in case he got emotional. And, feeling his eyes water up, he knew he had made the right decision.

Rayna led him into his room, and Leo set his bag on the chair. There was a plastic bag on his nightstand. He sat, and they stood looking at him for a moment.

"You rest for a little bit," Rayna said. "Driving with Leo will tire out anyone. I'll have dinner ready soon."

As they walked out, he slowly shimmied himself into a lying position. He turned and took the plastic bag off the table. And then he howled for her to come back in.

"You bought me diapers!" he shouted.

Clara came rushing to the bedroom's doorway.

"Your mother thinks I am a blabbering old man who pisses himself!" he said to her, mock angry.

Clara turned red and shook her head. Then they both started laughing together.

◈ ◈ ◈

HE SPENT THE FIRST WEEK INSIDE THE HOUSE, ONLY WALK-ING OUT TO THE COURTYARD TO PAT WILLIE AND SIT IN THE SHADE FOR A WHILE. Rayna and Clara came by every day to cook and keep him company, and he slowly felt his appetite returning. But not his energy. He felt down, listless, and knew it was less because of the procedure than because of a shocking sensation at the questions he was asking himself.

One day as he sat in the shade with Willie, he held his rosary and allowed the questions to come full throttle. What to do next? What is our next step? I could build out the playing fields behind the church, build a clinic for drug addicts, and build a school. But you know what you are going to have to do, Kevin? You are going to have to adapt again, get used to a new life, and not try to be a hero but be a builder again.

And you know what that means, Mullins. Fundraising. Back to that racket, using your charm, being a capitalist again, a participant in the great money machine.

The ball fields, he thought. That is where to start. Back in the day, the key was getting to their stomachs. Then Rayna's singing and dancing. And now, now that we've made it—sports for their kids. There are so many playing fields in other neighborhoods, but here, aside from the new one up the hill, where can the kids run around? Or a swimming pool? Good God, imagine that! I'd really have to shake down some philanthropists for that, but imagine all these kids learning how to swim. We'd be competing with the Aussies in the pool in the Olympics in a couple of generations!

Indeed, he recognized that the network of the generous in El Paso, once he got past his genetic distaste for fundraising, was extensive and increasingly active. Now that Juarez had settled down, the interest from across the border in helping in the city's reconstruction was surging. He had been fielding calls each week but had not felt strong enough yet to journey across the border again. But the day he did, he knew his first stop would be a former benefactress, a woman who had contributed to the extension of the church and had financed trips for parish children and a health clinic up the road.

◈ ◈ ◈

HERE, FROM THIS HOUSE PARTY ON THE MOUNTAINSIDE ON
EL PASO'S WEST SIDE, HE COULD LOOK OUT AND SEE LOMAS
DE POLEO, see Anapra's edge, see the pollution, know precisely
how different the evening is here compared with the evening a
few thousand meters away, and he felt even more apart, more
separated than he had during his hospital stay.

The hostess, whose husband had certainly done business
with the Zaragoza family, had regularly met with the various
actresses who had been passing through town over the past
few years to protest las desaparecidas. That was the extraordi-
nary thing to him—the spider's web of relationships stretching
across the border that uncannily connected the Juarez oligarch
with the American benefactress with the missionary priest.
Money—being robbed or wrested by the oligarchs, recycled by
the benefactors, and given back to the missionary priests—is
our great bond, Kevin thought.

When the hostess cornered him to discuss the sudden peace
in Juarez, he was tempted to put his hand in his pocket and
say his rosary while she rambled on. That always did the trick,
calming him down in places like this just as successfully as it
did during hairy moments in Juarez. But then he heard her say
something that sounded original.

"We need to see the factories finally get built out there near
you," she said. "All this planning and talk for years, and I don't
see it happening. I don't care how much people criticize the maquilas, their jobs are the only way to keep Juarez growing, to
build a middle class."

He stopped listening to her again so he could pause and
think on it. He had driven himself via the Santa Teresa crossing
to see if any construction activity had started since his surgery.

"On the way to your house I decided to drive the Camino

Real and experience the new border crossing again," he said. "And I thought it was spectacular."

A look of exaggerated shock came over the woman's face. Her teeth, he thought, are stunning.

"A big dome at the crossing, so freshly painted, and the guards, at least on this side, so much better organized and more courteous than downtown," he said. "As if coming over the Camino Real, the Royal Road, was exactly that, somehow more royal or noble."

He could tell she thought he was setting a trap for her.

"But you are exactly right," he said.

Her eyes darted.

"I stopped the car on the Camino," he said, "and got out and walked around the desert a bit. There is trash everywhere. All kinds of trash."

She smiled.

"Yes, yes, you see," she said. "The trash, too. We have got to clean the place up!"

He smiled back at her.

"Las bragas de las brujas," he said, but she paid no heed.

A waitress came by with the tiniest burritos he had ever seen, and he grabbed one but in the process unavoidably touched others with his fat fingers. The hostess squinted as she looked at the tray.

"Thank you for supporting our mission," he said to the woman before sticking the burrito in his mouth. "So many children in my parish have benefitted from your generosity."

They shook hands, hers seemingly the size of a desert pecan nut in his palm, and she walked him to the door.

As she opened it, she held it halfway open for a minute and blocked his exit.

"Here there is no distance between the good and the bad," she said. "We are all so close together, those who have and those

who suffer. We are the human family, and slowly we will all realize that."

He smiled kindly. He could tell life wasn't that simple for her,
just by the look of her face. He could tell she had her own very
different struggles.

"We all suffer," he said. "Far and wide."

She nodded slightly, oblivious, he realized, to his under-
handed attempt at empathy.

"Thank you again," he said.

As he walked out to his car, he decided to drive as far up the
mountainside as roads would permit.

The hill was steep, and the lots got wider the further up the hill
he drove. The bends in the road grew severe as he ascended. As he
drove over here earlier, he had thought he would feel anger. But
right now all he could think about was going home. His regular
trips to El Paso to determine the extent of his prostate cancer had
always been in the morning, so this evening trip had disconcerted
him. He had missed one of Rayna's suppers, and he didn't like
the odd and incommensurate sense of loss that accompanied the
thought. He felt safer back in Juarez, he realized, less under assault. These big houses and the party chatter had unnerved him.

But he felt vindicated, too. After all his debates with Father
Billy and Leo about what the developers were doing to Anapra,
tonight he felt he had been right to hold his opinion. The lesser
evil can become a good—that had been his refrain. Don't fight
the development, fight for little changes in these little lives. Let
the rich men have their roads and buildings; at least there will
be less dust in the lungs of Anaprans when it is done. At least
their bus rides to work will be shorter and there will be less pollution and less trash. Less trash. That was why the lady's words
had perked his ears, that was why he had ended up feeling an
odd affection for her.

At the peak of the street he made a U-turn and began the

big descent. He had to urinate but was learning to hold it now and suffer longer. I might even ask to use the bathroom at the beautiful border crossing, he thought. It was night now, the green and yellow lights over in Juarez the most beautiful sight he could imagine.

◈ ◈ ◈

WHENEVER HE ATTENDED A MASS AT THE CATHEDRAL IN DOWNTOWN JUAREZ, HE JOKED WITH RAYNA THAT HE WAS HEADING DOWNTOWN TO THE VATICAN FOR A FEW HOURS. Today he said it to her again, for he was heading downtown for the ordination of several new priests, among whom would be young Juan, the first one ever from the parish of Corpus Christi.

They lined up, each new priest with his padrino, or sponsor, by a door on the side of the Juarez cathedral downtown. Kevin, Juan's sponsor, could tell Juan was nervous, for when he shook his hand upon seeing him, Kevin had to then wipe the poor fellow's sweat off his own hand with his trousers.

As they stood there, it was the sunlight that first reminded him of his own ordination back in Sydney. The sun this March was still softer here in Juarez than in the full of desert summer, and it felt kind on his face. That was the sensation that triggered his memory of his own ordination.

"I remember feeling like I was going to poop my pants right about now," Kevin said to Juan, to try to lighten the mood.

As they proceeded inside, pair by pair, the hoots and hollers from the packed pews startled Kevin.

"Sounds like a bloody football game in here," he said under his breath. He looked up at Juan and saw joy in his face.

Yes, lad, this is what you've gotten yourself into, Kevin thought. If you serve them right, and crack the right jokes, they're gonna make a rock star out of you.

They took their seats at the front of the church, and as Kevin's bottom hit the seat, he remembered sitting for the first time at his ordination, too. That first relief, the first step over.

We've produced killers and dealers and coyotes and addicts and, now, a priest, he kept thinking over and over.

When it came Juan's turn to read his part in the eucharistic prayer, Kevin felt what he had been resisting since he had laid eyes on the young man an hour earlier outside the cathedral: a few tears beginning to form. Juan's first assignment was a parish a few neighborhoods over. A tough part of town, as Kevin liked to say, drug war or no drug war. He will be doing a funeral within a week, Kevin thought. A funeral for a murder victim within two weeks. What trials await him, what trials, he thought. Was growing up with it, growing up in Anapra, sufficient preparation? Better preparation even than what my order had tried to acquire for me in Chicago and Chile? Was seeing a man killed, which he no doubt had seen before, an adequate trial run for the trial of giving last rites to a dying man bleeding in the street?

Kevin wiped his eyes. I didn't get him into this, he said to himself. But I did. On a good day I charmed the bejesus out of these folks, and he no doubt wants to do the same, minister but also be on the big stage.

He put his hand in his pocket and thumbed the rosary as the Mass continued. But he slowly lost focus and began to pray, over and over, the same little prayer:

"God, let me preside up there in Rancho Anapra, let me last for years longer, and let the powers that be let me remain as long as my body permits; and if you fancy working a miracle right about now like Rayna says, make me young again like these young men, and let me do it all over again right up there in Rancho Anapra. Amen."

CHAPTER FOURTEEN

---◇---

Rayna

LEO NEVER BURST IN; HE WANDERED IN, MEANDERED **IN.** Rayna would be cooking or cleaning or talking with Kevin, and there Leo would be, silent, smiling, standing in the current of the moment so adeptly that Kevin wouldn't even acknowledge him anymore when he appeared.

Sometimes Leo would half raise his hand, not so much to speak, she had realized, but to seek permission to change the subject before he spoke.

"They got El Chapo," he said this time as he put his hand down.

This time Kevin reacted quickly.

"¡Imposible!" he half-shouted. "Leo, I heard that earlier out in the street and didn't believe it. You're the biggest skeptic in Mexico, and now you believe it!"

"No, no, es él, seguro que es él," Leo said steadily. No, it is him, it surely is him.

Rayna didn't have the fingers or toes to count the times Leo had expounded to Kevin—over coffee, rum, breakfast, lunch, and dinner—his theory that the violence would stop in Juarez once El Chapo's Sinaloa cartel finally wrested control of Juarez from the Juarez cartel. A secondary part of his theory was that the army and El Chapo's gang were synonymous, that El Chapo controlled the government, that El Chapo controlled ninety-five percent of the politicians and judges, that El Chapo was, at the end of the day, necessary and had to be appeased to restore peace in Juarez.

She loathed the conversations, the theories of this and that to explain why thousands of people were getting murdered, to explain why all these English and American commentators on the television kept calling Juarez the most dangerous place in the world. She never interjected—let men talk in the silly ways of men, she decided; let these two waste their time with their theories and explanations and complicated thinking. It is Satanás, not El Chapo or drugs or money, it is Satanás and it is all that simple. I'm shocked that at least Kevin doesn't grasp that simple fact, but Leo brings this silliness out of him when they are together.

So she tried to close her ears, but as they turned on the television, she noticed that they didn't sit down but stood in front of it, close to it.

She hated that she was intrigued, that they were distracting her from her work, but she sensed in the announcer's voice something different, some combination of shock and fear and awe and elation.

She let herself walk over and stood behind them looking at the photo of El Chapo—apprehended, disheveled, and thoroughly, absurdly common-looking.

They were both shaking their heads in amazement.

"He looks a little bit like you, Leo," she said, shocked that her thought came out before she could process it.

She had come to give and take with both of them in that man's way of theirs, and she knew that this only added to her appeal, to their interest in her company. But she instantly realized she had crossed the line. She didn't say it to tease Leo. She said it because Leo was standing right there, because this man who had a role in the catastrophe of the past few years didn't so much have the nose or the jaw or the brow of Leo but simply his normalcy, his everydayness, his stature and complexion.

She immediately tried to atone.

"I wanted to say, he just looks like any man in the street, he just looks like one of us," she said.

But she realized neither of them had heeded her anyway. They still stood transfixed, even more captivated than they had been when Francisco had been presented as the pope.

She lost interest quickly and retreated to the kitchen. In fact, she found Kevin and Leo more interesting than what was on the television.

Why are they reacting in this way? Are they in disbelief? I have always known, known firsthand, how boring and ugly and uninteresting these bad men are. They are always the ones who do the worst things, the ones who look like this man. What did they expect? A monster? A giant? A cowboy? And also, perhaps this is it, if he is in jail now, what happens to their theory? Wasn't he the key to peace? Will the peace come falling apart now? Are they realizing that?

But no, she thought, this is cosmetic, this is so the Americans can see progress. Now another one will rise up to replace him, one who looks like him and one who is as stupid as he is. That is why my theory is better than Leo's complicated nonsense. It is so easy, and it will go on, because of who is behind it. It is not, it never was, El Chapo. It is a thing, an existing thing, this evil. The police cannot squash it, not even the Americans can.

In his heart, Kevin knows the only way to squash it. Leo

knows the only way, too. What we have done, our way, is the only way.

But she left them alone.

◈ ◈ ◈

FOR SEVERAL YEARS NOW THE EASTER PROCESSION HAD BEEN ATTRACTING MORE AND MORE PARTICIPANTS, and the past year she felt she had never seen Anapra so unified. A few hundred people followed a donkey Kevin had borrowed through the streets past Corpus Christi and up a hill that stood in as Anapra's version of Calvary during the Crucifixion. The violence had lifted, and people seemed to change their demeanor overnight. More people were coming to church than ever, and she did not hesitate to pridefully tell anyone who would listen that Corpus Christi, and prayer, had played a role in the transformation of Juarez itself.

Leo heard her once and laughed, and she reprimanded him until he turned red in the face.

"You and your theories about the Sinaloa cartel winning, Leo, I mean de verdad, really, where is your faith?" she said to him outside the church one day as they prepared the costumes for the Easter procession. "You think it is just because one group gave in? You're as bad as Kevin not believing in the consequences of our praying!" Las consecuencias de rezar, that was how she said it, and she realized as soon as she said it that she had said a good one, that she was going to repeat the line to Kevin to get his reaction, to impress him. But Leo snickered, that noise that made her want to spank him on the bottom like one of her children when they were young.

They were laying out the Roman soldier outfits that some men from the church would wear as they escorted Christ up the hill, their version of Christ and their version of Calvary, to his mock death. But here the crucifixion ended in communal prayer and singing and dancing, not in abandonment.

She snickered back at Leo and continued organizing the outfits. The big wooden cross that Leo had built lay in the corner, and she stood over it and imagined what the real day had been like. Kevin had talked about that in his last homily, how we have carried the cross, how the cross is the perfect symbol for what we have lived, and now we are rising up again.

But now new crosses, she thought, kicking it slightly. Kevin's health; my stomach acting up; the struggles of my children and grandchildren. The daily, little crosses, not the big one of the past years. But still not easy. Still, the crosses will be less hard to carry so long as we keep going together, keep building this parish with Kevin healthy again.

She turned and saw him coming through the courtyard. Kevin healthy again, she repeated. And if his superior thinks we don't need him now, if he thinks he has spent enough time here and it's time for him to go minister somewhere else, well, I'm going to cross the border illegally and go to Omaha or Hong Kong or wherever his boss lives and forbid it myself.

◈ ◈ ◈

THE PRESS WASN'T SAYING IT, BUT EVERYONE KNEW. Or, at least the women of Juarez knew. Women were disappearing again.

Kevin's surgery had made her realize this life they had constructed, this occasional heaven, would not last forever. She walked out into the courtyard and looked up at the hill above Corpus Christi where Kevin and Leo did their daily walks. She peered out over the wall and saw them—Kevin and Leo walking up, puffing, stopping, starting again. I am getting them in shape, she thought.

She stood watching for several minutes, and Willie got up and walked over to her and nudged her leg.

Why can't we just freeze this life now, she thought, just freeze it like this forever?

Kevin wouldn't tolerate such talk from her. She had grown wistful a few times in front of him lately, never emotional, but reflective, and he'd change the subject like summer lightning in the desert.

But look at them, my two man-children, she thought. I have built my life around an Australian priest and a handyman.

But women are disappearing again. The thought kept nagging her, zipping in and out of her head for days now.

Now it wasn't just the prostitutes that they were dumping in the desert. It was women of all sorts—women dragged off buses, dragged out of their homes, dragged into cars off the street. All the "smart" men said the new peace in Juarez was a result of the victory of the Sinaloa cartel over the Juarez cartel. But they weren't so smart, she thought. Or they were looking at it through their own eyes, as men always did. Women were disappearing in droves before the drug war had consumed Juarez; it kept happening all during the war even though we lost track of it; it is still happening, only now there is room for it in our brains again.

She knew her daughters were prime targets, young, pretty women who dressed like the young, pretty women just across the border.

The night before, she had tossed and turned in bed, tortured by the thought. We have saved money, she thought. Kevin and Leo cannot live without me, I know it, but perhaps we will just take a break. Head south for a while.

But then she realized she was playing tricks with herself. She was making up excuses, shielding herself, protecting herself. Something inside couldn't stop thinking that this was all going to change very soon. That it was too good. That she needed to be prepared to start a new life again.

◈ ◈ ◈

SHE DIDN'T LAMENT THE FACT THAT SO MANY PARENTS FELT THE NEED TO SEND THEIR KIDS TO AMERICA IN WHAT-EVER WAY THEY COULD; she lamented that they felt the need to do so at all, that they hadn't found a place like she had found. On days when the paranoia about it all changing receded, this was what she allowed herself to think.

"You couldn't pay me to send one of my children to America!" she said to Kevin one day as he sat eating lunch and watching coverage of the border crisis consuming the American media in the summer of 2014. Children, the press said, were crossing illegally by the thousands, though she had yet to see it and no one around Anapra knew anything about it. We live on the border, she thought, and there have been plenty of crossings, but I don't know anyone that desperate right now, now that the peace has come, to head over to America.

He had told her a few weeks prior that he was going to take a little vacation and had told her just the day before that he was going to do so in Chile, not in Australia as she had assumed. She had spent the night wanting to ask him why there, why Chile, but instead, the onslaught of news about the border crisis was consuming every conversation.

It seemed to her that people here, despite living their lives amid the new peace, at least relative peace, of Juarez, couldn't imagine life being worse elsewhere. It had become a habit: tell yourself you are living in hell. But the description of life for the poor in Honduras and the flight of their children through Mexico somehow appalled her and some other Anaprans she had discussed it with—not because of their plight in and of itself but because their desperation seemed even worse than the Juarez version at the height of the killings.

"Sending your children away like that—I just couldn't do it!" she said again.

"Nor I, Rayna, nor I!" Kevin said. "What would we do without your children and grandchildren? We'd be bored stiff. You couldn't pay even me to go live over there, and I'm a missionary! I'd leave the order like I threatened to do when they were going to pull me out of here. I remember when we discovered that Mario and Jose were coyotes, I wondered who they were smuggling across. Who thinks life is better anywhere other than here? Or better anywhere else? That is one thing I have learned in my travels. Chicago, Chile, Brisbane, here. Life is life."

They smiled momentarily, and then their faces grew blank. Here it is again, she thought, that type of momentary silence that never used to make her uncomfortable. But now, as they spent more and more time in this home together and as the broadcasters reported less the tragic news of here and more the tragic news of elsewhere, for some reason the domestic silences had started to unnerve her.

"The funny thing is, Rayna, I don't know anyone who would," he said, picking up the same topic, she knew, because he, like she, had not thought of anything else to discuss.

Clara usually was here with them at lunchtime, with Jenny Violeta either feeding or napping or in need of changing, and whatever they were doing with her at the time inevitably filled their conversation. She was pleased that Jenny Violeta's arrival had coincided with his surgery and recovery, for she had expected him to turn into an unbearable grouch when he told her that his surgeon had advised a couple of months of doing nothing at home as the best way to recover.

She had concocted the plan to have him care for Jenny Violeta as much as he could—at first at least have him sit with her while she slept in her tiny crib atop the couch; then feed her; then change diapers.

She had waited to assign him the last task until she had noticed him moving about with ease, and at first he had looked at her with absolute horror when she had told him he was now ready for diaper duty.

But she had nudged him over to the couch, where she and Clara showed him how it was done. He simply nodded, but the next time she told him it was time, he stood up, assembled the diaper cream, wipes, and fresh diaper beside him atop the sofa, and rather adequately completed the task without even holding his nose in the air once.

She chuckled at her recollection, not realizing she was doing so.

He stood up, and as he walked to the bathroom—less and less, she was happy to observe—he turned back to her and said, "When I get back, you can tell me what's so funny!"

But when he came back and made that face that said he was ready for her answer, she felt a sudden sadness overcoming her, so much so that she stood up and turned and walked to the other bathroom closer to the kitchen.

As she walked, she didn't turn back so he could see her face, but she did manage to say, "I'll be right back."

She walked in, closed the door, and breathed deeply. She wasn't going to cry, she knew; the pain in her gut wasn't stabbing but merely gnawing; she immediately composed herself once she stood there for a few seconds.

And as she looked in the mirror, she smiled. She had thought of her line. I'm getting as good as these fellows, as good as Father Kevin and Leo, she thought to herself. As good a dodger, as quick-witted when it comes to the evasive one-liner that can instantly rescue you from the hole you feel you are about to get trapped in.

She walked back out, and he sat there looking at her as she sat back down.

"Even though I don't have a prostate either," she said, "I find I have to go to the bathroom more often as I age."

◈ ◈ ◈

SHE HAD FELT THIS SENSATION THE NIGHTS HE HAD BEEN IN THE HOSPITAL IN EL PASO. She was seeing Juarez differently—the streets, the faces, the dogs, the buildings, the entire surrounding landscape of desert and mountain. It affected her gait—she found herself not stumbling but feeling like she was always about to stumble, like the dirt road was going to give out from under her just as she was about to place her foot down on it.

Now that he was in Chile, away on what he called his vacation, she felt it again. Why would he go on vacation to a place as hard as he said it was, even if it is so beautiful? Did I not realize all along that he really is crazy?

Then she would catch herself. You are being jealous, she said. You are jealous of people you don't even know. There is no plan he is hiding from you. He would not do that. He said just a few weeks ago that he hopes to keep working here until he dies.

She knew her daughters noticed. Clara, in particular, came by the house more often, bringing Jenny Violeta, who herself didn't even look like herself without Kevin's arms and chest and grin as the backdrop, without him holding her.

She noticed it in Clara, too.

One day they were sitting watching a telenovela, and both suddenly looked at each other and started laughing, knowing how much Kevin hated them. Rayna used to joke that Clara's children were going to be bilingual but speak with British accents, given how Kevin always insisted on having the BBC news on the satellite.

One afternoon, during a commercial, Clara looked at her and shook her head.

"Ahora entiendo por qué se llaman 'padres,'" Clara said. Now I understand why they call them fathers. Rayna had never, never conflated padres of the clerical sort with real padres. But a priest, a Padre, had never fed and coddled one of her babies. And Clara had never known the love and steadfastness of a real father. So it was surely logical for Clara to see the word differently than she did.

"Nunca creía en Dios, la verdad," Rayna said suddenly. I never believed in God, really. She didn't say she had never truly believed in God until Kevin became her pastor and her friend, for that dependent clause was obvious.

"And it amazes me how different your life is than mine, your life and the way you see the world," she said to Clara, not realizing that she and her daughters never spoke about profound things like this. "The way you see the world is shaped more by your life in this parish than by your life in this city that Kevin says they call the most violent place on earth."

"Sí, Mamá," Clara said. "Tienes toda la razón." You are completely right.

The TV show returned, and Rayna reached for the clicker and turned it off. She felt the stinging in her stomach again, catching herself from wincing so as not to worry Clara.

"Qué desgracia," she said, looking at the television. What a disgrace.

"Voy abajo, a rezar un poco," she said, standing up. I'm going down the hill, to pray a little bit.

Clara looked at her with a start, with shock. Rayna knew her daughter knew that her mother was not the sort to go down to the church in the middle of the day to pray. Rayna knew Clara knew, all of the children knew, that the last time she did that sort of thing was when she was conning (no, not conning, she

thought, that is too harsh a word, perhaps simply trying to impress) the priests into bringing Cristina back to her.

Rayna laughed for a moment.

"No, no, stay here with the baby," she said, firmly. "I'm just
going to go down, make sure everything looks okay. I'll be right
back up."

She took a drink of seltzer to calm her stomach, stopped to
watch Jenny Violeta sleeping, and then smiled at Clara as she
walked out.

Kevin is with his old people now, she thought as she walked
down the hill. She laughed this time at her reaction when he
had first told her he was going back to Chile on his vacation, at
how she had grown instantly suspicious and then overwhelm-
ingly jealous. The man needs to rest, relax. Why is he going back
there? Is it just to get out of the heat? Or are they going to send
him back there again? Or does he want to go back there again?
Does he care about them as much as he cares about us?

All those questions which hit her then came back now as
she walked. It was a half hour before she had tamped down her
paranoia. It kept surging, she realized. It just won't go away even
though I know my fears have no basis. He will never leave here.

She could see Corpus Christi once she turned the corner,
standing across from the bustling S Mart store just down the
hill. When they had announced that they were going to build
an S Mart in Anapra, she had twold Leo and Kevin in the living
room one day, and they couldn't help stop giggling. How many
times they had had the debate about what constitutes progress,
she thought. Not a debate really but a discussion, a lecture by
Kevin on how only capitalism, even the kind that powered the
maquilas and paid for the S Marts, was still the only way to
transform Anapra.

"These are the rules," he liked to say, "and we have to play
within the rules."

That afternoon they had recalled together how Anapra had no water when Kevin had arrived, and how most shacks had no plumbing and sewage systems.

"Ten thousand murders later and now the folks who run S Mart see a market here, Leo!" Kevin had said. "They value Anapra's collective pesos enough to build a store here! Think about that! Did you think that was possible fifteen years ago?"

Rayna stopped at the corner and laughed to herself. Steaks, burgers, processed chicken, pasteurized milk, baby formula— they used to have to go all the way downtown to buy anything of the sort. Now it was all right here, right in front of Kevin's church.

She walked up to the gate and reached into her pocket but realized she had forgotten the key.

You are out of sorts, she thought. You really are.

She walked behind the church, a new playing field now completed with boys running up and down kicking a soccer ball. The empty field beyond it—she now imagined what he told her he was imagining—fields and a swimming pool and a clubhouse there someday soon.

And suddenly she felt stronger, happier. Her stomach pain even went away.

My grandchildren, I can see them diving into that swimming pool, she said to herself. She focused her eyes on it, on her vision, on the teeming children playing all sorts of games out there in front of her.

I can hold this place together no matter what comes, she thought. We have won, and we will keep winning; they will keep winning even after he and I are someday gone. There will be battles, there will be crosses, but the winning will keep on.

And she turned and walked over to the S Mart. The baby needed more formula, and she also wanted to see people, feel the activity.

And as she walked the aisles alongside mothers pushing babies in carts and men sent out with lists written by their wives, she remembered what he had said a few months ago about saints, about how they were going to make Pope John Paul II a saint.

"The saints are all around us," he had said. "I've met more people in Anapra that I would make a saint than the church has canonized in her history. I'd never be pope because I'd be canonizing half the population. Living and dying in a holy way, that's the test, Rayna. The saints are all around us."

She paid the clerk and walked out with her bags and headed up the hill. Maybe he is right, she thought. The miracles are all around us, the miracles are here. That's what he said, and I found it so disagreeable. But maybe it was just a different way of speaking.

She stopped thinking as she walked home, and tried to observe the people and dogs and huts the way she imagined he would. She tried to capture his awe.

As she arrived at her shack, she heard Jenny Violeta crying, the hungry cry no doubt. She walked in and handed Clara the formula and stood there and watched as she fed her daughter.

Clara suddenly looked at her with tight eyes.

"Mamá, ¿qué haces?" she asked. What are you doing?

"Nada," Rayna said. Nothing. "Just thinking about what I have to do before Kevin comes home next week. I need to do a full shopping trip. I need to deep clean the house. He is going to have a busy year."

"And you are, too, Mamá," Clara said. Tú también.

Rayna nodded, half there but half not.

She heard his voice again, she heard it and she knew that no matter where he was, she would always hear it, and she hoped that Clara and Jenny and everyone else would always hear it in the same way, so clear and sure, saying things like this, saying things like now. The saints are all around us. The saints are always here.

The author wishes to thank

Jim Shepard, Bill Anderson, Jon Graham and
Richard Rosen; Alberto Gonzalez and Tom
Jordan; Cappy Hill, Kent Kildahl, and the
Vassar College library; Ron Shapiro and SNI;
Tom and Connie McEvoy; Isaac Vasquez
and Charles Dodds; and Paul Hardart, Andy
Klemmer, Sott Resnick, and Diane Sokolow.

Also, special thanks to Jessie Borkan for her devotion
to this project, and to Therese Ratliff and Daniel Smart
for their support, conviction, humor, and faith.

The Skids many years ago provided the fitting title
for this story, and sacred background noise during
many a day spent inside the fine minds and hearty
souls of Kevin Mullins and Rayna Hernandez.

Ezekiel, Lukas, and Ali, the saints are all around
us. Special gratitude to Dr. Kurt Newman,
and to the NICU nurses and surgical team
at Children's National Medical Center.

Un eterno agradecimiento to the Cathedral
High School Class of 1996 in El Paso, Texas,
and to infinite Leo, Tice, and the Candy
Man. And to Antonio Gimenez.

Sweet Virginia, you are always here.

READING GROUP GUIDE

1] Early in his ministry, Kevin feels he is being tested in the Mexican desert, but his perspective changes during the story. What does he learn about himself as a person and priest? About the church? About Juarez and the people there? What makes him stay in Juarez despite the risk to his own life and his superior's order for him to leave?

2] In the narrative, Rayna is transformed from a victimized person alienated from the church into a woman with an important role in parish ministry and a new understanding of herself as an active agent of peace and healing in Juarez. What changes her relationship with the church and her connection to her own role as a believer and a citizen?

3] At one point, Kevin realizes that there is a "spider's web of relationships stretching across the border." He thinks of this in terms of the connections between Juarez and El Paso, but what could it also mean with regard to the broader relationship between the United States and Mexico? How does U.S. policy affect the people of Mexico? What responsibility, if any, might Americans have toward people of other nations?

4] Violence against women and girls in Juarez permeates the story. In what way is Kevin's partnership with Rayna an example of the ways in which the church can support women and girls? How might you participate more concretely in making the world a safer place for the powerless among us?

5] Rayna believes that violence and suffering in Juarez are caused not by the drug cartel leaders and manipulative Mexican oligarchs, but, rather, by "Satan's work." In contrast, Kevin, Billy, and Leo blame problems on broken social structures and corrupt people. How do their understandings of evil shape these characters' actions? What difference might your understanding of evil make in the way you respond to life's events?

6] The book ends with Rayna's repetition of phrases Kevin has used: "The saints are all of us. The saints are always here." Who are "saints"? What do these phrases mean for Christians? What do they mean in the context of Juarez? What do these phrases contribute to your understanding of the story itself? In what ways might you be challenged by these words?

Parish Themed Discussion Points

1] Kevin and Billy represent two priests with different visions of church. What are their respective visions of the church, and how do we see this through the way they embrace their priestly ministry? Which do you see operating in your own parish? Do we need both?

2] Kevin and Rayna develop a deep friendship that helps both of them grow and shapes the life of the community in significant ways. How does their mutual ministry demonstrate a creative partnership between ordained and lay persons? How is it a model of shared ministry between a man and a woman?

3] Rayna brings flowers into the church, a symbol of her attention to the life of the senses. Kevin resists the flowers at first but then realizes that they are "proof of God" and preaches at a funeral about "flowers and Mexico and hope and survival." What is the role of beauty in Christian life and parish hospitality? How is beauty connected to survival? How is it connected to social justice?

4] Rayna tells Kevin, "Faith is about us, not me." What does it mean for the church to be about mutual support and community transformation rather than individual salvation? How might a parish live this out in concrete ways?

5] Kevin, Leo, and Rayna are awed when Jorge Mario Bergoglio of Argentina is elected pope, the first from the Southern Hemisphere and the Americas. How did the resignation of Pope Benedict XVI and the election of Pope Francis affect the people of Anapra? How has Francis' papal ministry affected your own local ecclesial community?

In this gem of a book, Greg Jordan quietly draws the reader right into the scene with three compelling characters as their relationship deepens—a committed missionary priest, his housekeeper, and the parish handyman. They develop a parish community in the face of daunting and deadly challenges in an impoverished Mexican barrio on the border where poverty, drug wars, violence, and exploitation dictate every day. The story is salted with their rich personal reflection. Jordan puts the reader right with them, saints living season by season with hope.

◈ **REV. OTTO HENTZ, SJ,** *Professor of Theology, Georgetown University*

This intense, riveting story grabs hold of you and won't let go. Back in my Hollywood days, this is the kind of eloquent and evocative book that I would have loved to turn into a compelling film. Gregory Jordan's grippingly vivid writing has a real cinematic feel to it as he presents very human, flawed, contemporary saints.

◈ **GERARD THOMAS STRAUB,** *author of*
   The Loneliness and Longing of Saint Francis

Greg Jordan's terrific non-fiction account is not just stunning, first-rate reporting on the Catholic response to poverty and violence in Juarez, "the most dangerous place on earth," but an inspiring and fascinatingly intimate look at a Mexican parish from the perspectives of both its John Wayne of a pastor and his wise, resilient housekeeper. In its psychological complexity, richness of detail, and discerning sympathy for its main characters, *The Saints Are Coming* reads like a novel worthy of Graham Greene.

◈ **RON HANSEN,** *author of Mariette in Ecstasy, Atticus,*
   and A Wild Surge of Guilty Passion

If Pope Francis signals the transformation of the Catholic Church, then this book—a powerful story of courage and mercy, of gutsy faith—embodies what Francis so perfectly calls "a poor Church for the poor." Greg Jordan propels us into the midst of this gripping story of danger and redemption with the tenacity of a seasoned journalist.

◈ MARK SHRIVER, *author of* A *Good Man:*
Rediscovering My Father, Sargent Shriver

Conversion is a slow and complex process, however fundamental a part of the spiritual life it may be. Read this book: you'll find yourself immersed in your own spiritual transformation.

◈ JOAN CHITTISTER, OSB, *author of* The Breath of the Soul

Gregory Jordan tells a moving tale of human dignity, faith, and love in the everyday lives of people struggling to survive in Borderland. Without ignoring the political realities and moral ambiguities, he finds genuine hope in the midst of despair.

◈ MARK C. TAYLOR, *Chair, Department of Religion, Columbia University*

Greg Jordan's *The Saints Are Coming* examines the intricacies and possibilities of the relationship between the faith of the heart and the works of the hand. Like his subjects, the priest and the housekeeper, Jordan exhorts us to go in with our eyes wide open, to learn about lives and worlds that it would be easier to ignore. And he generously and empathetically reminds us that if you can see, you must act.

◈ KAREN SHEPARD *author of* The Celestials *and* Don't I Know You?